THE DEFINITIVE GUIDE TO EDITING WITH

DaVinci Resolve 12.5

by Paul Saccone

The Definitive Guide to Editing with DaVinci Resolve 12.5

Paul Saccone

Blackmagic Design

www.blackmagicdesign.com

To report errors, please send a note to training@blackmagicdesign.com.

Series Editor: Patricia Montesion

Editor: Bob Lindstrom

Cover Design: Blackmagic Design

Interior Design and Compositor: Danielle Foster

ISBN 13: 978-0-9961528-3-9

Contents

Foreword

Welcome to *The Definitive Guide to Editing with DaVinci Resolve 12.5*

I think one of the most exciting things about DaVinci Resolve is that it gives you a true professional video editor plus the same incredible color correction tools used in Hollywood on high-end films and television shows, all in one software solution. We recently added professional editing to DaVinci Resolve with version 10 and the response from editors has been incredible. Since then, we've been turning it into the world's best professional editor.

Best of all, DaVinci Resolve is absolutely free! We've made sure that the free version of DaVinci Resolve actually has more features than any other paid editing system. That's because at Blackmagic Design we believe everybody should have the tools to create professional, Hollywood-caliber content without having to spend thousands of dollars.

I hope you'll enjoy using DaVinci Resolve and we can't wait to see the amazing work you produce!

—Grant Petty
Blackmagic Design

Getting Started

Welcome to *The Definitive Guide to Editing with DaVinci Resolve 12.5*, the official Blackmagic Design authorized training book that teaches editors and students how to edit in DaVinci Resolve. All you need is a Mac or Windows computer, the free download version of DaVinci Resolve 12.5, and a passion to learn about editing.

In this book, you will edit a project from start to finish in Resolve 12.5. You learn how to import and organize media; edit and trim in the timeline; add transitions, effects, and titles; and export a finished project. You'll understand the essential editing functionality while acquiring skills that you can develop as you grow with Resolve.

About DaVinci Resolve 12.5

DaVinci is the world's most trusted name in color correction and is used on virtually all Hollywood feature films, TV shows, and commercials. With DaVinci Resolve 12.5, Blackmagic Design has added a complete set of professional editing and trimming tools so you can now edit and color correct complete projects using only one piece of software!

Within this single application you have access to editing, asymmetric and dynamic trimming, multicam, audio mixing, filters, effects, animation tools, titling, and much more. DaVinci Resolve 12.5 also features the same incredible color correction tools and legendary image quality relied upon by Hollywood professionals. Now you can freely move between editing and color correction at any time with a single click.

DaVinci Resolve 12.5 lets you work in a comfortable, familiar way while also providing an innovative and powerful toolset to help you cut and finish projects more efficiently than ever before.

The DaVinci Resolve Quality Difference

DaVinci Resolve has become the #1 tool for professional Hollywood colorists because it processes images using a unique, floating 32-bit YRGB color space. It manipulates luminance independent of color, which lets you create looks and effects that are literally impossible to create on other systems. In addition, Resolve works natively with your camera's RAW files so you can produce the highest quality "first generation" masters when you output content. With the innovation of DaVinci Resolve 12.5, editors can realize that same level of quality from start to finish and apply the same tools that high-end colorists have relied upon for years.

Which Version of Resolve is Right for You?

DaVinci Resolve 12.5 is available at no charge for Mac and Windows and all of the lessons in this book are designed to work with this free version. DaVinci Resolve 12.5 Studio, and DaVinci Resolve 12.5 Studio with Control Panel include additional, advanced features that you can use on Mac, Windows, or Linux systems.

DaVinci Resolve 12.5: This free version of DaVinci Resolve includes everything you need to edit and color grade SD, HD, and UHD (Ultra High Definition) projects. This version is recommended for individual editors and colorists working on 2D projects.

DaVinci Resolve 12.5 Studio: This version adds support for greater than UHD resolutions, such as 4K and beyond, along with motion blur effects, temporal and spatial noise reduction, HDR grading, automatic lens correction, lens flares, film grain, lens blur, 3D stereoscopic tools, and remote rendering. Also included are multi-user collaborative workflow tools that allow an editor, multiple editing assistants, and colorists to all work on the same project at the same time. This version is highly recommended if you're working within a collaborative studio environment. DaVinci Resolve 12.5 Studio is available for purchase at $995 (U.S.).

DaVinci Resolve 12.5 Advanced Panel: Includes DaVinci Resolve 12.5 Studio, along with the award winning DaVinci Resolve hardware control surface. Designed with input from professional colorists, the DaVinci Resolve Advanced Panel lets colorists manipulate multiple parameters simultaneously, giving them more control and creative options than are possible using a standard mouse and keyboard. This version is recommended for professional colorists and costs $29,995 (U.S.)

What You Will Learn

The lessons in this book take you through an entire project following a real-world workflow. You'll start by importing and viewing clips. Then you'll organize them, put together a rough cut, and refine your edit using professional trimming tools. You'll also mix audio, add effects and titles, and color grade your project for a perfect-looking production before outputting your final timelines to various file formats.

These lessons are meant to teach practical technique, not theoretical observations about editing. As you work through these lessons, you'll learn real-world skills that you can apply to real-world productions.

Lessons 1, "Setting Up a Project," through 4, "Working in the Timeline," build upon each other, so you must complete each lesson in order. In them, you prepare your media for editing.

Lesson 5, "Mastering Trimming Options," begins by importing a project that contains material you use in Lessons 5 through 9; Lesson 11, "Primary Color Correction;" Lesson 12, "Using the Delivery Page;" and Lesson 13, "Managing Projects and Media."

Lesson 10 is a standalone multicam lesson.

System Requirements

This book supports Resolve 12.5.2 for OS X and Windows. If you have an older version of DaVinci Resolve, you must upgrade to the current version to follow along with the lessons. Fortunately, DaVinci Resolve 12.5.2 is a free upgrade from the previous version of DaVinci Resolve so you can download it now from the Blackmagic Design website.

Download DaVinci Resolve 12.5

To download the free version of DaVinci Resolve 12.5.2 from the Blackmagic Design website:

1. Open a web browser on your Windows or OS X computer.
2. In the address field of your web browser, type: www.blackmagicdesign.com/products/davinciresolve.
3. On the DaVinci Resolve landing page, click the Download button.
4. On the download page, click the Mac OS X or Windows button, depending on your computer's operating system.
5. Follow the installation instructions to complete the installation.

When you have completed the software installation, follow the instructions in the following section, "Copying the Lesson Files," to download the content for this book.

Copying the Lesson Files

The DaVinci Resolve editing lesson files must be downloaded to your OS X or Windows computer to perform the exercises in this book. After you save the files to your hard disk, extract the file and copy the folder to your Documents folder.

To Download and Install the DaVinci Resolve Editing Lessons Files:

When you are ready to download the lesson files, follow these steps:

1. Connect to the Internet and navigate to: https://www.blackmagicdesign.com/dvres/editing-with-resolve.

   The download will begin immediately.

   The **DaVinci Resolve Editing Lessons Files.zip** file is roughly 2.5 GB in size and can take up to 30min to download to your computer using a standard broadband connection.

2. After downloading the zip file to your OS X or Windows computer, open your Downloads folder, and double-click DaVinci Resolve Editing Lessons Files.zip to unzip it if it doesn't unzip automatically.
3. Drag the DaVinci Resolve Editing Lessons Files folder from the Downloads folder to your Documents folder.

You are now ready to begin Lesson 1: Setting Up a Project.

Acknowledgments

We would like to thank the following individuals for their contributions of media used throughout the book:

Citizen Chain

Jitter Bug Riot

1 Setting Up a Project

Blackmagic Design's DaVinci Resolve is the only software that lets you both edit and color correct projects from start to finish, all within one integrated software tool. DaVinci Resolve has been designed to handle major Hollywood feature films, episodic television shows, and commercials, along with indie films, corporate and event videos, and even student films. This book teaches you how to edit your projects using the professional nonlinear editing tools in DaVinci Resolve 12.5.

Whether you use the application on a Mac or Windows computer, you'll learn how to take a project from the initial setup to the final output. You'll become familiar with the standard menus and buttons, as well as essential keyboard shortcuts that will accelerate your workflow.

Let's begin by setting up a project; exploring the basic layout of the Resolve windows, buttons, and menus; and finally importing the clips that you'll use throughout this book.

TIME

- **This lesson takes approximately 35 minutes to complete.**

GOALS

- **Create a profile**
- **Start a new project**
- **Explore the media page**
- **Import clips**
- **Play clips**
- **Color manage a project**
- **View clip metadata**
- **Add custom metadata**

Creating a Profile

At this point you should have installed Resolve 12.5 on your computer, downloaded the content for this book, and located that content in your Documents folder.

1. To open Resolve, do one of the following:
   - In OS X, in the Dock, click the Resolve icon.
   - In Windows, in the Start menu, click the Resolve icon.

The first window that appears depends on whether or not you have previously installed Resolve on your computer.

If you have never installed Resolve, skip directly to the next section of this lesson, "Starting a New Project."

If you previously installed DaVinci Resolve 12.0 or earlier, a login window appears, and you will be given the opportunity to set up a new account or log in to an existing account.

> **NOTE:** If you've previously opened Resolve 12.5 on the current computer, you may already have an account. However, for use with this book, you should create a new account by following this exercise.

In the login screen you can create and manage an account with a unique user profile. An account profile has its own individual settings, preferences, and projects to support each user's login screen.

2. To create a new account, in the center of the window, double-click the New User icon.

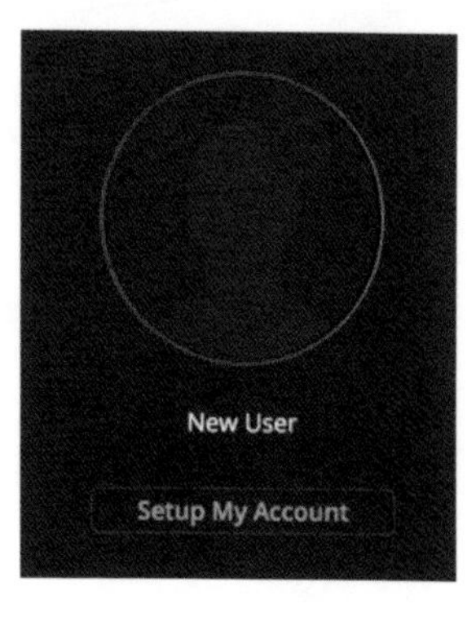

3. In the New User Set Up window, enter a user name, and if you wish, enter a password to protect the account. Then click the Setup New User button.

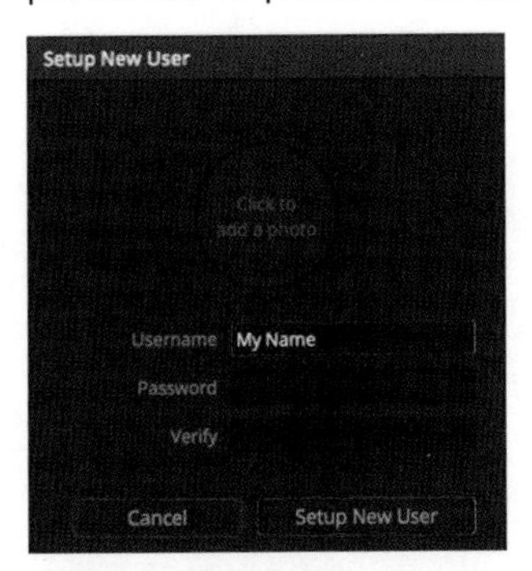

4. In the login screen, click the Log In button.

   The Project Manager window opens. Here you'll find listed all the projects belonging to the current account. You'll create a new project in the next exercise.

> **TIP:** To delete a user profile, you can right-click a user name in the login window. From the pop-up menu that appears, choose Delete User, and then click Yes.

> **NOTE:** You can set up DaVinci Resolve as a multi-user application that allows multiple individuals using the same computer to personalize the tools and configurations they want when they open Resolve.

THE DAVINCI RESOLVE WORKFLOW

DaVinci Resolve is organized as a series of interface pages—Media, Edit, Color, and Deliver—that correspond to the order of most traditional editing workflows.

- **Media:** Used for importing footage, organizing media, creating bins, adding metadata, and backing up or cloning camera original media.
- **Edit:** Here you'll find bins, timelines, and all the professional editing tools you'll need to assemble your show. The Edit page also includes multicamera tools, an audio mixer, and clip metadata information.
- **Color:** This page contains DaVinci Resolve's world-class color correction and creative grading tools, including primary and secondary correctors, keyers, trackers, Power Windows, and much more.
- **Deliver:** Here you can master to tape, create files for the web, and even output masters for theatrical distribution. You can also roundtrip files with ProTools, other popular NLEs, and various visual effects applications.

DaVinci Resolve is both powerful and flexible because you don't have to use its pages in order and you don't have to work in other applications (unless you choose to.) You can freely move between pages to import and manage media, edit in the timeline, color and add effects, or generate files for output in any order at any time, and all within the Resolve environment.

Starting a New Project

Projects represent a single job and they contain the timelines and clips that link to the media on your hard drives. Currently, an empty project with the default title, Untitled Project, is displayed in the Project Manager. To begin editing, let's create a new project that contains all the clips you'll use in the following exercises.

1. At the bottom of the Project Manager window, click the New Project button.

2. In the Create New Project dialog that appears, enter the project name **DaVinci Resolve Editing**, and click Create.

   The DaVinci Resolve Editing project is added to the Project Manager.

3. In the Project Manager, double-click the DaVinci Resolve Editing thumbnail to open the project in the media page.

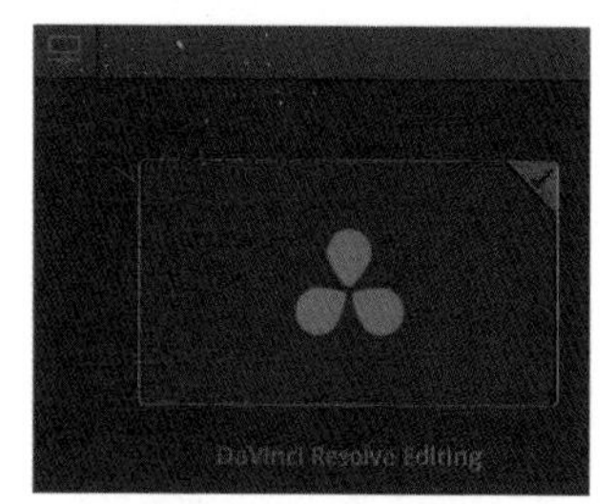

   Resolve uses default values for project settings such as deck capture, playback, and resolution. You can customize these values in the Project Settings window.

4. Choose File > Project Settings to open the Project Settings window.

   In this lesson, you'll use clips with a frame size of 1280 x 720 pixels running at 24 frames-per-second (fps). Let's adjust your project settings accordingly.

5. From the "Timeline resolution" pop-up menu, choose "1280 x 720 HD 720P."

   The frame rate is already set correctly at 24 fps, so no other setting change is required for this project. If you were using a Blackmagic Decklink card, or USB or Thunderbolt video interface to output to a broadcast monitor, you would also set Video Monitoring to 720P. However, for this project, you are done with the Project Settings window.

6. In the Project Settings window, click Save to save your changes and return to the media page.

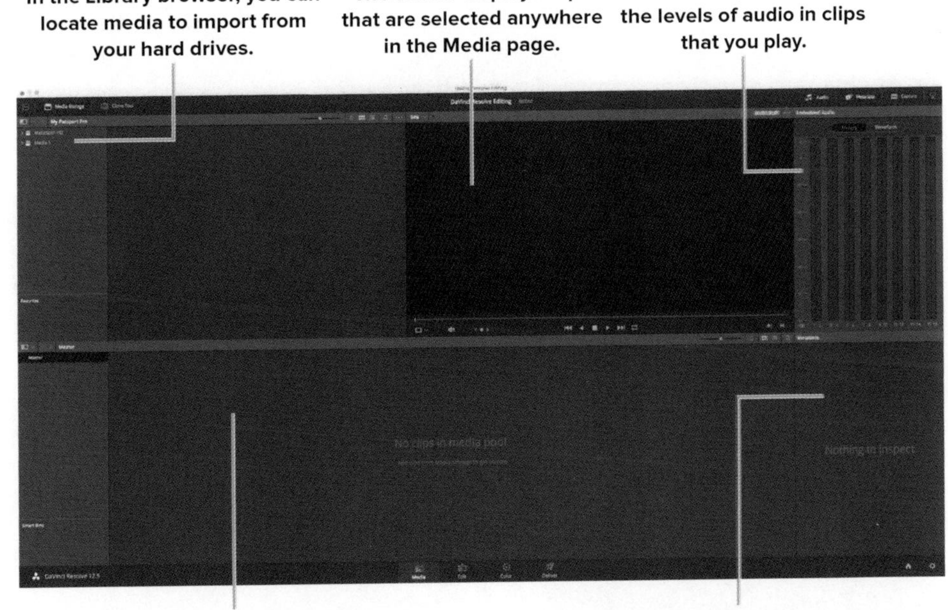

The Media page is the first Resolve window you'll generally use to import media from your hard drives. You'll also perform tasks here such as media management and clip organization, switching between proxy and camera original media, and troubleshooting clips that appear offline. In the previous figure, you can see all of the panels in the Media page.

The media page is divided into five areas:

- Library browser shows all of the connected drives on your system.
- Media Pool contains all of the media for your current project, organized in bins. You can import files from the drives in the library browser into the media pool in your project.
- Viewer for previewing video
- Audio meters for checking audio levels
- Metadata Editor for viewing, adding, or editing clip metadata

Importing Clips

When you are ready to import clips into a project, you'll use the Library browser. In this browser, you can navigate to any folder or hard drive where you keep your media. When you import clips into your project, they are stored in bins in the media pool.

> **NOTE:** The following steps assume that you have copied the DaVinci Resolve Editing Lessons Files folder to your Documents folder. If you copied the files to a different location, use the Library browser to navigate to that location.

1. In the Library browser sidebar to the left, click the icon of your computer's internal hard drive.

2. In the right panel, double-click folders to locate your Documents folder.
3. In the Documents folder, double-click the DaVinci Resolve Editing Lessons Files folder.

   The library displays three folders in the DaVinci Resolve Editing Lessons Files folder. You'll import clips for this project from the first two folders.

4. Double-click the 01 Video Clips folder.

   The right panel of the library displays a thumbnail-sized image icon for all of the clips you want to import. You can skim over each icon to preview more frames in the clip.
5. Position your pointer over one of the icons.
6. Move the mouse pointer left and right over the icon.

   As you move the pointer left and right, Resolve displays various frames from the clip as if you were fast forwarding and rewinding through it.

   After you're finished previewing clips, you can choose to import one or more clips.
7. Choose Edit > Select All to select all of the clips displayed in the library, or press Cmd-A (OS X) or Ctrl-A (Windows).
8. In the library, right-click any clip, and from the pop-up menu, choose "Add into Media Pool" to import the clips into the Media Pool.

> **TIP:** You can also drag clips directly into the Media Pool from the library, the OS X Finder, or Windows Explorer.

All of the selected clips are added to the Master bin in the Media Pool, the default location for all imported clips. Note that the clips are not copied, moved, or transcoded when you import them. With Resolve's non-destructive processing, the files remain unaltered and in their current locations on your hard drive.

Importing Folders

Instead of selecting each of the clips you want to import and adding them all to the Master bin, you can import an entire folder and automatically create a custom bin.

1. In the upper area of the library, click the back arrow to view the contents of the DaVinci Resolve Editing Lessons Files folder.

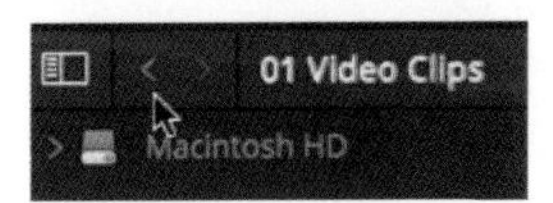

2. Drag the 02 Music and Sound Effects folder into an empty area in the Media Pool bin list below the Master bin.

> **TIP:** Subfolders within a folder that you drag into the Media Pool are imported as part of the bin.

Dragging the folder into the Media Pool sidebar creates a separate bin with the folder's name and nested in the Master bin. All of the clips contained in the folder are included in the bin.

Reviewing and Scrubbing Clips

You might want to review and check your clips after you've imported them, especially if you're editing a project that was shot by someone else and you're unfamiliar with the footage.

1. In the Media Pool sidebar, select the Master bin.
2. In the bin, click any video clip icon of the interview.

Clicking a clip icon in the library loads that clip into the viewer, where you can see a larger version of the icon. More importantly, the viewer allows you to play and shuttle through the clip using the jog bar and transport controls.

> **NOTE:** Due to screen and window size differences, the order of clips in your bin may appear slightly different from the figures shown in this lesson.

3. In the jog bar, drag the playhead to shuttle quickly through the clip.

   Dragging the jog bar's playhead to shuttle through a clip provides the same preview speed that you enjoyed when skimming over the icon in the library, and it also allows you to see a larger frame. Still, to edit clips most efficiently you need to know their contents intimately. For that purpose, nothing can replace just sitting down and watching a clip play from start to end.

4. Under the viewer, click the Play button, or press the Spacebar to play the clip.

   The clip plays at the project's frame rate

5. Under the viewer, click the Stop button, or press the Spacebar again to stop playback.

   Other buttons under the viewer allow you to play a clip in reverse, and move the playhead to the beginning or the end of a clip.

   When previewing video clips that contain audio, you can display an audio waveform overlay of the sync sound.

6. From the Options menu in the upper-right corner of the viewer, choose Show Zoomed Audio Waveform.

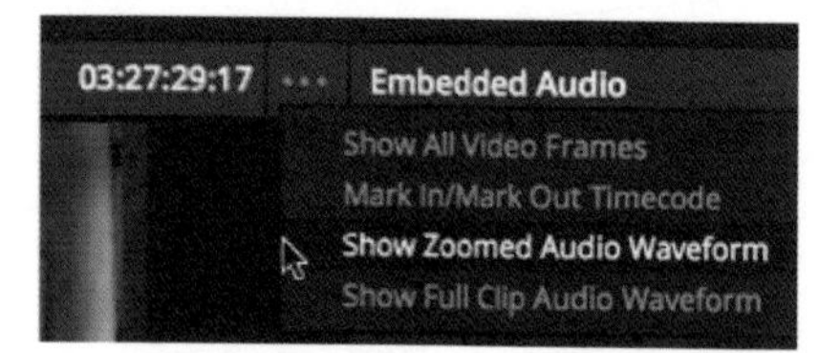

   A waveform appears at the bottom of the viewer. The red playhead bar in the waveform indicates the current frame.

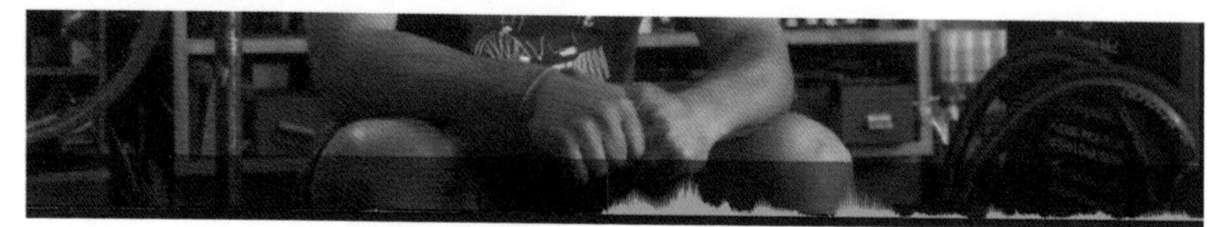

7. From the Options menu, choose Show Zoomed Audio Waveform again to hide the overlay.

NOTE: Having the option to view the audio waveform overlay can be helpful when trying to find a clip location that has a distinct sound or lack of sound.

Playing Audio Clips

Clips that contain audio content only are displayed differently in both the bins and the viewer.

1. In the 02 Music and Sound Effects bin, click the clip with the musical note icon, **Marin Headlands Biking Song**.

This clip contains only audio, so the icon displays a musical note. The viewer shows the audio waveform. When you're editing, this display makes it easier for you to find loud audio points within the clip. By shuttling through the clip using the jog bar, you can play the audio-only clip.

2. In the jog bar, drag the playhead slowly to shuttle through the clip and listen to the audio.

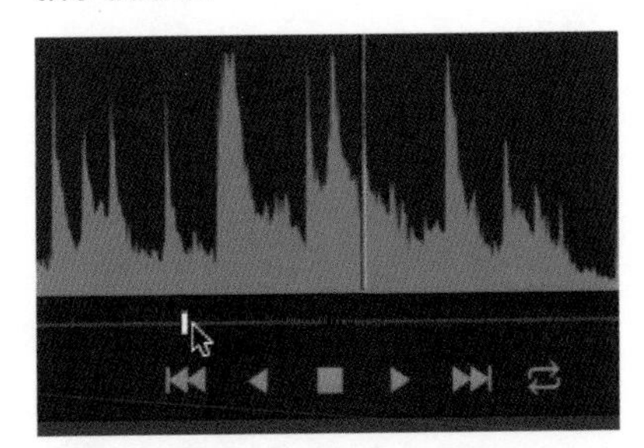

The viewer shows a detailed section of the clip's waveform. Above the viewer you can see a zoomed-out waveform of the entire clip. As you shuttle through the clip, a white outline in the zoomed-out waveform identifies the region of the clip currently visible in the viewer.

TIP: Press Shift-S to disable the audio scrubbing sound when you move the playhead.

3. Click anywhere in the zoomed-out waveform above the viewer.

When you click in the waveform overview at the top, the playhead jumps to that location, which allows you to quickly and accurately locate any point within an audio clip. Of course, you also can play audio clips using the same buttons and keyboard shortcuts that you use to play video clips.

Color Managing a Project

The clips you use in a project can come from a variety of cameras that may have different color and contrast characteristics. This is especially true of the content you have here which was shot with a Blackmagic Design digital film camera. Digital film cameras use a wider dynamic range than traditional video cameras, and if left as-is will have a flat, low-contrast appearance in the viewer.

To give all of your footage a more natural and consistent look while editing your project, you can unify the footage appearance using DaVinci Resolve's project color management system to select the appropriate color space for your clips and output display.

1. Select the Master bin, and click any clip icon in the bin to load that clip into the viewer.

The clip in the viewer wasn't recorded with low contrast, but the computer doesn't know how it was recorded and therefore assumes that it is a standard video file. You can apply the DaVinci Color Management system to ensure that every color from every source, at every workflow stage identifies the correct colorspace of the source, establishes a common colorspace in which to work, and coordinates all color differences to match the final viewing device. DaVinci Color Management takes the heavy lifting out of this color management pipeline.

2. Choose File > Project Settings.

The first step in setting up a color-managed project is to enable the type of color management you want.

3. In the Master Project Settings window, click the "Color science" pop-up menu to view its options.

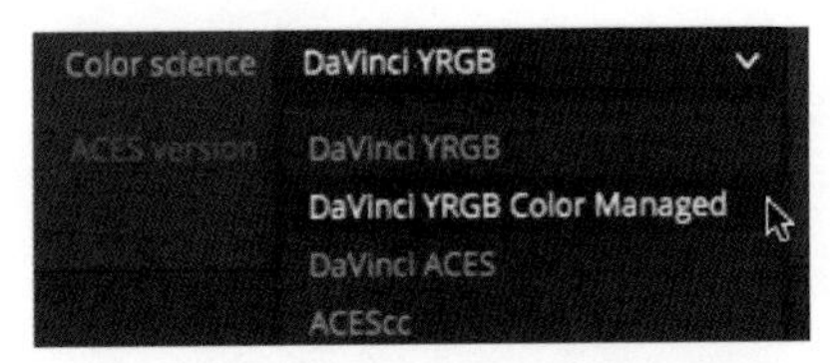

In the "Color science" pop-up menu, you can choose to apply either DaVinci's Color Management or ACES (Academy Color Encoding Specification).

> **NOTE:** As a general rule, use DaVinci Color Management. ACES is a good alternative but useful primarily when your production pipeline has prescribed an ACES workflow for final distribution on film.

4. Choose DaVinci YRGB Color Managed.

   The DaVinci YRGB Color Managed option allows you to set specific color space profiles for your source clips and your output destination.

5. Click Save to save the Color science setting, and close the Settings window.

   The default output color space is set to Rec 709 (the HDTV specification), but you still must assign the Input color space for your source clip.

> **NOTE:** You can change the output color space profile in the Color Management section of the Project Settings window.

6. Select all of the video clips in the Media Pool.

   All of these video clips came from the same camera, a Blackmagic Design Production Camera 4K, so they can all be set to the same color space profile.

7. Right-click (or Ctrl-click in OS X), and from the contextual menu, choose Input Color Space. Then select Blackmagic Design 4K Film.

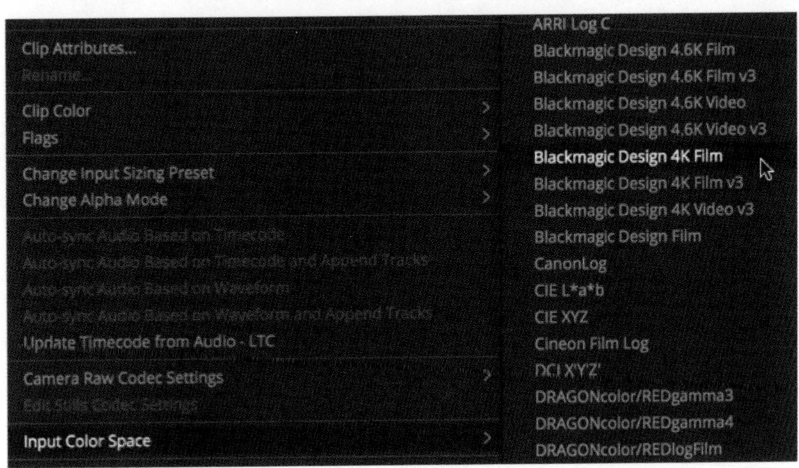

The viewer updates to reflect the new color space that you set in all the clips. You now have consistent, normalized images from which to begin editing. Remember, these clips are not color corrected. They are just set to a common color space baseline that you can build upon, which you will do in a later lesson.

Viewing Clip Metadata

Clips can contain more than just sound and images. Many cameras can add metadata, which is extra information about the clip such as the scene, shot, and take. Metadata can be useful when you're editing because it can help you better identify which clips you want to work with. This metadata includes all of the settings captured by the camera as well as any custom information you choose to add.

1. Select the Master bin and hover the mouse pointer over any clip icon.

   When you place the mouse pointer over an icon, a metadata badge appears in the lower-right corner.

2. Click the icon's metadata badge.

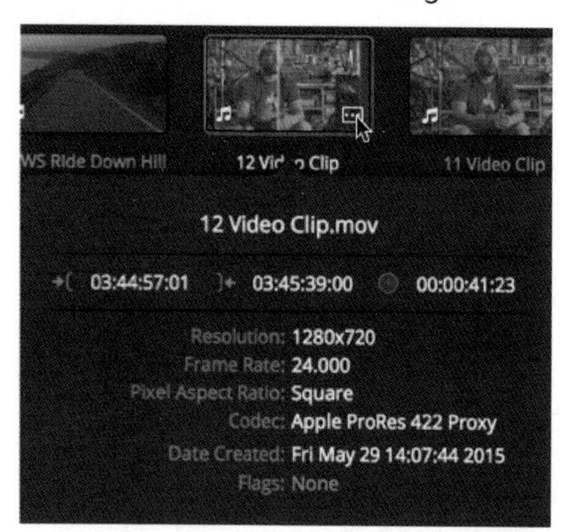

   A metadata pop-up displays basic information about the clip.

3. Press the Esc key to close the metadata pop-up display.

   You can view additional metadata by loading a clip into the viewer.

4. In the Master bin, click the same clip to load it into the viewer.

Detailed information about the selected clip is displayed in the Metadata editor in the lower-right corner of the Resolve window.

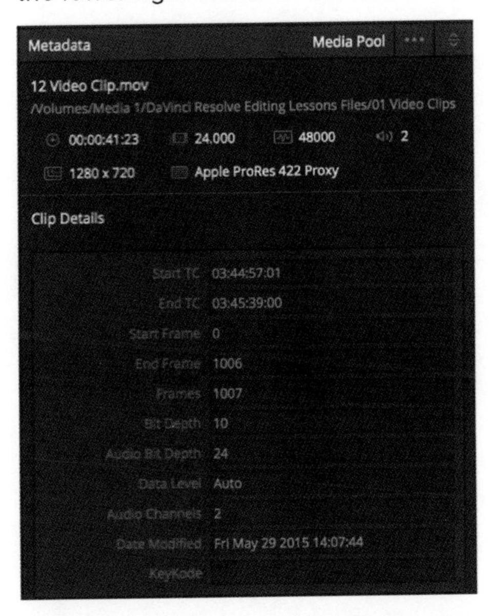

The upper section of the Metadata editor displays the clip name, the clip's location on your hard drive, frame size, frame rate, and other basic information. This upper section is always visible in the Metadata editor. The larger lower section shows clip details, but it can show additional custom information.

5. In the upper-right corner of the Metadata editor, from the pop-up menu, choose Shot Scene.

In the pop-up menu you can choose from multiple sets of metadata. Each set contains additional fields and checkboxes in which you can add custom information that may be helpful in organizing your clips. You'll notice that the Shot Scene group is empty. In the next exercise, you'll add some metadata to clips to make it easier to locate them.

Adding Custom Metadata

Standard metadata that is captured or created automatically by the camera is certainly helpful when organizing clips, but adding your own metadata is equally important. In most jobs you'll organize content by scenes. Because your camera knows nothing about scenes, you need to add that metadata. In the current project, you are dealing only with one scene, so adding that information is a not as important as adding information that identifies the different types of clips within the scene.

1. In the Master bin, select the **11 Video Clip** icon.

This is one of the three interview clips that you'll be using. It's a good idea to identify it as an interview clip, so let's add that information as a keyword.

2. In the Keyword field of the Metadata Editor, enter **interview**.

Two other interview clips could also use that "interview" keyword.

3. In the Master bin, select **12 Video Clip**, and attach the same keyword to it.
4. Locate the **13 Video Clip** in the bin and repeat the step. Be careful to spell the word correctly (or at least the same) in all three clips.

5. Choose File >Save Project, or press Cmd-S (OS X) or Ctrl-S (Windows) to save your work.

Now you have interview clips tagged with some important information about their content. You'll be able to use this information as you work with the clips in upcoming lessons. Next, you'll learn ways to view the metadata as you begin your edit on the Edit page.

2 Using Bins

Resolve uses four pages to roughly organize your workflow. In the first lesson, you used the Media page to import clips and add metadata. In the next nine lessons, you'll switch to the Edit page to organize your clips, assemble a timeline, and add effects.

In this lesson, you'll focus on organizing the clips that you imported. You can create custom bins, which are similar to folders, to group clips to your liking, or use the automated grouping capabilities found in Smart Bins to take advantage of metadata. Whichever method you choose, the goal is to help you quickly locate the clips you'll need when you begin to edit.

TIME

- **This lesson takes approximately 25 minutes to complete.**

GOALS

- **Explore the edit page**
- **Make new bins**
- **Create smart bins**
- **Rename bins**
- **Save custom bin views**
- **Change clip names**

Exploring the Edit Page

Media, Edit, Color, and Deliver—these four buttons near the bottom of the Resolve interface represent the four primary stages of a project workflow. Clicking one takes you to a page containing the specific tools and resources you need to complete that stage of your project.

Although while creating a project you may often bounce between pages as you work, each page helps to structure your workflow, and to organize the deep and powerful Resolve toolset into well-organized, accessible layouts. For this book, the primary page you will work in is the Edit page. So let's get a better overview of the Edit page layout.

1. Open the DaVinci Resolve Editing Project that you created in Lesson 1, if necessary; and then at the bottom of the Resolve window, click the Edit button to switch to the Edit page, or press Shift-4.

The Edit page has four primary sections focused on editing clips into a timeline.

The Media Pool contains all of the media in the current project organized into bins.

Source and Timeline Viewers show images for the selected source clips on the left and the timeline on the right.

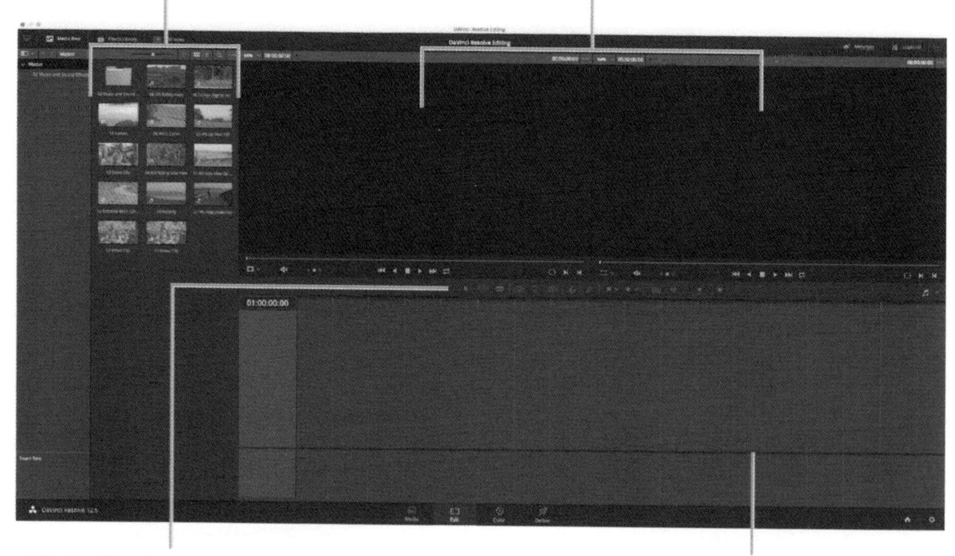

The toolbar buttons running along the top of the timeline let you choose various editing tools.

The timeline displays a graphical representation of your edited clips.

You can allocate more or less room to each panel of the Edit page by resizing them.

2. Place the mouse pointer under the Source Viewer's transport controls.

3. Drag down slightly to increase the size of the viewers and decrease the size of the timeline.
4. To increase the size of the browser, place the mouse pointer on the right edge of the browser, just before the source viewer and drag slightly to the right to provide more room for the clip icons in the bin.

5. To return to the default layout, choose Workspace > Layout > Reset UI Layout.

Making New Bins

For most of this lesson, you'll concentrate on the media pool and the bins created there. Bins are containers for all your clips. Although all the clips that you import will go into the default Master bin, relying entirely on a single bin results in a single overloaded, unwieldy bin of clips.

A better strategy is to create custom bins to categorize and organize your clips more specifically to make it easier for you to find them.

1. In the media pool, select the Master bin.

> **NOTE:** The Media Pool with all of its bins and clips is visible on both the Media and the Edit pages. The organization that you apply on one page is duplicated on the other page.

All of the video clips currently in the Master bin would be easier to work with (and faster to locate) if they were organized by content. For instance, you could place all of the scenic shots in a Scenic bin to distinguish them from the interview clips that you would place in an Interview bin.

2. To create a new bin, choose File > New Bin, or press Cmd-Shift-N (OS X) or Ctrl-Shift-N (Windows).

   A new bin with the default name Bin 1 is created and added to the media pool. Let's change the name to make it fit your project. The names of new bins are immediately available for editing.

3. Type **Headlands** as the name of the bin.

   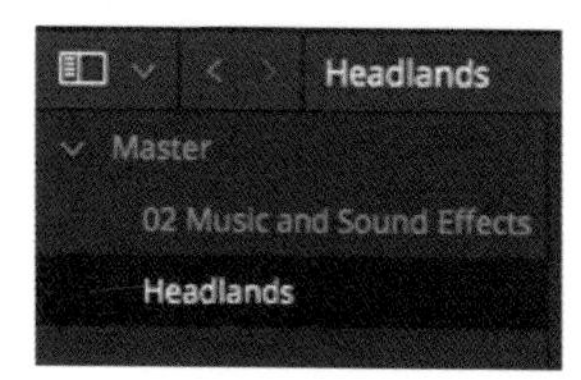

   All new bins you create appear inside the Master bin. With a new bin created and named to suit your project, you're ready to start organizing clips into bins.

4. Select the Master bin, and then click the first video clip thumbnail in the bin to select it.

   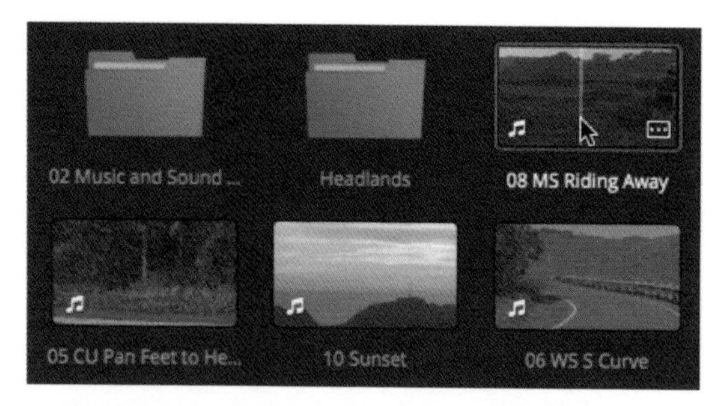

5. Hold down the Shift key and click the last video clip thumbnail in the Master bin.

All of the video clips in the bin are selected, as shown by a red selection outline. The 02 Music and Sound Effects bin and the new Headlands bin are not selected. To move only the scenic headlands clips into the Headlands bin, you need to deselect the three interview clip.

6. Cmd-click (OS X) or Ctrl-click (Windows) the three interview shots to deselect them.

> **NOTE:** Due to differences in display and window size, the order of clips in your bin may appear different from the figures shown in this lesson.

The remaining selected clips were shot in the Marin Headlands, so you will want to organize them into the Headlands bin.

7. Drag the selected clips onto the Headlands bin folder icon. When the Headlands bin icon highlights, release the mouse button.

8. In the Media Pool sidebar, click the Headlands bin to view its contents.

You've now successfully moved clips from one bin to another. Although the process is simple, it is also very labor intensive. But you have a more efficient way to organize clips that you'll explore next.

> **TIP:** To delete a bin, select it and press the Delete key. All of the clips in the bin will be removed from Resolve but remain unchanged on your hard drive.

Creating a Smart Bin

Smart Bins use metadata to automatically find and show your footage. For example, if you create a Smart Bin for the word "interview," that bin will automatically show you all of the project footage that has the word "interview" in its metadata. Best of all, a Smart Bin's content will continually update as new footage is added to your project. That means you don't have to manually organize footage when using metadata and Smart Bins.

1. Right-click in the sidebar area of the Media Pool under the words "Smart Bins."
2. From the contextual menu, choose Add Smart Bin.

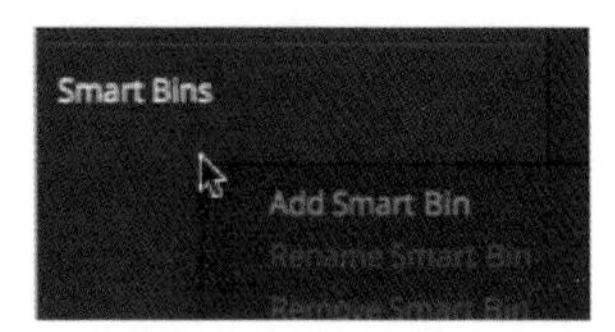

The Create Smart Bin dialog appears. In this dialog you set up the rules that determine which clips are automatically added to this Smart Bin. The criteria choices are many, enabling you to create smart bins that group all of the clips from specific camera types, file types, or timecode ranges; those containing specific keywords; and any combination of those criteria.

3. In the Create Smart Bin dialog, in the Name field, enter **Interview**.

4. In the Media Pool Properties menu, choose Shot & Scene because this is the metadata set that was in use when you entered the keyword.

5. Set the Shoot Description menu to "Keywords," and leave the final Menu set to "contains".

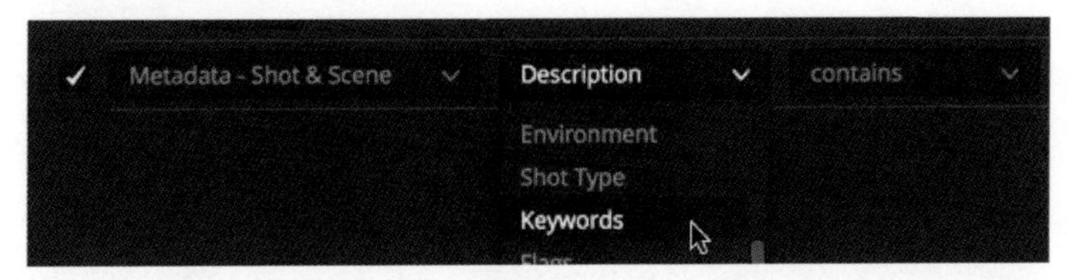

6. In the text entry field, type **interview**, and click Create Smart Bin.

> **NOTE:** The Smart Bin search is not case sensitive, so as long as you spell the keyword in the same way, the Smart Bin will find all instances of that metadata.

The Smart Bin appears at the bottom of the Media Pool and updates to include all clips that contain the keyword "interview." In the future, when you add the "interview" keyword to new clips in this project, those clips are automatically added to the Interview Smart Bin. That's the beauty of the Smart Bin. It collects clips based on whatever criteria you identify and continually keeps your clip organization updated.

Renaming Bins

Whether it's a Smart Bin or a bin that you created manually, you can change a bin's name at any time. The process is different for the two bin types, so let's first learn how to rename a standard bin.

1. In the media pool, select the Headlands bin.
2. After pausing for a second, click the name again.

After the second click, the name is ready for renaming.

3. Type **B-Roll** as the new bin name, and press Return (OS X) or Enter (Windows) to change the name.

You can change the name of a smart bin in the same dialog in which you set the criteria.

4. Double-click the Interview Smart Bin to open the Edit Smart Bin dialog.

In this dialog you can change the Smart Bin's name as well as update the criteria used to place clips in the Smart Bin. To change the bin name, you activate the Name field for editing and then type the new name. However, this Smart Bin doesn't require renaming, so let's leave the dialog without making any changes.

5. Click the Cancel button to close the dialog without making changes.

> **TIP:** You can also rename a bin by right-clicking the bin's name, and from the contextual menu, choosing Rename Bin.

In a larger project you will certainly have more than just a few bins of clips, so give the naming and organization of your bins and clips some advance thought. Making sure that you name bins in a clear and descriptive way sets the foundation for your clip organization. Will you organize them based on scene numbers, content type, or camera? Defining an organizational strategy ahead of time—and making sure that your co-workers understand those naming conventions—can support a much smoother workflow throughout the edit room.

Saving Custom Bin Views

The Edit page also provides you with a Metadata Editor, and can display the metadata for all of your clips using a List view in the bins.

1. Select the B-Roll bin.
2. At the top of the bin, click the List view button.

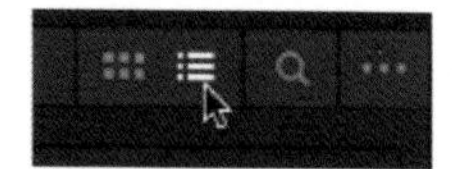

The bin switches from showing the clips as icons to showing clips in a text list.

3. To provide the List view with more room, click the Show sidebar button to hide the sidebar.

List view displays the same metadata that you could view in the Metadata Editor. Each bit of information is listed in a column for every clip in the bin.

4. Drag the scroll bar at the bottom of the Media Pool to scroll the List view to the right until you see the Audio Ch column.

In every project, some of the columns in List view will be more important than others. To ensure that you can see the information you need most, you can move columns so they are prioritized in the order you want.

5. Drag the Audio Ch heading to the left edge of the bin until the bin begins to scroll.

6. When your mouse pointer is between the File Name and Reel Name columns, release the mouse button.

The Audio Ch column is now positioned between the File Name and Reel Name columns.

You can also sort columns, and therefore the clips, based on the information found in a column.

7. Click the heading for Start TC so the small arrow next to the name points up.

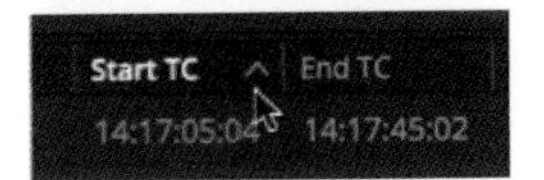

Clicking the heading for any column sorts that column based on its criterion. Clicking the Start TC heading sorts the bin contents in ascending order based on the starting timecode number for each clip. A small arrow pointing up is shown next to the column heading name to indicate that this column is used for sorting as well as indicating the order of the sort.

> **NOTE:** Icon view sorts clips based on the sort order that you select in List view. The first clip in the List view is placed as the first clip on the left in Icon view. Clip icons are then arranged left to right and top to bottom based on the List view order.

You can also choose which columns to show and hide for all your bins by selecting them from a list.

8. Ctrl-click (OS X) or Right-click (Windows) any column heading to display the bin headings, contextual menu.

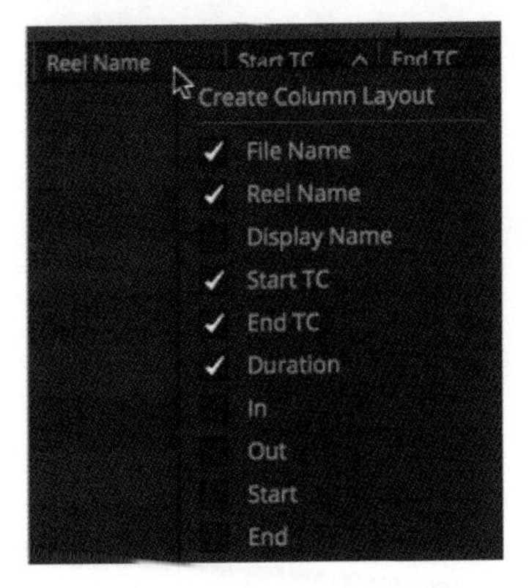

The contextual menu lists all of the columns that you can display in a bin. The headings with a check mark are the currently displayed columns.

9. From the contextual menu, choose File Name, Reel Name, Frames, Type, File Path, Format, Codec and Flags to uncheck and hide all of those columns in the bin.
10. To add a column, right-click over the headings area, and from the bin headings contextual menu, choose Display Name.

    The columns you unchecked are removed and the Display Name is added to the bin's List view. You can now use the Display Name column to rename clips.

    After making these changes, you have a nice slimmed-down number of columns that shows you only the essential information you might want to see. You can save as many different bin views as you want and recall them from the menu at a later time. To save a bin view you can use the same contextual menu.
11. Ctrl click (OS X) or Right-click (Windows) one of the bin column headings, and from the contextual menu, choose Create Column Layout.

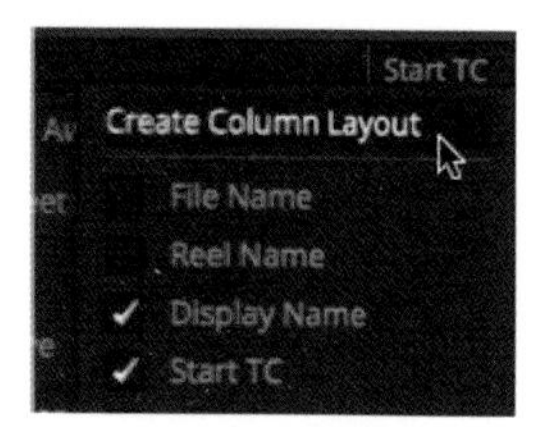

12. Type **Basic View** as the Column Layout name, and click OK.

You now have a bin with all of the desired columns displayed. In the next exercise you'll use the Display Name column to change the names of a few clips.

Changing Clip Names

Although most of the file names for the clips you are using are clear and descriptive, the default filenames produced by most cameras are often cryptic. Resolve lets you create custom names, called *Display Names*, that are used throughout the software while you're editing and grading. The Display Name column displays the original filename by default, but you can also use it to rename your clips in Resolve to something more descriptive. (Don't worry, changing the Display Name does not change the filename on your hard disk.)

1. At the top of the bin, click the Show sidebar button to display your bins.

2. Select the Interview Smart Bin, and in the List view, double-click **11 Video Clip** to load it into the source viewer.

The first clip is shown in the Source Viewer and a filmstrip of the clip is displayed at the top of the bin. Let's keep the shot number and replace the clip name with the name of the person being interviewed.

3. Click the first clip's Display Name, and in the Display Name field, type **11 Sasha G**, the name of the interview subject.

4. Double-click the second clip in the List view to load it into the Source Viewer.

   You can scrub through the filmstrip at the top of the List view to quickly review a clip's contents.

5. Move your mouse pointer back and forth over the filmstrip to see more of the clip in the Source Viewer.

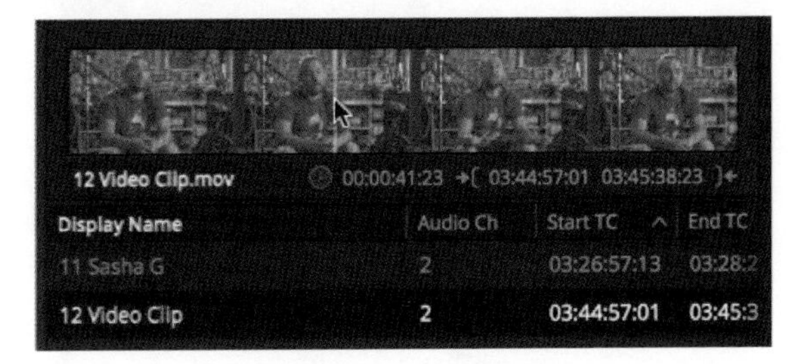

This clip is a similar angle of the interview. You should give it a similar name to describe its contents.

6. Click the second clip's Display Name, and type **12 Sasha G**.

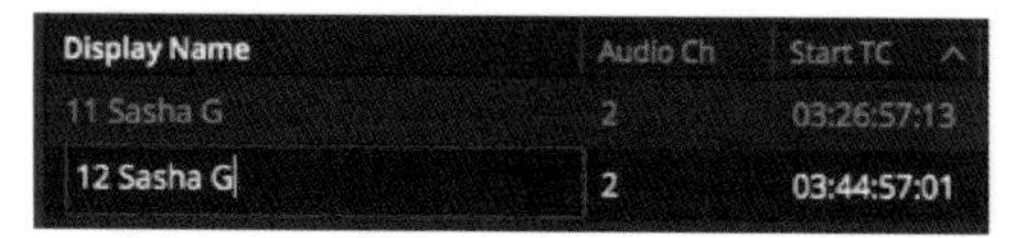

Let's add a name and number to the remaining clip in the Interview bin.

7. For the remaining clip in the Interview bin, enter **13 Sasha G Side View** to differentiate it from the first two interview clips.

8. To make sure the Display Names are used throughout Resolve, choose View > Show Display Names.
9. Choose File > Save Project to save your work

You have now set up all the bins and are ready to begin editing your interview. In the next lesson, you'll use the bins and clips that you've organized to create a short interview scene using the Edit page and its functionality.

3 Marking and Assembling Clips

With your content imported and organized, you are ready to start editing. The goal of this lesson is to teach you how to assemble your clips into a timeline, and how to do it quickly. DaVinci Resolve is designed to help you realize that goal through a variety of editing functions and customizable keyboard short cuts.

The first step is to create a rough cut, which is an assembly of the clips on your timeline in the basic order you want them to appear. Once you have the beginning of your timeline in place, you'll explore some of the specialty editing functions in Resolve that can help you be more creative as you develop your story.

TIME

- **This lesson takes approximately 40 minutes to complete.**

GOALS

- **Mark clips**
- **Create a timeline**
- **Make the first edits**
- **Drag clips to the timeline**
- **Use the toolbar edit buttons**
- **Cut in video only**
- **Perform a split edit**
- **Backtime a three-point edit**

Marking Clips

A large part of the editing process is selecting your shots. Not only are you selecting which clips to include in your project, but you are also selecting the range to include within each clip. You identify that range within a clip by setting starting and ending points with *In* and *Out markers*.

1. Open the editing project you created in Lesson 1, and click the sidebar button to view the contents of your hard drives.

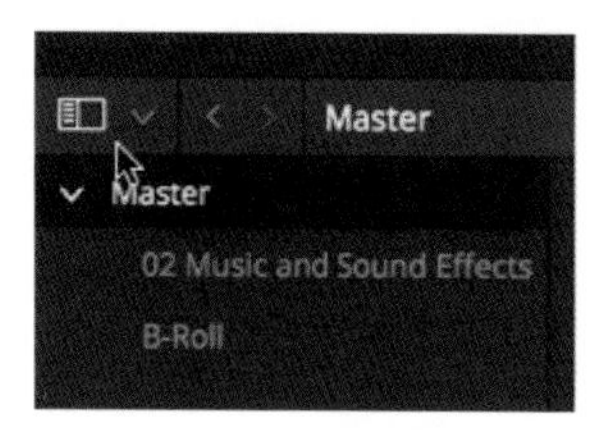

2. At the bottom of the sidebar, select the Interview smart bin.
3. Click the Icon View button to display the icons for the three interview clips.

4. In the bin, select the **11 Sasha G** clip, and press Return (OS X) or Enter (Windows) to load the clip into the source viewer.
5. Press the Spacebar to play the clip.
6. Press the Spacebar to stop clip playback when you hear the interview subject say, "So, bicycles have stories to tell."
7. Press the Left and Right Arrow keys to nudge the position of the playhead to just before the word, "so."
8. Under the Source Viewer, click the Mark In button, or press the I key to create an In point.

NOTE: If you don't mark any points in the source viewer, the entire clip will be used in the edit.

9. After marking an In point, play the clip for roughly 10 more seconds until the man says, "Some of them have lots of miles left to travel." Then press the Spacebar to stop playback.

10. Click the Mark Out button under the source viewer, or press the O key to create an Out point.

> **TIP:** You can press Option-I (OS X) or Alt-I (Windows) to clear an In point; press Option-O (OS X) or Alt-O (Windows) to clear an Out point; and press Option-X (OS X) or Alt-X (Windows) to clear both the In and Out points.

A clip can contain only one set of In and Out points, but you can mark as many clips as you like without losing the In and Out points that you've placed in other clips.

11. In the bin, select the **13 Sasha G Side View** clip, and press Return or Enter to load the clip into the source viewer.

12. Play the clip until you hear the subject say, "Each bike is slightly different."
13. Press the Left and Right Arrow keys to position the playhead just before the words, "Each bike."
14. Click the Mark In button, or press I to mark an In point.
15. Play the clip for roughly 20 more seconds until the man says, "It's a reflection of the person themselves." Then press the Spacebar to stop playback.
16. Click the Mark Out button, or press O to place an Out point.

    Even though you have marked a second clip, the first clip retains the In and Out points that you set previously.

17. Double-click the **11 Sasha G**. clip in the bin to load it into the source viewer.

The first clip loads back into the Source Viewer with the In and Out points exactly where you set them. Marking clip ranges before you edit them can be helpful when you are working with a producer or director. (It allows them to pick the clip ranges they particularly like without micro-managing your entire editing process.) With the clips marked, you can begin editing them into a timeline.

Creating a Timeline

Before you can start editing, you must create a timeline into which you place clips in the order that you want to show them. Resolve projects can contain one or more edited timelines that you save into the Master bin. However, as you experiment with multiple versions of your timeline, it can be helpful to keep them together in their own bin. This can make it easier to go back and compare them or locate the exact cut you want.

1. In the Media Pool sidebar, select the Master bin, and choose File > New Bin to create a new bin within the Master bin.
2. Name the new bin **Rough Cuts**, and press Return or Enter.
3. With the Rough Cuts bin selected, choose File > New Timeline, or press Cmd-N (OS X) or Ctrl-N (Windows).

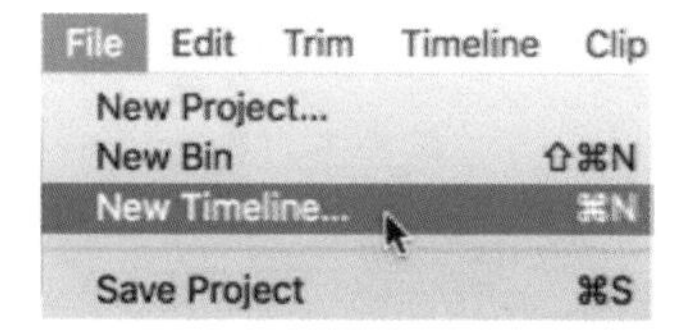

When the New Timeline dialog appears, you can give the timeline a new name.

4. Name the timeline **First Rough Cut**, and click Create New Timeline.

An empty timeline is added to the timeline editor and an icon for that timeline is added to the Rough Cuts bin. You are now ready to add clips to your timeline.

Making the First Edits

The first edit you make is often the easiest because nothing is in the timeline to obstruct it. You've already marked the In and Out points for two interview clips, so all you have to do is edit them into the timeline. For the first two cuts, you'll use the edit overlay to perform an *Append edit*. The edit overlay provides the simplest way to see all of the editing types that you can use in Resolve

1. With the **11 Sasha G.** clip still visible in the Source Viewer, drag it from the Source Viewer into the Timeline Viewer but do not yet release the mouse button.

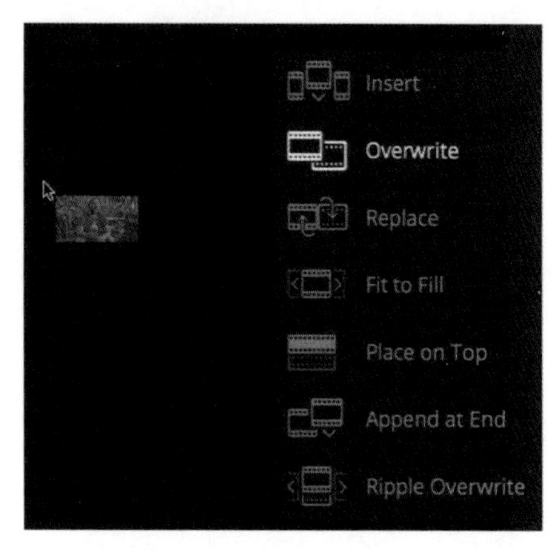

The edit overlay appears in the Timeline Viewer, displaying seven edit functions from which to choose:

- **Overwrite**: Replaces a clip (or part of a clip) in your timeline using the new clip.
- **Insert**: Embeds a new clip in the timeline by splitting existing clips.
- **Replace**: Substitutes a clip in the timeline with a new clip.
- **Fit to Fill**: Changes the speed of a clip to fit a specified length.
- **Place on Top**: Positions one clip on top of another for blending or composting.
- **Ripple Overwrite**: A hybrid replace/insert edit
- **Append at End**: Adds new clips after the last clip in the timeline.

An Append At End edit is a common edit to use when first assembling clips because it always adds the new clip to the end of the last clip in the timeline. That's how you'll use it here to start off your timeline with two clips.

2. In the edit overlay, position the mouse pointer over Append at End, and release the mouse button.

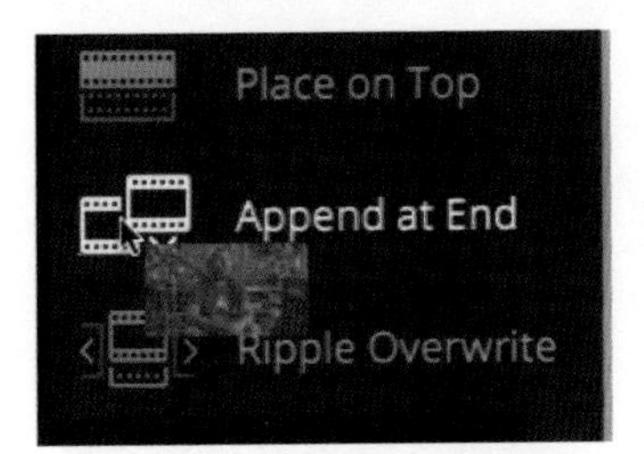

A video and audio segment is added to the timeline consisting of the In and Out range that you marked.

The timeline displays an orange vertical bar to represent the playhead. The playhead's location in the timeline corresponds to the current frame displayed in the Timeline Viewer. After you make an edit, the playhead is placed at the end of the newly added clip.

3. Drag the playhead to the beginning of the timeline.

Dragging in the Timeline Ruler causes the playhead to move in a manner similar to dragging in the jog bar under the Source and Timeline Viewers.

4. Press the Spacebar to play the timeline.

   The timeline plays the clip and stops playback when the clip ends. When you are working on a larger timeline, it's very helpful to know when the playhead reaches the actual end of the timeline and not one or two frames shy of the end. To help with this, a jagged overlay indicator appears on the right side of the frame when the playhead is at the end of the timeline.

   This overlay indicates that the playhead is on the last frame in the timeline. This is where you will want to append a new clip.

> **NOTE:** Positioning the playhead at the start of the timeline displays an overlay that has a straight edge instead of a jagged one.

5. Select the Interview Smart Bin, and load the **13 Sasha G Side View** clip into the Source Viewer.
6. Drag the clip from the Source Viewer into the Timeline Viewer, and from the edit overlay, choose Append at End.

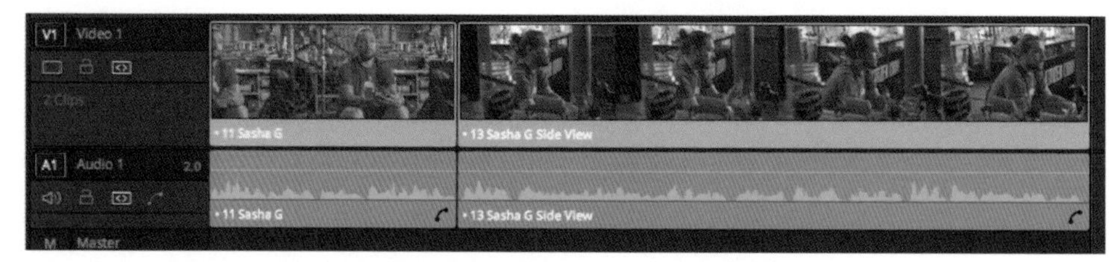

   The new clip is added to the end of the clip in the timeline.

   To play your timeline, you want to move the playhead back to the start. Rather than requiring you to drag the playhead to that location, Resolve provides handy keyboard shortcuts to jump to the start or end of the timeline.

7. Press the Home key to move the playhead to the start of the timeline.

> **TIP:** Some Apple Mac keyboards do not have Home and End keys. In that case, press Fn-Left Arrow to move to the start of the timeline and Fn-Right Arrow to move to the end.

8. Press the Spacebar to play the timeline to its end.

Marking clips, positioning the playhead, cutting in clips, and playing the results are the fundamental steps in editing a timeline together. However, Resolve does provide other methods of cutting clips into a timeline that you'll sometimes find more expedient.

Dragging Clips to the Timeline

When you want to add a series of clips to the timeline, one right after the other, you can do so quickly by dragging them into the timeline as a group.

1. Select the B-Roll bin.
2. Double-click the last clip in the bin, **10 sunset**, to load it into the Source Viewer.

To mark the In and Out points, you'll reference the precise timecode numbers that are displayed above the source viewer.

> **NOTE:** Timecode numbers are displayed above the source and timeline viewer in hours, minutes, seconds, and frames. Each time segment is represented by two digits separated by either a colon or semi color (such as HH:MM:SS:FF or 01:00:00:00)

The timecode number to the left of the viewer shows the duration of the In to Out points. When no marks are present, it displays the total duration of the clip.

The timecode number to the right side of the viewer displays the current playhead position.

To jump to a specific timecode, you can click the viewer that you want to work in, and then type the timecode's hour, minute, second, and frame values.

> **TIP:** When typing timecode numbers, you can use a period to quickly add a pair of zeroes. That is, typing 010203. places the playhead at timecode 01:02:03.00.

3. Click in the Source Viewer to activate it.

   The file name above the viewer appears in red when the viewer is active.

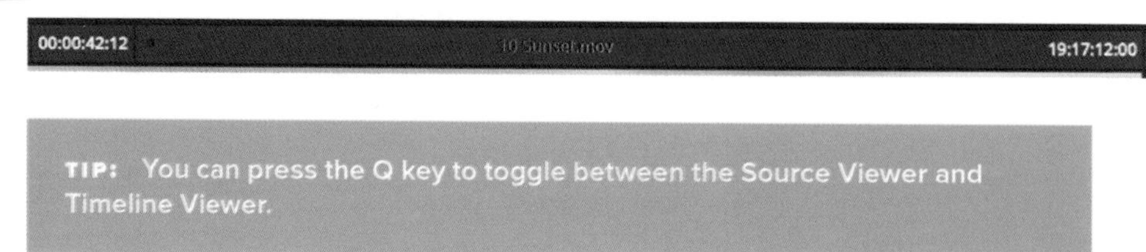

> **TIP:** You can press the Q key to toggle between the Source Viewer and Timeline Viewer.

4. Type **191720.** (period), and then press Return or Enter to move the playhead to 19:17:20:00. This frame is where you'll place the In point.

5. Press I to mark an In point.

   Now you'll mark an Out point, but instead of typing an exact timecode, you'll type the number of seconds forward that you want the playhead to move.

6. Type **+5**, and then type **.** (period). Press Return or Enter.

The playhead jumps forward five seconds. This is the location for your Out point.

> **TIP:** When using a keyboard without a number pad, press Shift-= (equals sign) to enter a + (plus sign).

7. Press O to mark an Out point.

> **TIP:** You can press the – (minus) key to move the playhead backward.

For the next two clips—**09 MS Parking** and the third to last clip, **08 MS Riding Away**—you'll use the timecode values listed below to mark In and Out points.

8. Load the **09 MS Parking** clip into the source viewer.
9. Type **190939.** (period) to mark your In point. Then move the playhead forward four seconds and mark an Out point.

10. Load the **08 MS Riding Away** clip into the Source Viewer.
11. Type **18265210** and press Return or Enter to mark your In point. Then move the playhead forward three seconds and mark an Out point.

With all three clips marked, you can now add them to the timeline. Instead of adding each one individually, you can select all three and drag them into place.

12. Select the last clip in the bin (**10 Sunset**), and then Shift-click the third to last clip in the bin (**08 MS Riding Away**) to select all three clips.

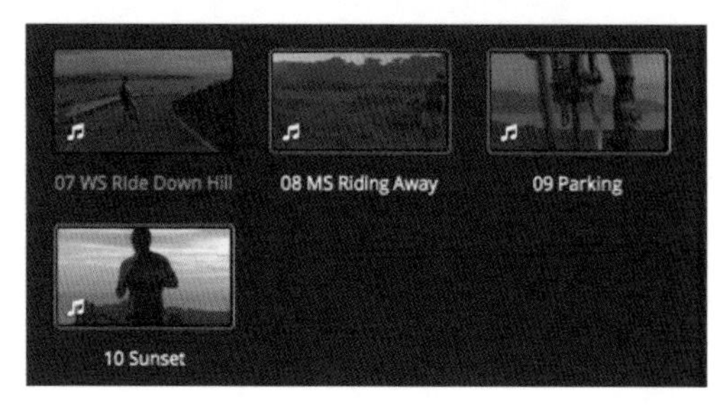

The three clips are outlined in red to indicate that they are selected.

13. Drag the clips from the bin to the end of the last clip in the timeline, and release the mouse button.

> **TIP:** When the mouse pointer is close to the end of the timeline, it will snap into place.

With the clips edited into the timeline, you can back up and play the timeline to review your results.

14. In the timeline ruler, click just before the three clips that you added, and press the Spacebar to play the timeline.

You now have two techniques for editing clips into a timeline. But there is another way that may be the fastest method yet.

Using the Toolbar Edit Buttons

Resolve offers more editing options than just dragging clips into the timeline or onto the edit overlay. The toolbar located under the Source Timeline Viewers provides three buttons that enable the most common editing types: *Overwrite*, *Insert*, and *Replace*. Let's edit a couple of clips into your timeline using the toolbar's insert edit function.

1. Double-click the sixth clip in the B-Roll bin, **06 WS S Curve**, to load it into the Source Viewer.

2. Type **172115.** (period), and press Return or Enter to mark your In point.
3. Move the playhead forward five seconds, and mark an Out point.

   Let's place this clip between the last interview shot and the first scenic bike riding shot. To do so you'll position the timeline's playhead between those two clips. You can click the Previous Edit and Next Edit buttons to move the playhead forward or backward to the edit you want. The location of the playhead determines where the source clip will be edited into the timeline.

4. If your playhead is still at the end of the timeline (from the previous exercise), click in the Timeline Viewer to activate it, and then press the Up Arrow to move from edit point to edit point until the playhead is between the last interview shot and the first bike riding shot in the timeline.

   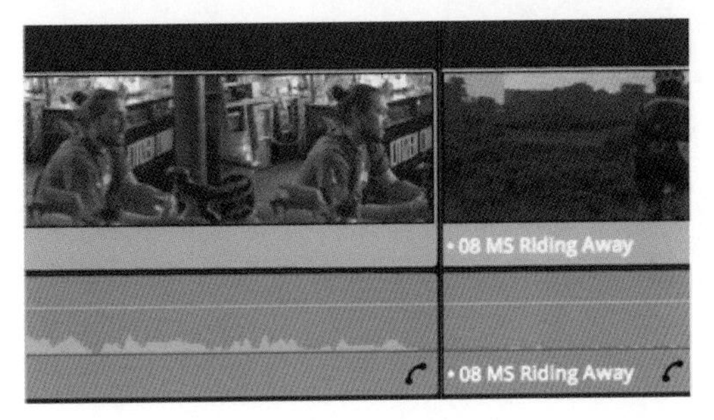

   The Timeline Viewer shows the first frame of the bike riding clip. By clicking the Up Arrow key (Go to previous edit) and Down Arrow key (Go to next edit), you ensure that the playhead is positioned exactly on the first frame of the upcoming clip, perfect for cutting in a new shot.

5. In the toolbar, click the Insert button, or press the F9 key.

> **TIP:** You can remap keyboard functions using the Keyboard Mapping section in the Project Settings window.

The Insert edit splits the timeline clip at the playhead position and places the new clip at that point in the timeline. The overall duration of your timeline is now longer by the duration of the newly added clip. Let's perform another Insert edit using another source clip.

6. From the B-roll bin, drag the **03 Up Over Hill** clip into the Source Viewer. Type **162937.** (period), and press Return or Enter. Press I to mark your In point.
7. Move the playhead forward four seconds and mark your Out point.

Next, you will position the playhead where you want to insert the clip, and then use the Insert button to edit the clip.

8. Click the Previous Edit button, or press Up Arrow, to place the playhead in the timeline between the last interview shot and the **06 WS S Curve** shot.
9. In the toolbar, click the Insert button.

Again the Insert Edit splits the clip at the playhead position, inserts the new clip, and pushes the remaining clip to the right.

Cutting Video Only

The Overwrite editing function is another commonly used edit you'll employ often throughout a project. It can be found in the edit overlay and in the toolbar. You'll use it here to overwrite a portion of a clip in the timeline.

1. Double-click the first clip in the B-Roll bin, **01 WS Side View GG Bridge**, to load it into the Source Viewer.

2. Type **141716.** (period), and press Return or Enter. Then press I to mark an In point.
3. Move the playhead forward three seconds, and mark your Out point.

   You'll overwrite this clip to cover up a three-second portion of the second interview shot. But you don't want to overwrite the audio. You want to continue to hear the voice of the interview subject while viewing this bridge shot. This is often called a *cut-away* because the clip temporarily cuts away from the main action.
4. Click in the Timeline Viewer to activate the timeline, and then click the Previous Edit button, or press the Up Arrow, until the playhead is located between the first two clips in the timeline.

   The Timeline Viewer shows the first frame of the second clip.

   The timeline has destination controls that display which video and audio tracks from the source clip are edited into the timeline. By default, the destination controls are enabled in both the V1 and A1 source tracks, as indicated by the orange outline around the track number.

5. Click the A1 destination control to disable it.

The deselected control displays no outline when it is disabled. Any audio source material on A1 will not be edited into the timeline.

6. In the toolbar, click the Overwrite button, or press F10.

Only the video content of the clip is edited into the timeline. Using the Overwrite edit caused a three-second section of the second interview clip to be covered up by the new clip. The audio from the interview, however, remains and can be heard even when the cut-away plays.

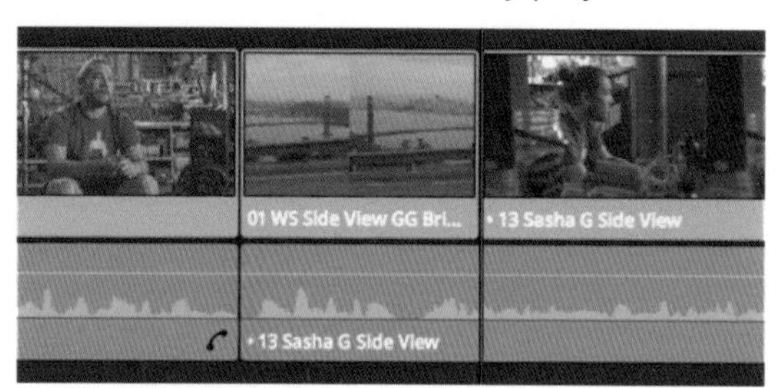

7. Press the Home key to position the playhead at the start of the timeline.
8. Press the Spacebar to play the timeline to the end of the second interview shot.

   Using an Overwrite edit is the most common method for making video-only cut-aways, but it's not the only method. Resolve can layer video tracks on top of one another. This feature comes in handy when creating effects, but it can also be used to create a simple cut-away.

9. In the B-Roll bin, double-click the **07 WS Ride Down Hill** clip to load it into the Source Viewer.

10. Type **175749.** (period), and press Return or Enter. Press I to mark an In point.
11. Move the playhead forward four seconds, and mark an Out point.

    For this cut-away, you'll perform an edit similar to an Overwrite edit by using the Place on Top editing function. The source clip will cover up (overwrite) the middle of the **13 Sasha G Side View** clip using a second video track.
12. In the Timeline Ruler, drag the playhead to the point where the interviewee says, "It's just very interesting to me."

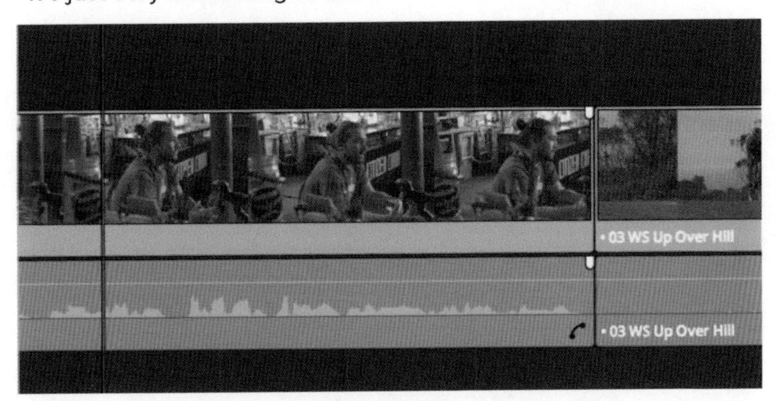

13. Because you want to use only the video from the source clip, make sure that the A1 destination control in the timeline is still disabled.
14. Drag the clip from the Source Viewer over the Timeline Viewer and move the mouse pointer over "Place on Top" to highlight it.

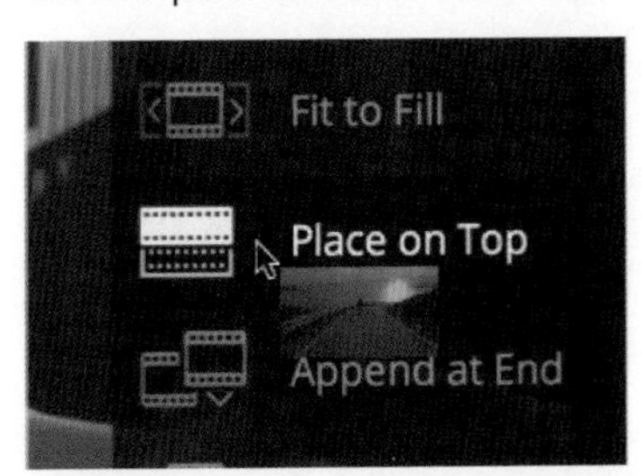

15. Release the mouse button to perform the Place On Top edit.

16. Drag the playhead to the start of the second interview shot in the timeline, and play the timeline to review the new cut-away you just added.

    A place on top edit automatically places the source clip onto the first empty track above the clips in the timeline, starting at the point of the playhead. It makes it easy to superimpose titles and other clips that you may want to composite over another clip. In this case, you used it to create a simple cut-away.

Performing a Split Edit

You have one more interview clip to add to the timeline. This clip will be placed after the second interview clip, so you'll position the playhead there.

1. With the timeline active, click the Next Edit button, or press the Down Arrow, until the playhead is located at the first frame of the **03 WS Up Over Hill** shot.

   Now find the clip you want to use in the Interview bin.

2. At the bottom of the Media Pool sidebar, select the Interview smart bin.
3. Load the **12 Sasha G** clip into the Source Viewer.
4. Drag the playhead under the Source Viewer to locate the man saying, "I've thought about it before." This point is located somewhere around 03:45:12:00.
5. Mark an In point just before the man says, "I've thought about it."

   You are about to do something special with this Out point. After this interview clip, you'll transition to all the bike-riding shots that you added earlier. To make a smoother transition between the two distinct types of footage, you'll continue to play the audio from the interview as the first bike-riding shot plays onscreen. To do this, you'll place two Out points, one for the video and one for the audio, thereby performing what is known as a *Split* edit.

6. Press the Spacebar to play the clip until the man says, "But you know after it's been proven in practice," stopping at around 03:45:28:00.

   This is where you want the video to cut to the bike-riding shots.

7. Under the Source Viewer, right-click the playhead.

8. From the contextual menu, choose Mark Split > Video Out.

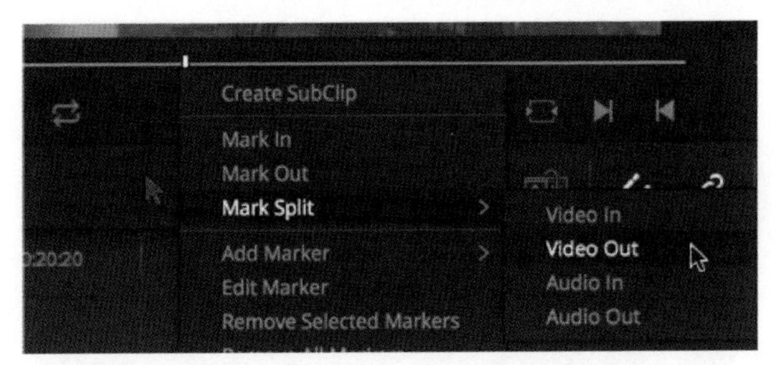

When you set the video Out point using the pop-up menu, the jog bar displays a double line. The upper blue line indicates the video Out point, and the bottom green bar indicates the audio Out point.

9. Press the Spacebar to begin playback, and stop when the man says, “The most wonderful machine in the world, I think.” This is where you’ll want to end the audio.
10. Right-click the playhead under the Source Viewer.
11. From the contextual menu, choose Mark Split > Audio Out.

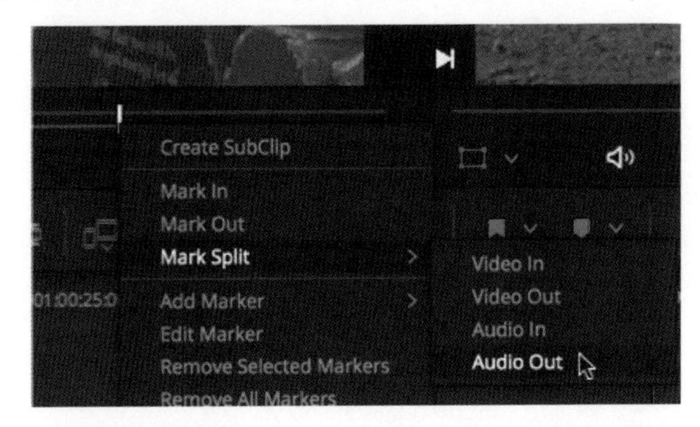

With the In point and two Out points set, you are ready to edit in the clip.

12. Click the A1 destination control to enable it, if necessary.

13. In the toolbar, click the Insert Edit button, or press F9.

Now let’s review your edit.

14. Drag the playhead just before the third interview clip in the timeline, and press the Spacebar to play through it. Stop playback when you see the bicyclist coming up over the hill.

You still have a little bit of cleanup to do. Currently you have no video playing during the extended audio from the last interview. In the next exercise, you'll fill in that gap using your last bike riding shot.

Backtiming a Three-Point Edit

After inserting your split edit, all of the biking clips were pushed to the right, leaving a big gap that you need to fill with video. It's a unique situation because you know exactly how long the source clip has to be: it needs to match the length of the gap. To fill it, you'll use a *Three-point edit*. Actually, you've been using Three-point edits throughout this lesson by marking an In point and Out point on your source clips and using the timeline's playhead as an In point. This time, you'll mark an In point and an Out point around the gap in the timeline and use a single mark on the source clip to make your edit.

1. In the timeline, click the A1 destination control to disable it. You want to edit in only the video from your source clip.

2. In the timeline, drag the playhead to the middle of the gap.

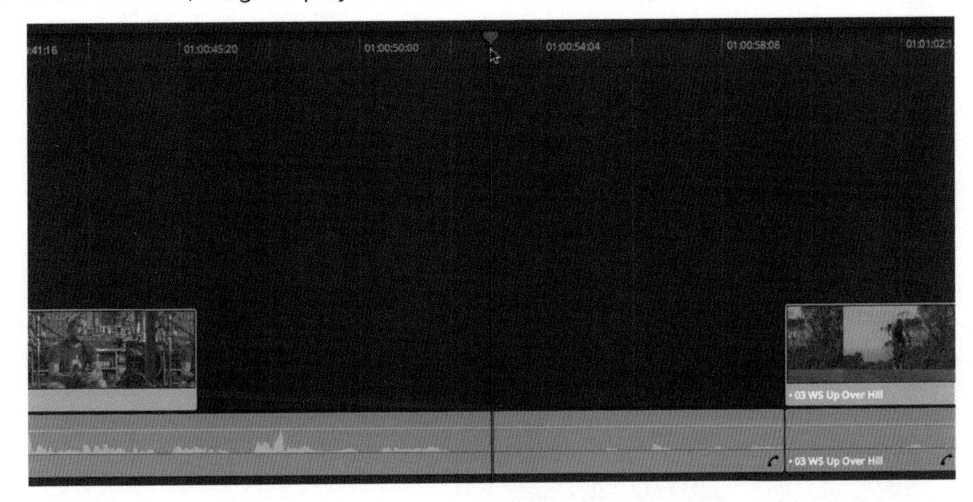

You are interested only in the duration of the gap on the video track, so you must disable the timeline's audio track. To disable tracks in the timeline for operations such as copying, deleting, or automatically marking a region, you disable the Auto Select button to disable and exclude all tracks that you don't want to involve in the operation.

3. On track A1, click the Auto Select button to disable selection on that track.

4. Choose Mark > Mark Clip, or press X, to mark the clip.

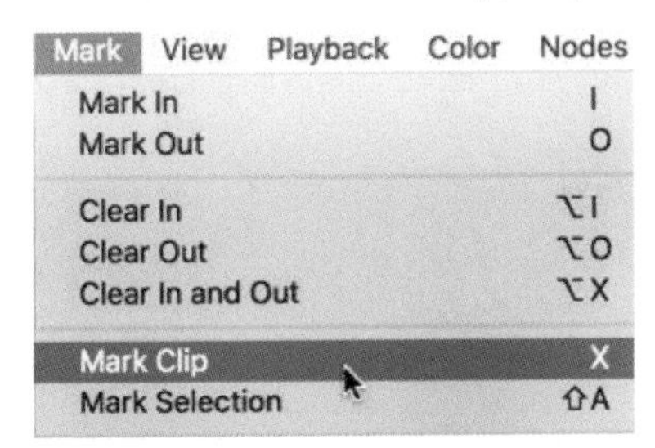

Mark Clip places In and Out points based on the start and end locations of a clip or a gap in the timeline. With In and Out points placed in your timeline and an Out point located on your source clip, you are ready to edit the clip into the timeline.

5. In the Media Pool sidebar, select the B-Roll bin.
6. Load the **05 CU Pan Feet to Head** clip into the Source Viewer.

   This clip is mostly a shot of the pedaling bicyclist that pans up toward his face at the end of the clip. You aren't interested in using the pan up to the face, so that makes it easier to know exactly where you need to end this clip.

7. Type **170433.** (period), and press Return or Enter. Then press O to mark an Out point.

   This locates almost the last second of pedaling before the camera begins to pan up, so it is a perfect location for your Out point. In this case, you won't need to set an In point. Almost all of the source clip before your Out point is of the same pedaling feet, so it's almost arbitrary where it begins. You can, however, preview where the In point will be if you are curious about it

8. At the bottom of the View menu, choose Show Preview Marks.

   With preview marks turned on, you can see an artificial In point, a *preview mark* (sometimes called a *phantom mark*). It is placed there to help you visualize where the In point will be when you add this clip based on the marks in the timeline.

9. Under the Source Viewer, drag the playhead to the preview mark.

   Dragging to the preview mark allows you to double-check where the input will be. This point looks perfectly fine for this edit.

10. In the toolbar, click the Overwrite button, or press F10.

    The video from the source clip fully fills in the gap. The starting point for your source clip is automatically calculated based on the duration that you set using the Mark Clip operation.

11. On A1, click the Auto Select button to enable selection on the track.

12. Choose View > Show Preview Marks to hide the preview marks.

13. Drag the timeline playhead to the middle of the third interview clip, and press the Spacebar to review your three-point edit, which in this context is also called a *Back-timed edit*.

Whether the clip shows someone crossing the finish line or scoring a goal, when the start of the clip is less important and the ending of the clip is critical, using the Out point instead of an In point to make a Back-timed edit comes in very handy.

4 Working in the Timeline

Most of your editing time will be spent in the timeline, which is much more than a graphical representation of your edits. Once you start putting together a project, the timeline quickly becomes the hub of all activity. You zoom up and down it, move segments around in it, split clips in half, and delete segments from it. Knowing how to manipulate the objects in your timeline will make you a more capable editor. In this lesson, we'll look at some of the timeline tools and techniques that you'll use on a daily basis.

TIME

- **This lesson takes approximately 25 minutes to complete.**

GOALS

- **Navigate the timeline**
- **Move clips in the timeline**
- **Perform a Ripple Overwrite edit**
- **Swap clip positions**
- **Delete clips from the timeline**
- **Split clips**

Navigating the Timeline

Before you can begin modifying clips in the timeline, you must know how to move around within the timeline.

1. To zoom in on an area of the timeline, drag the toolbar's Zoom slider to the right.

2. When the timeline is zoomed in, you can display the start of the timeline by dragging the scroll bar below the timeline view all the way to the left, or press the middle mouse button and drag right in the Timeline window.

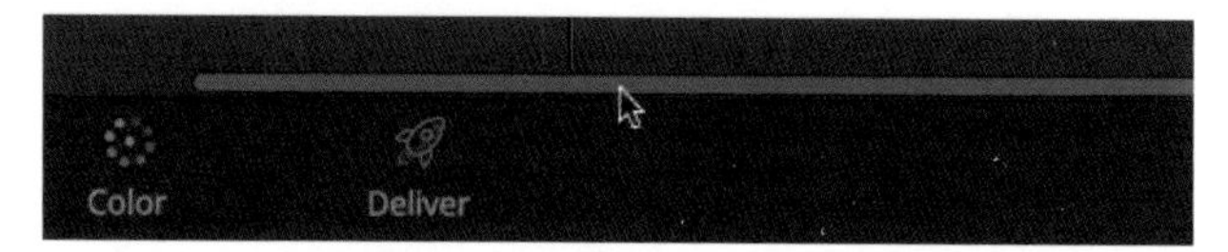

The Timeline window will pan as you drag.

3. To see the entire timeline, press Shift-Z.

> **TIP:** Pressing Shift-Z acts as a toggle. Press the combination once to zoom all the way out to see the entire timeline. Press it again to return to the previous zoom level.

4. To zoom into the timeline in incremental steps, press Cmd-+ (plus sign) (OS X) or Ctrl-+ (plus sign) (Windows)

Throughout this book, feel free to move around and zoom into the timeline to perform any exercise more efficiently. Although the exercises will sometimes explicitly suggest zooming in and out, at other times feel free to change the timeline view to see items more clearly.

Moving Clips in the Timeline

Now that you know how to navigate within the timeline, your next step is to learn how to move and manipulate clips that you've edited into the timeline. Despite your best efforts, a little revision is often necessary. Sometimes you will make mistakes in editing, or find that what looked correct a few days ago now seems unacceptable. It happens. After clips are edited, moving clips to a new timeline location is a common necessity that you'll address multiple times a day when editing.

1. In the timeline, on track V2, place the playhead over the **07 WS Ride Down Hill** clip, and click the clip to select it.

The selected clip is outlined in red.

To understand exactly what you are working on in this section of the timeline, you should view the content in the wider area of the selected clip to see what comes before and after.

2. Choose Playback > Play Around/To > Play Around Current Clip.

Choosing Play Around Current Clip backs up the playhead before the start of the selected clip and plays past the end of the clip. Doing so gives you a better sense of the overall area you are going to change. The selected clip you just viewed could be better placed if you move it to cover up the awkward cut between the two interview clips.

> **TIP:** The Play Around commands use the pre-roll and post-roll times identified in the project settings to determine how many frames to play before and after the current clip or frame.

3. Drag the **07 WS Ride Down Hill** clip to the right until it snaps above the starting point of the last interview clip.

> **TIP:** You can move the playhead one frame at a time by pressing , (comma) to move one frame left or . (period) to move one frame right. Pressing Shift-, (comma) or Shift-. (period) nudges the playhead 10 frames to the left or right, respectively.

You can also move clips onto other tracks. In some cases, a clip may be perfectly positioned in time, but you want to change the track that it's on.

4. Shift-drag the **07 WS Ride Down Hill** clip in the timeline to move it onto track V1. By holding down Shift, you won't change its position in time.

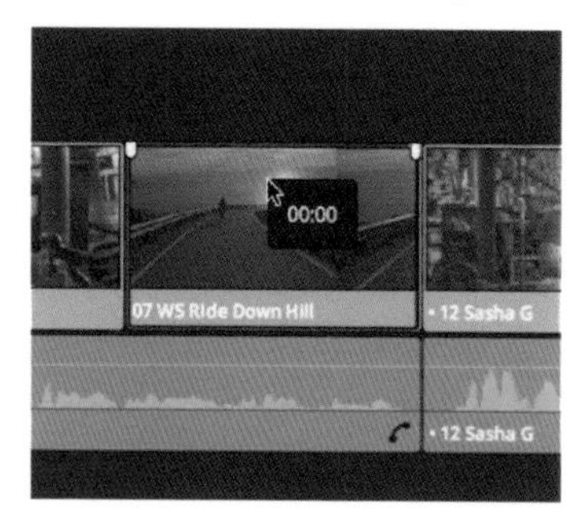

The result is visually the same as having the clip on V2. The benefit of placing it on V1 is that it will be easier to refine the cuts using the Resolve trimming tools.

5. Drag the playhead over **08 WS Riding Away** (third clip from the end).

6. Choose Timeline > Select Clips Forward > Select Clips Forward on This Track, or press Y, to select all three clips from the location of the playhead forward (to the right of the current clip).

7. Drag the selected clips to the right. Use the Offset pop-up as a guide to move them three seconds (+3:00).

> **TIP:** When a clip is selected, you can type a positive or negative timecode offset to move the clip by a specific length earlier or later in the timeline.

While moving the clips, you'll notice that they automatically snap to the playhead. This is the same *snapping* behavior that makes it easier for you to position clips against other clips or move the playhead at the start of a clip. Sometimes, however, snapping can interfere with your ability to precisely place clips. Let's undo your previous step and turn off snapping to see the difference in positioning.

8. Choose Edit > Undo, or press Cmd-Z (OS X) or Ctrl-Z (Windows).
9. In the toolbar, click the Snap button to disable snapping, or press N.

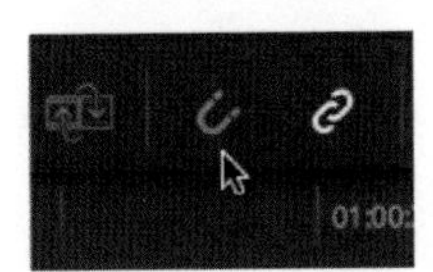

10. Once again, drag the selected clips to the right by +3:00.

    With snapping turned off, the clips move smoothly and do not snap to the playhead.

11. Enable snapping again by clicking the Snap button, or pressing N.

You've had snapping turned on for all your exercises to this point. The feature is very useful when you're trying to place clips back to back or positioning the playhead at the start of a clip; so in general, you'll want to leave it on. However, you've now seen one situation in which it's best to disable it.

Performing a Ripple Overwrite

You'll now need to fill in the gap that you created in the previous exercise. You could easily overwrite the gap with a clip, but instead let's use a Ripple Overwrite edit. This type of edit will allow you to precisely mark the gap and still mark an In and Out in the source clip. Using four marks may mean that one marked range could have a longer duration than the other. Ripple Overwrite can compensate for the duration difference. Let's see how it works.

1. Position the playhead in the center of the gap, and press X to set In and Out points.

2. Select the B-Roll bin, and load **02 Extreme WS S Curve** into the Source Viewer.
3. Play the clip from the start to the end.

   This clip has a very clear point at which it needs to start (just before the rider appears on screen) and a very clear point where it must end (before he rides off screen).
4. Mark an In point at 15:50:24:00, just before the bicyclist appears onscreen.

5. Type **+4.** (period), and then press Return or Enter, and mark an Out point. This Out point will be placed just as the bicyclist rounds the first curve.

The four-second duration you marked for the source clip is longer than the three-second gap marked in the timeline. The Ripple Overwrite feature combines two editing functions into one to make the longer source clip fit into the smaller timeline gap. Ripple Overwrite will perform an overwrite to fill the three-second gap marked in the timeline; then it will insert the remaining one second of source content, pushing the clips in the timeline further down to make room.

6. In the timeline header, make sure V1 and A1 are both enabled so your edit will include both audio and video content.
7. Drag the clip from the Source Viewer into the Timeline Viewer, and from the edit overlay, choose Ripple Overwrite.
8. Back up the playhead in the timeline and play over the edit to review the clip that you have added.

The gap is filled and additional space is made to fit the longer duration of the source clip.

Swapping Clip Positions

Dragging clips in the timeline from V2 onto V1 overwrites the clips in the timeline. At times, however, you don't want to overwrite an existing clip's content, but just change the clip's position. This is often the case when swapping the position of two clips.

1. Under the Timeline Viewer, click the Previous Edit button, or press the Up Arrow, to move the playhead between the **06 WS S Curve** clip and the **02 Extreme WS S Curve** clip.

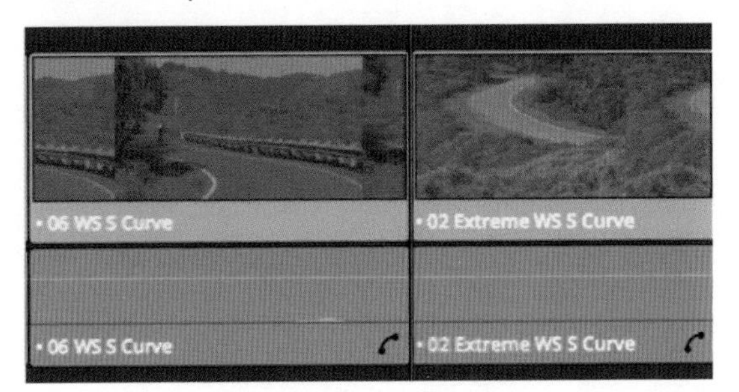

2. Choose Playback > Play Around/To > Play Around Current Frame, or press / (slash).

   The Play Around Current Frame command backs up the playhead and plays past the cut so you can see how the two shots work together. Often you'll just want to try out an edit to see if you can improve an already acceptable sequence of clips. Let's see how it looks when you swap the position of the two clips.

3. In the timeline, select **02 Extreme WS S Curve**.

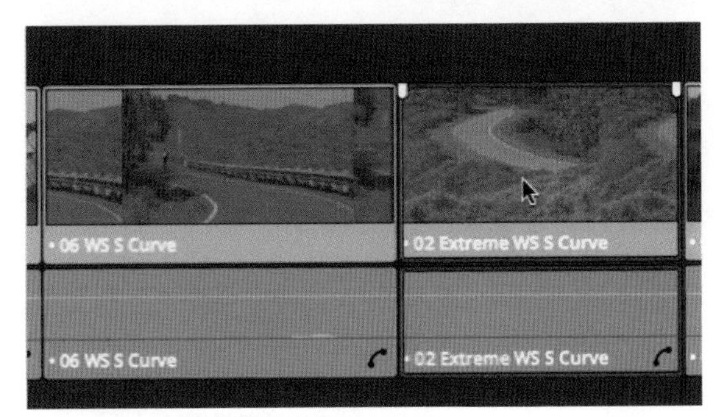

4. Cmd-Shift-drag (OS X) or Ctrl-Shift-drag (Windows) the selected clip to the left, until it swaps position with **06 WS S Curve**.

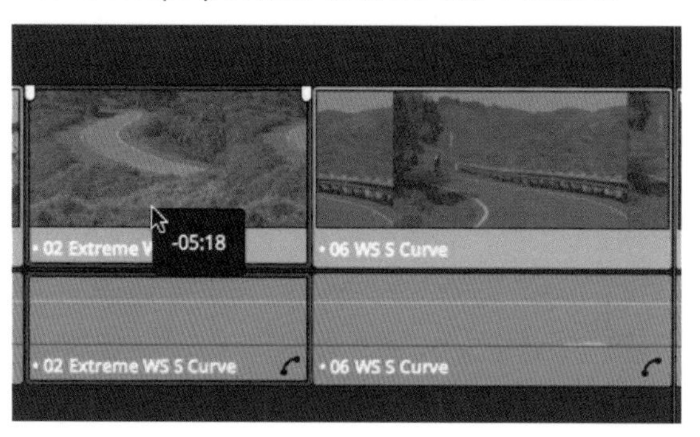

Holding down these modifier keys while dragging a clip inserts it into the new position without overwriting existing clips. You now know a number of ways to flexibly move clips around in the timeline.

Deleting Clips from the Timeline

Almost as important as knowing where to place clips in the timeline is knowing when and how clips should be removed. Deleting a clip seems like it should be straightforward, but not all deletions are alike.

1. In the timeline, select **03 WS Up Over Hill**.

To remove a selected clip from the timeline, you can press the Delete key.

2. Press Delete.

The clip is removed, or *lifted*, from the timeline but not deleted from its bin or your hard drive. In addition, a gap is left where the clip used to be. If you don't want to leave a gap, you can delete that as well with a different type of deletion.

3. Choose Edit > Undo, or press Cmd-Z (OS X) or Ctrl-Z (Windows) to undo the deletion and restore the clip to the timeline.

> **TIP:** When you perform the following deletion, make sure that the A1 Auto Select button is enabled from the previous lesson. If Auto Select is not enabled, the gap will not be removed when you delete the clip.

4. Select **03 WS Up Over Hill**, and press Shift-Delete (OS X) or Shift-Backspace (Windows).

   This time, the clip is removed and the gap is closed by moving all the clips that followed it to the left. This is called a *Ripple Delete*.

Deleting Video or Audio Content Separately

What if you want to delete only the audio content from clips in the timeline and leave the video content in place?

1. In the timeline, position the playhead over the last interview shot.

2. Play the timeline and listen carefully to the audio during the last five scenic bike-riding shots.

   You can hear directions being called out on many of the clips, along with some wind noise that isn't desirable. You'll want to keep the video of these clips but remove their audio. You already know that when you select these clips, Resolve will automatically select both the video and its associated audio. To remove the breeze and crew noise, you'll need to unlink the two tracks so you can select the video separately from the audio.

3. In the toolbar, click the Link/Unlink button, or press Cmd-Shift-L (OS X) or Ctrl-Shift-L (Windows).

The Link/Unlink button is no longer highlighted, indicating that the function is disabled. The association between video and sync audio content is no longer recognized, so you can move and delete them independently.

4. Select the audio track of the last clip in the timeline.

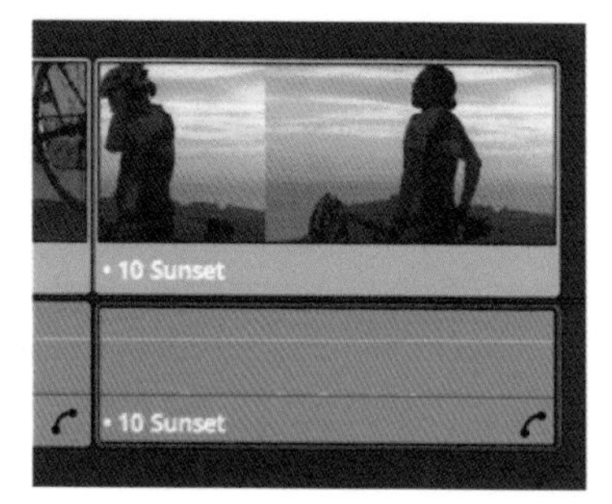

Only the audio is outlined in red.

5. Press Delete to remove the audio track.

The audio is now removed from the timeline, but the video track remains.

6. In the toolbar, click the Link/Unlink button, or press Cmd-Shift-L (OS X) or Ctrl-Shift-L (Windows) to re-enable the link behavior.

That's an efficient way to unlink audio and video, but you can do it even faster using key combinations.

7. Locate the last audio clip in the timeline (**09 Parking**), and select it by Option-clicking (OS X) or Alt-clicking (Windows).

Even with the Link/Unlink button enabled, holding down the modifier key during selection will temporarily disable the link between audio and video. Let's select the remaining audio that you want to delete.

8. In the timeline, select the audio in **02 Extreme WS S Curve** by Option-Shift-clicking (OS X) or Alt-Shift-clicking (Windows).

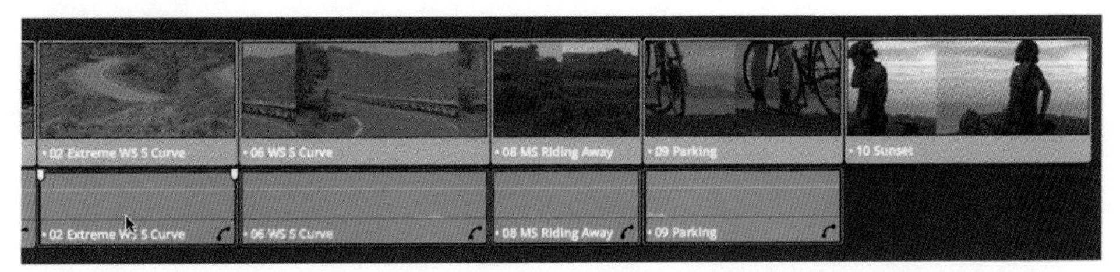

9. You now have a tight bike-riding timeline without any unwanted audio.

Splitting Clips

Often during interviews, you'll get lots of "umms," "errs," and halting speech that interrupts the flow of the interview. While you may not want to remove the entire audio clip, you can improve the flow of the interview.

1. Position the playhead in the middle of the **12 Sasha G** clip, roughly around 01:00:44:00.

2. Press the Spacebar to play the timeline, and stop playback when the audio from the interview stops.

   You can hear a lot of stuttering right around the point where you cut to the scenic bike shot. The interviewee stumbles a bit over the word "it's" and tosses in a few "ahhs." You can fix this. But to plan your audio cleanup in detail, it helps to slowly play backward and forward within the area.

3. With your right hand, position your index finger over the J key, your middle finger over the K key, and your ring finger over the L key.

   The JKL keys act as transport controls that allow you to play backward, pause, and play forward, respectively.

4. Press J to play the clip backward until you get to the middle of the interview clip. Then press K to pause playback.

   You can press the J, K, and L keys to move over the clip to find the spot where the stuttering begins.

5. Hold down the K and L keys at the same time to play forward at half speed until you hear the second time he says, "it's."
6. Hold down the J and K keys at the same time to play backward at half speed until the playhead is just before the first time he says, "it's."

   You can make it even easier to find the exact location by zooming in to the timeline.
7. In the toolbar, drag the Zoom slider to the right until you have a clear and detailed view of the area that you are playing.

TIP: Press Shift-Z to zoom out and display the entire timeline.

8. Use the combination of J-K and K-L to move backward and forward until you find the space between the two times the interviewee says, "it's."
9. When you are close to the space between the two "it's," you can move the playhead a single frame backward and forward by holding down K and just tapping J or L to precisely place it.

   Your goal is to find a spot in his speech where he begins to stutter on the word "it's," and then you can cut it out. To remove the stuttering, you must split the clip using the Razor Blade tool.
10. In the toolbar, click the Razor Blade tool, or press B.

11. Using the razor blade cursor, click the audio clip at the playhead location to create a cut.

This identifies the start of the area you want to remove. You can now press the JKL keys to locate the playhead to the end of the area that you want to remove.

12. Using the JKL keys as you did earlier, place the playhead just before he says, "the most wonderful machine in the world." Get as close to the word "the" as you can without cutting it off.
13. Using the razor blade, click the audio clip at the playhead location to create another cut.

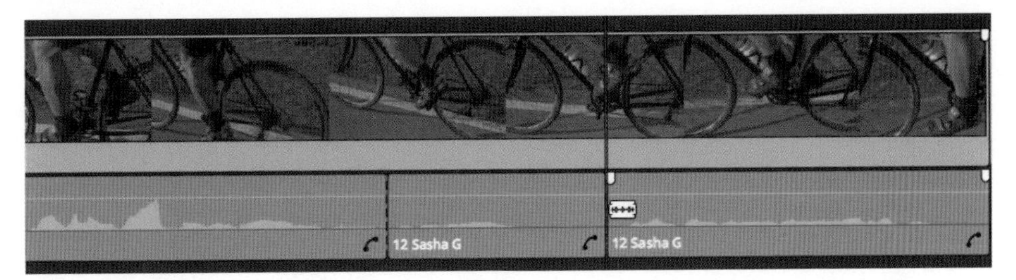

By adding cuts to the clip, you have identified a section that you can remove.

14. In the toolbar, click the Selection tool, or press A, so you don't accidentally create new cuts with the razor blade.

15. In the timeline, select the audio section that you want to remove.

Earlier in this lesson you learned that pressing the Delete key will remove a clip and leave a gap. In this case, you don't want the long pause that a gap would create, so you can press the Shift-Delete (OS X) or Shift-Backspace (Windows) combination to remove the clip and close the gap.

Remember, however, that Auto Select on A1 and V1 is enabled. As a result, when you delete the audio content Resolve will remove video content to maintain sync between the audio and video in the clip. If you want to delete only the audio without deleting anything from the video track, you'll need to disable the Auto Select button for V1.

16. In the timeline header, click the V1 Auto Select button to disable it.

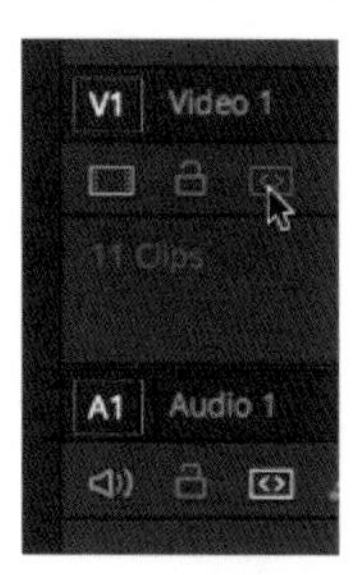

17. Press Shift-Delete to remove the audio segment and close the gap.

    You have tidied up the audio portion of the interview without altering the video clip of the biker.

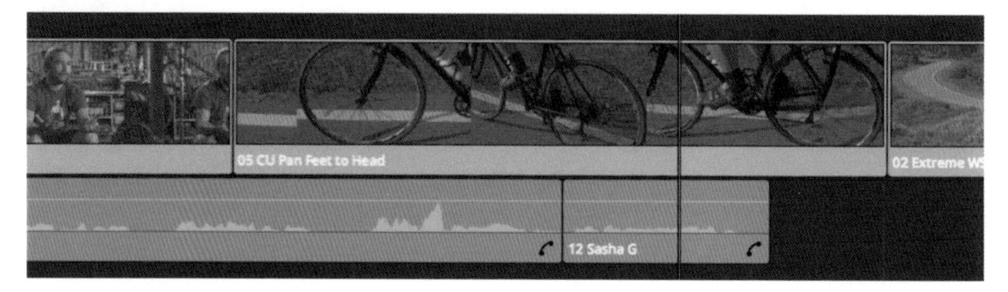

18. Position the playhead in the middle of the last interview clip, and press the Spacebar to play the timeline until the interview ends.

The result of splitting the clip may or may not be perfect. It all depends on how precisely you selected the cut points. For further practice, you can undo the last few steps and retry the edit, or proceed to the next lesson, where you'll learn about additional trimming options and how you can further refine edits you've already made.

5 Mastering Trimming Options

Editing is as much about timing as it is about shot selection. You've already learned about selecting shots and placing them in an order to best tell your story. But what if you cut off an extra turn of a subject's head? What if you extended the action to last a half second longer? How might even small changes impact the shots before and after the edit?

When critically refining the start or end of a clip in a timeline, you may be dealing with a few seconds or even just a few frames. That refinement process is called *trimming*, and those trims can make the different between a good sequence and a great sequence. Resolve includes precision trimming tools that allow you to try out multiple edit choices and review them quickly to address your creative questions.

In this lesson, you'll import a project for trimming, and then examine each cut point in your timeline, shorten and lengthen clips, and figure out the best trimming method to enhance your storytelling.

TIME

- **This lesson takes approximately 50 minutes to complete.**

GOALS

- **Import projects and relink media**
- **Perform a ripple trim**
- **Perform a roll trim using the JKL keys**
- **Select tracks to trim**
- **Slip a clip to change content**
- **Slide a clip to change position**
- **Use match frame**
- **Trim with the selection tool**

Importing Projects and Relinking Media

Resolve creates a database to track all of your editorial colleagues who are working with projects on your computer. If one editor creates a project and another editor on the same computer wants to perform additional work on it, however, the project must be imported into the new editor's project manager. This requirement also exists when transferring projects from one computer to another. Projects created by other editors or on other computers must be imported and the media must be relinked on a different system.

> **NOTE:** You'll be working with this project in multiple upcoming lessons. To accelerate your learning, each lesson has a starting timeline that you can load into the timeline viewer. For the most part, the timelines pick up roughly where you left off in the previous lesson, sometimes with a few minor adjustments to make the upcoming lesson more effective.

1. If Resolve is open, choose File > Project Manager to open the Project Manager window. If you are opening Resolve, log in to your account and into the Project Manager window.
2. Right-click in an empty area of the Project Manager window, and from the contextual menu, choose Import. Then, in the Open dialog, navigate to the DaVinci Resolve Editing Lessons Files folder, and select **DaVinci Resolve Lessons 5-13.drp**.

   The project is imported but the media may not yet be linked to the clips. This can occur when media is copied or moved from one computer to another or when folder names are changed. If necessary, you can easily relink the media to all of the clips and timelines in a project.
3. Open the imported project. If your media is offline (as indicated by the presence of thumbnail icons), in the Media Pool sidebar, select the Video Clips, Rough Cuts, and Music and Sound Effects bins.

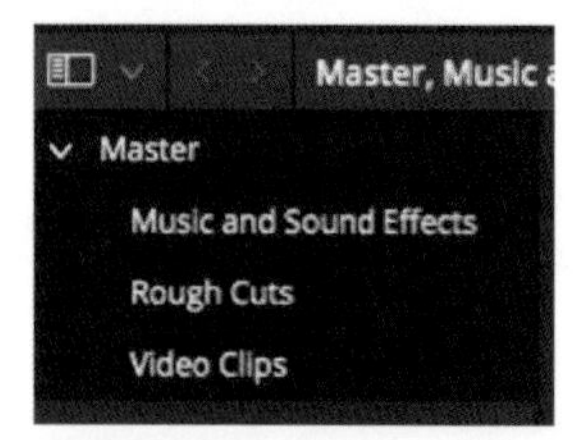

> **TIP:** You can import timelines and media from Final Cut Pro 7, Final Cut Pro X, or Avid Media Composer by choosing File > Import AAF, EDL, XML.

4. Control-click (OS X) or Right-click (Windows) any of the bins, and from the contextual menu, choose Relink Clips for Selected Bins.

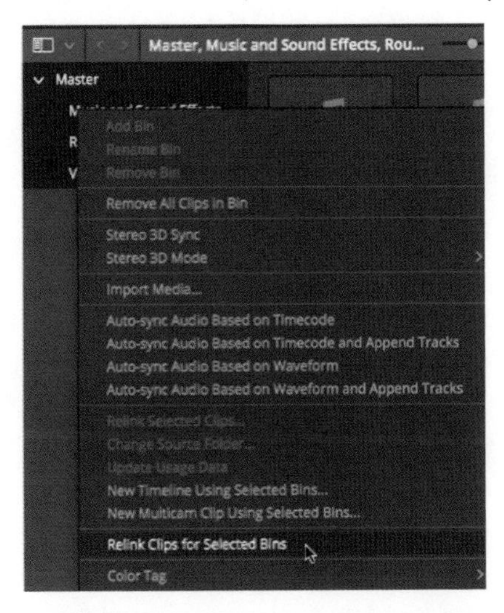

5. In the Find dialog, navigate to the DaVinci Resolve Editing Lessons Files folder and select it. Click OK. Relinking the bins automatically relinks all of the clips and timelines in those bins.
6. When all of the clips are relinked, click the Edit button to switch to the edit page.
7. In the Rough Cuts bin, double-click the Trim Rough Cut timeline to load it into the Timeline Viewer.
8. Play the timeline to review the cuts you will work with in this lesson.

Ripple Trimming in Trim Mode

Resolve includes a powerful Trim Edit mode that you can use to shorten and lengthen clips in the timeline. Once you have a rough cut assembled, the next task is to step through the timeline cut by cut and refine each edit by adding and removing frames. The tools and techniques used in Trim Edit mode make this refinement process fast, precise, and flexible. Let's look at a section of your timeline to decide how trimming could improve it.

1. Press Shift-Z to view the entire timeline in the window.
2. Position the playhead at the start of the **02 Extreme WS S Curve** clip.

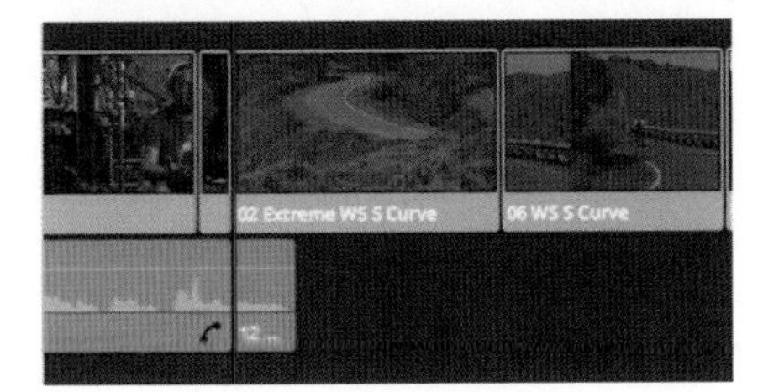

3. Play the timeline to view the next three clips: **02 Extreme WS S Curve**, **06 WS S Curve**, and **08 MS Riding Away**.

You'll encounter two issues here that you must address separately. The first issue concerns the length of the first clip. In this very long shot, the bicyclist rides all the way off screen. You can remove a few seconds to shorten the clip and end it with the bicyclist still on the road. This will eliminates unnecessary action that makes the clip too long.

4. In the toolbar, click the Trim Edit Mode button, or press T.

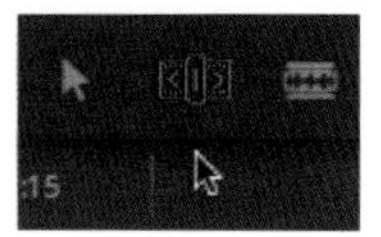

With the Trim Edit Mode button selected, you can no longer use the cursor to select clips and move them in the timeline. The primary purpose of the cursor is now to select a cut point and the side of that cut point that you want to trim.

5. Position the Trim Edit Mode cursor at the end of the **02 Extreme WS S Curve** clip.

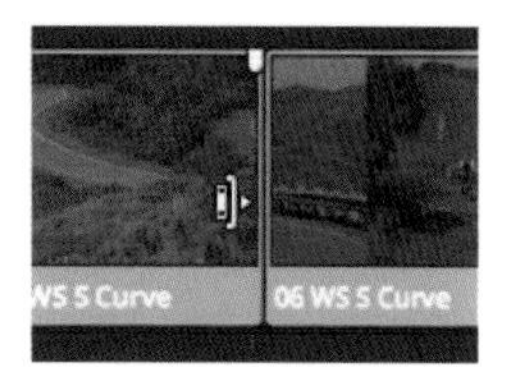

The cursor changes to the Ripple Trim cursor that is used to lengthen or shorten a clip duration. When the cursor is on the left of the cut, it will trim the end, or *tail*, of the cut.

6. Drag the tail of the cut slightly to the left and hold the cursor there for a moment.

As you drag, the Timeline Viewer splits to show you the last frame of the outgoing clip on the left and the first frame of the incoming clip on the right. This two-frame, side-by-side display is designed to show how the action and framing from the two sides of a cut will match up...or not.

7. Continue dragging left until the bicyclist is at the top of the first curve, or until the tool tip reads -04:00.

When removing frames, the ripple trim pulls in all the clips after the trim point to close the gap (much like the Ripple Delete that you performed in the previous lesson). When you remove frames using the Ripple cursor, you not only shorten the clip, but you also shorten the overall duration of your show.

8. To review the trim point, choose Playback > Play Around/To > Play Around Current Frame, or press / (slash)

   Let's look at the reverse situation in which you add frames. The start of the **08 MS Riding Away** clip is too late. The bicyclist goes by too quickly for your pacing. You can improve the pacing by giving the viewer more time to identify what is onscreen before it is over. Using the Ripple Trim tool, you can add frames to the start of this clip.

9. Position the Trim Edit Mode cursor over the beginning, or head, of the **08 MS Riding Away** clip.

   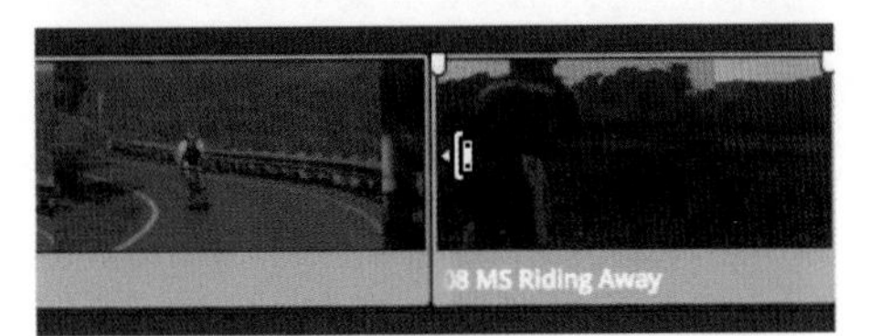

   When the cursor is on the right side of the cut, you can trim the head of the clip.

10. Drag the head of the clip to the left until the bicyclist is just barely onscreen.

    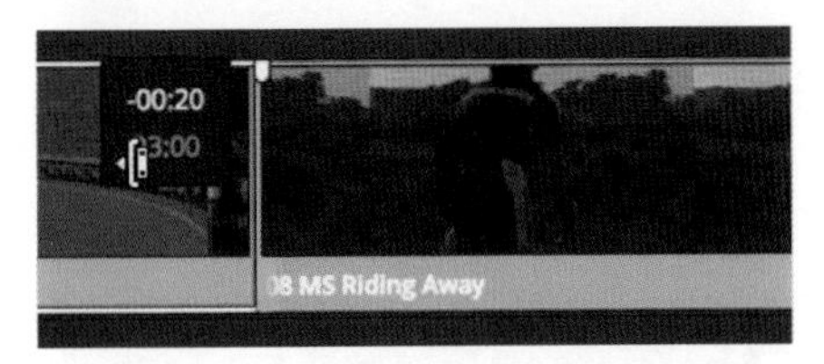

> **TIP:** When dragging to trim, the cut point may snap to the playhead and make it difficult to precisely position the trim. When this happens, press the N key to disable snapping as you trim.

11. To review the trim point, choose Playback > Play Around/To > Play Around Current Frame, or press / (slash).

    Adding frames during trimming requires that you have access to additional frames from the captured clip that were not included within the In and Out points as the clip was edited into the timeline. Those unused portions of each clip placed in the timeline are known as *handles*.

    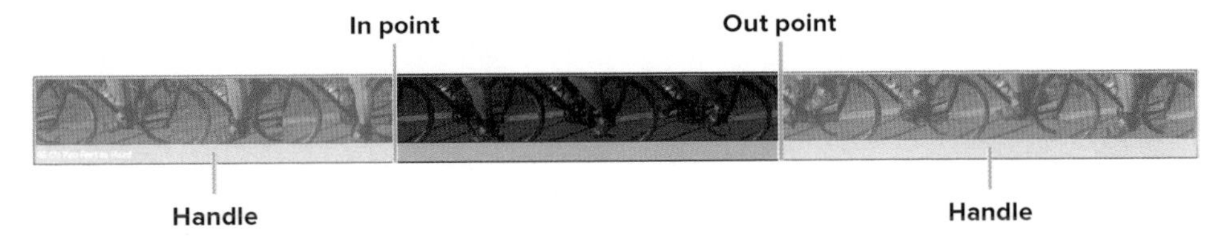

    If you edit the entire length of a clip into the timeline, you will not have handles available to extend the clip, so you will be able only to remove frames when you trim.

Trimming Using Numbers

When you are trimming just a few frames, instead of dragging the cut point, it is more precise to use the number pad to enter the exact number of frames you want to add or remove.

1. In the timeline, once more position the playhead between **02 Extreme WS S Curve** and **06 WS S Curve**.
2. Click the Ripple Trim cursor to select the head of **06 WS S Curve**.

The Ripple Trim cursor now points to the left, indicating that you will trim the head of the cut.

3. Type **+ 10**, and then press Return (OS X) or Enter (Windows).

Ten frames are removed from the head of the **06 WS S Curve** clip. Using a positive number to remove frames may seem a bit counterintuitive, but the positive and negative values are based on the timeline direction. Frame 0 in the timeline is to the left and values increase as you move to the right.

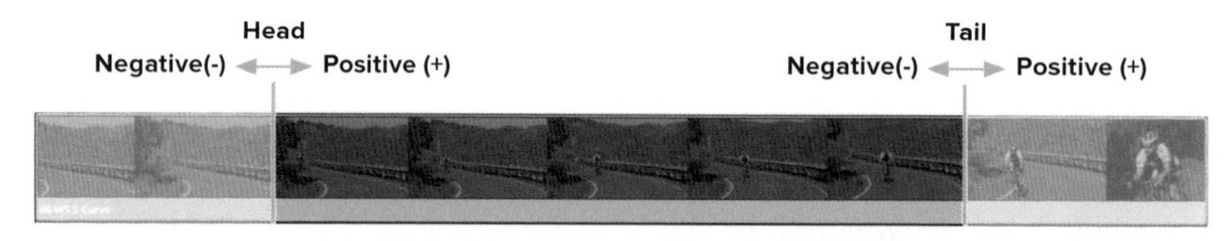

TIP: In Trim Edit Mode, you can use the "nudge" keyboard shortcuts of , (comma) and . (period) to trim the selection left or right a single frame, respectively. Pressing Shift-, (comma) and Shift-. (period) trims left or right by 10 frames.

4. To review the cut, choose Playback > Play Around/To > Play Around Current Frame, or press / (slash).

These quick trims can be repeated very rapidly until you reach the exact frame you want.

5. Type **+ 15**, and press Return or Enter. Then press / (slash) to play your trim results.
6. Click the Selection tool, or press the A key, to leave Trim Edit Mode.

Whether you use the number pad or drag to trim is really your choice. Although the number pad may be faster, it is also less visual. When trimming by dragging you are better able to see the frames, but you sacrifice speed. Whichever method you feel most comfortable with in any given situation is the right choice for you.

Roll Trimming Using the JKL Keys

Whereas a ripple trim alters a single side of a cut point, roll trims simultaneously trim the tail of the outgoing clip and the head of the incoming clip. Instead of performing a rolling trim by dragging or using the number pad as you did for the ripple trim, you'll apply a new technique called *dynamic trimming*.

1. In the timeline, position the playhead between the **05 CU Pan Feet to Head** and **02 Extreme WS S Curve** clips.

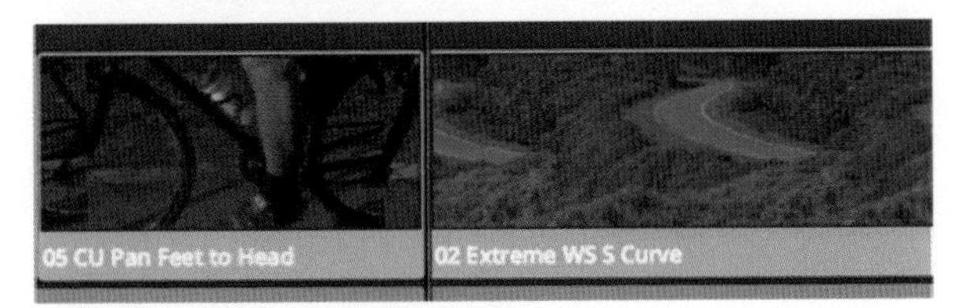

2. In the toolbar, drag the Zoom slider to zoom in on these two clips

3. Click the Trim Edit Mode button, or press the T key, to enter Trim Edit Mode
4. Place the pointer over the cut point to enable the Rolling Edit cursor, and click the cut.

Instead of trimming with the mouse or entering frame numbers, you'll use dynamic trimming, pressing the JKL keys to adjust the cut point. This technique is similar to the method you used in Lesson 4 to split an audio clip.

5. Choose Trim > Dynamic Trim Mode, or press W, to enter Dynamic Trim Mode

The words "Dynamic Trim" appear in the toolbar and the playhead turns yellow. Pressing the JKL keys will now trim as you play forward, in reverse, and at half speed.

6. Hold down the K and L keys to play forward at half speed until you see the bicyclist appear onscreen in the **Extreme S Curve** clip. Release the keys to stop.

Let's play the transition to see your results.

7. To review the cut, choose Playback > Play Around/To > Play Around Current Frame, or press / (slash)

> **TIP:** Once one side of a cut point is selected using the Ripple or Roll cursor, pressing the U key toggles between each side of the edit to select that side for trimming.

You can continue to refine the cut by pressing the J and K keys to play slowly backward, or holding the K key and tapping J or L to move one frame at a time. If you don't yet feel comfortable using the JKL keys, don't worry. You'll get more practice in the next exercise.

Selecting Tracks to Trim

So far in this lesson you've had to trim only video clips. What happens when you select a clip that includes sync audio?

1. Press Shift-Z to view the entire timeline, and then position the playhead between the **11 Sasha G** and **01 WS Side View GG Bridge** clips.

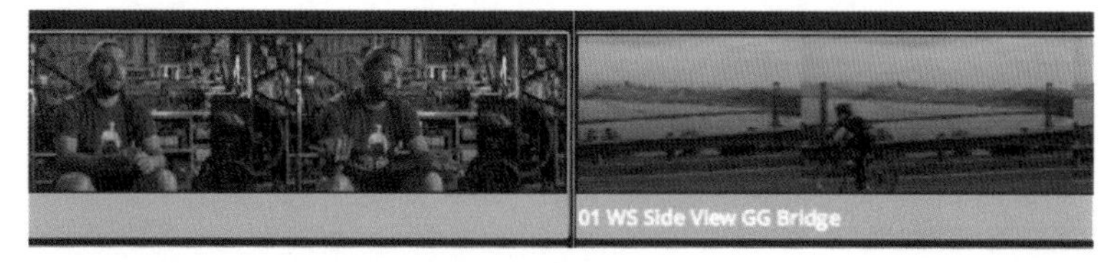

2. In the toolbar, drag the Zoom slider to zoom in on these two clips.

> **TIP:** Press Command-+ (plus sign) or Cmd- - (minus sign) (OS X) to incrementally zoom in to the timeline; and press Ctrl-+ (plus sign) (OS X) or Ctrl- - (minus sign) (Windows) to incrementally zoom out of the timeline.

3. Click the Trim Edit Mode button, or press T, to enter Trim Edit Mode, if necessary.

4. Place the pointer over the video cut point to enable the Rolling Edit cursor, and click the edit.

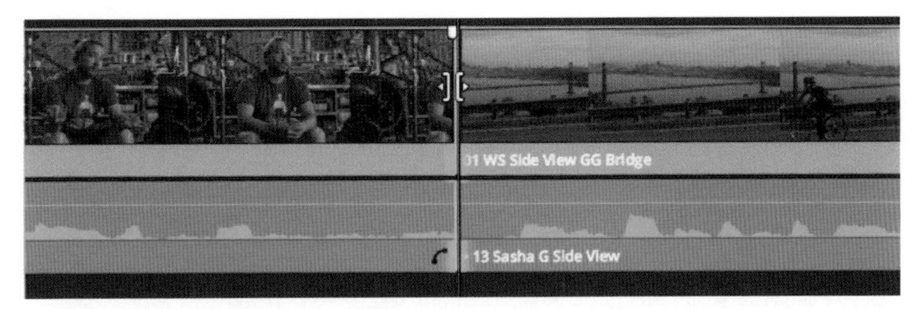

Even though you selected the edit between the two video clips, both the video and audio cut points were selected. The audio and video are from the same interview clip, so they are linked. This behavior is similar to moving clips in the timeline with the Link/Unlink button enabled.

5. In the empty timeline area above the video track, click to deselect the edit point.
6. Click the Link/Unlink button to disable it.

TIP: You can also hold down the Option key (OS X) or the Alt key (Win) to temporarily select the video edit point without disabling the unlink/link button.

7. Place the pointer over the video edit point to enable the Rolling Edit cursor, and click the edit point.

   With the link function disabled, only the video edit point is selected.
8. If dynamic trimming is no longer displayed in the toolbar, press the W key to enable it.
9. Hold down the K and J keys to play backward at half speed until the playhead is in the middle of the interview clip. Then release the keys to stop trimming.

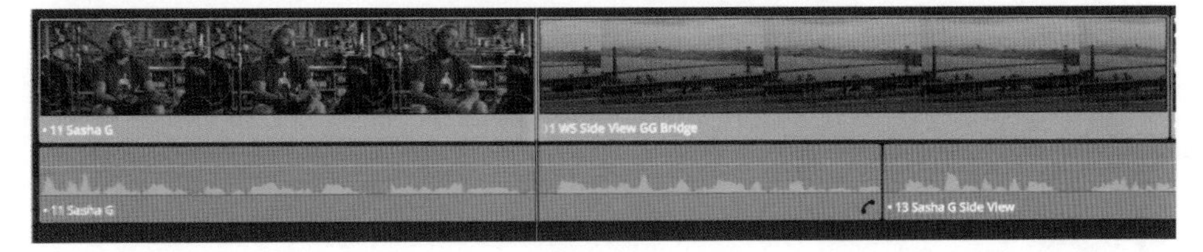

10. Choose Playback > Play Around/To > Play Around Current Frame, or press / (slash).

    At one point, the interviewee says, “Some of them have lots of miles left.” This is a good point to place the scenic Golden Gate Bridge cut-away.

11. Press J-K and L-K to play backward and forward until the playhead is located right after the man says, "miles."
12. When you find the right location, press W to disable dynamic trimming. Doing so ensures that you won't accidentally trim a clip when trying to play the timeline using the JKL keys.
13. Click the Link/Unlink button to enable linked clips, and then click the Selection tool to leave Trim Mode.

Keeping audio and video in sync is always a concern (and a chore) for editors. The link/unlink function is invaluable in assisting you with that effort. Although it's necessary to disable it in some situations, as shown above, it's good practice to enable it at all other times.

Slipping a Clip to Change Content

As you refine your timeline, making a clip longer or shorter isn't always going to be the best refinement. Occasionally, you'll want to shift frames earlier or later within a clip without changing its duration or position in the timeline. This trim is called *slipping a clip*.

1. In the timeline, position the playhead over the **01 WS Side View GG Bridge** clip.

2. Enable Trim Edit Mode, and place the mouse pointer over the upper-middle region of the segment.

The placement of the mouse pointer is important to activate the Slip cursor. With the cursor ready, you're ready to slip the clip.

3. Drag to the left to slip the clip until you see the bicyclist coming around again.

As you drag, the viewer changes to a *4-up display* that allows you to compare all relevant outgoing and incoming frames. The upper two frames show the incoming and outgoing frames of the clip being slipped. The lower-left frame shows the unchanging outgoing clip's last frame, and the lower-right frame shows the unchanging incoming clip's first frame. This display enables you to compare and match the action of all three clips that will be altered by the slip.

> **NOTE:** Depending on the window and the size of your display, you may need to stop dragging a clip, reposition the mouse, and then resume dragging.

As you slip the clip, you'll see the bicyclist ride in the opposite direction (right to left). The next time he rides from left to right, the camera pans with him, ending on the Golden Gate Bridge. This region of the clip is a nicer shot to include in this cutaway.

4. Drag to the left until the initial start of his uphill climb is visible in the upper-left display, and end with the Golden Gate Bridge visible in the upper-right display.

5. Place the playhead before the slipped clip, and then play the timeline to review your edit.

> **TIP:** With the Trim Edit Mode enabled, click the middle of the clip to select it, and then press the , (comma) or . (period) key to slip one frame left or right, respectively. Hold down Shift in combination with those keys to slip 10 frames at a time.

Slipping a clip is most often used more subtly than you have done here. You'll find that you frequently will slip clips just a few frames to get the perfect match with the surrounding clips.

Sliding a Clip to Change Position

Sliding a clip is almost the opposite of slipping. Sliding retains a clip's frames and duration but moves it to change only its position in the timeline.

1. In the timeline, position the playhead over the **05 CU Pan Feet to Head** clip.

2. With Trim Edit Mode enabled, position the mouse pointer over the blue clip label region of the segment.

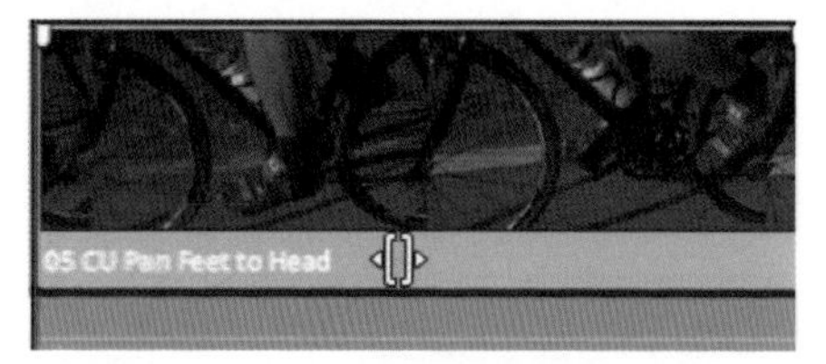

When the pointer is over the bottom of the clip, it changes to a Slide cursor.

3. Drag the clip to the right to slide it until it snaps to the first audio cut below.

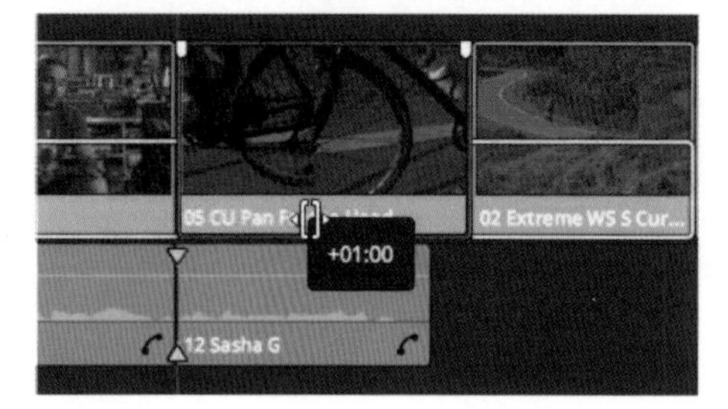

Dragging to slide a clip displays a 4-up viewer arrangement similar to the one you saw with the slip tool. The difference is that the upper frames stay the same because they represent the first and last frames of the clip that you are sliding. The lower frames change to show you the new adjacent frames changing as you slide.

4. Play the timeline to review your edit.

> **TIP:** With Trim Edit Mode enabled, you can click the middle of a clip to select it, and then press S to toggle between the Slip and the Slide cursors. You can also press the , (comma) or . (period) keys to slide one frame left or right, or use them in combination with the Shift key to slide 10 frames at a time.

5. Click the selection tool, or press A, to exit Trim Edit Mode.

No exact method exists for creating the perfect slip, slide, ripple, or roll trims. Sometimes you will trim large sections and sometimes just a few frames. With experience, you will find that you'll use all of these techniques at some point, but ultimately favor one technique over another. It's all a matter of personal taste and workflow.

Using Match Frame

At any time—not just while trimming— you may want to view the available handles for a clip in the timeline. Instead of searching through hundreds of clips in multiple bins, you'll find it much easier to use the match frame function to load and view that clip in the source viewer.

1. In the timeline, position the playhead between the **13 Sasha G Side View** and **07 WS Ride Down Hill** clips.

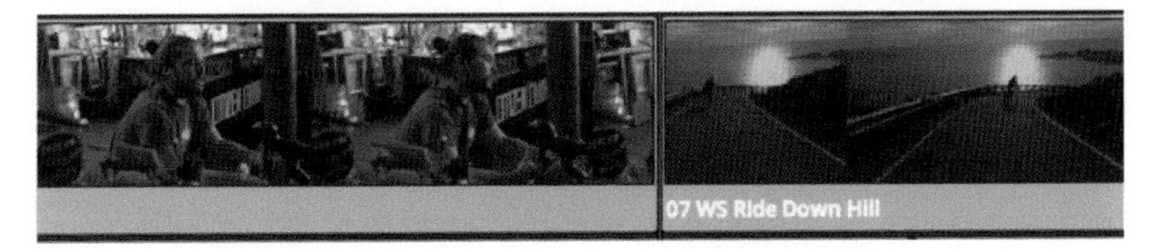

2. Choose Playback > Play Around/To > Play Around Current Frame, or press / (slash), to listen to the transition between the two cuts.

   Cutting dialogue too tightly makes it sound artificial. In the current interview, the subject changes topics abruptly, which unintentionally creates an artificial feel. Trimming to create a pause can often make awkward dialogue sound more natural.

   The audio trim you're about to perform requires that you understand the content. The incoming audio that needs a pause comes from the third interview. And at present, the interview video begins a bit later than the audio itself due to the inserted cut-away.

   You need to push the incoming audio left in the timeline to create a pause or gap between the two audio segments. Just moving the clips to create a gap would require that you insert new video. So, if you want to push things down in the timeline without adding a new clip, performing a ripple trim seems like the best choice.

3. Click the Trim Edit Mode button, or press T, to enable that mode.

NOTE: Make sure link/unlink is still enabled.

4. Place the pointer over the start of the cut-away video to enable the Ripple cursor, and then click the edit.

5. Drag to the left until the tool tip pop-up reads -1:00.

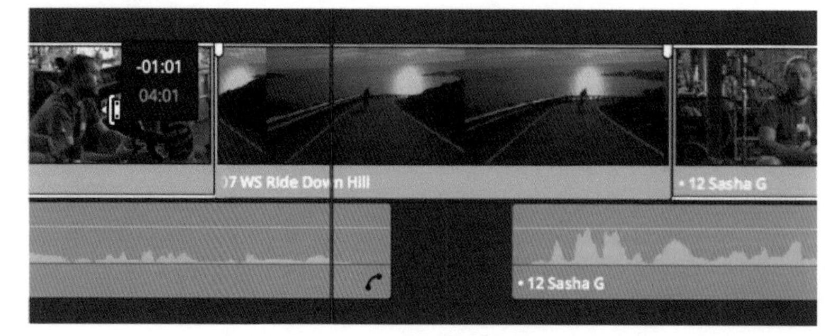

   You've added one second to the cut-away using a ripple trim, which also forced the interview clip farther to the right in the timeline. Because the interview clip and the audio are linked, the audio is also pushed right to remain in sync.

6. Position the playhead in the middle of the second interview clip, and play through the trim you just made to hear the pause that was inserted.

   That's a much more natural transition. Often, you'll need to fill in empty audio gaps with room tone from the interview. If you don't, audiences will easily detect a noticeable sound difference between the ambient audio heard in the interview and the absolute silence of the gap. The best way to fill in such a gap is to insert audio from the same interview, but taken from a moment when no one was speaking. This technique inserts room tone that matches the rest of the interview audio.

7. Just after the gap, drag the playhead over the audio clip.

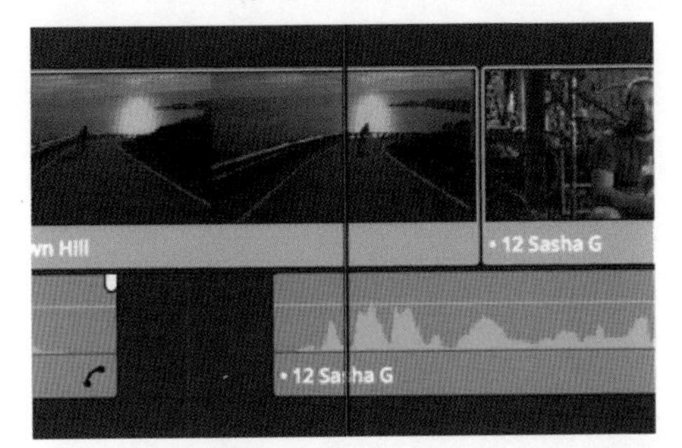

   You'll use the Match Frame function to load the source clip for this audio into the source viewer. To make sure that you match to the audio track and not the cutaway video track, you'll need to disable the Auto Select button on the V1 track.

8. On track V1, click the Auto Select button to disable the feature.

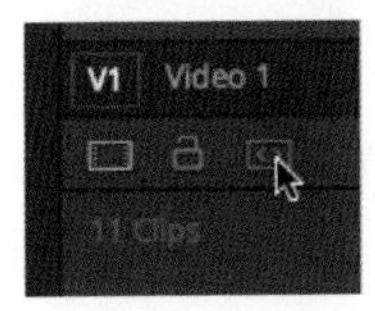

   Now the only clip under the playhead on an auto select track is the audio track.

9. Under the timeline viewer, click the Match Frame button.

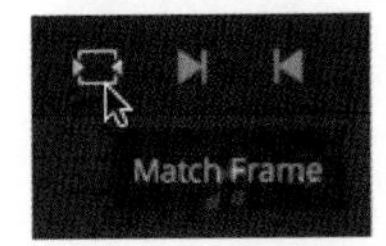

> **TIP:** You can also Option-double-click (OS X) or Alt-double-click (Windows) the segment that you want to match frame.

The source clip is loaded into the Source Viewer. You should now search the clip for a spot that has at least one second of quiet room tone. Such a moment can usually be found at the very start or end of a clip.

10. Under the Source Viewer, click the Jump to First Frame button to position the source playhead at the start of the clip.

You've already used the JKL keys to move and trim slowly through a clip. Now you can use them to quickly locate a moment of silence.

11. Tap the L key twice to play through the source clip at double speed. Tap the K key to pause when you think you have located a one-second-long area of complete silence.

One such area is found at the end of the clip, after the man says "I think." You can mark an In point as close to the ending of his word as possible by using the timecode listed in the following steps. (While taking care not to include any vocal sounds.) However, if you've found a different one-second area of silence feel free to use yours.

12. Mark an In point at 03:45:31:10.

Whether you use this In point or one of your own, you can now edit that one second of room tone into the gap.

13. Place the timeline playhead in the middle of the gap, and press X to mark an In and Out point around the gap.

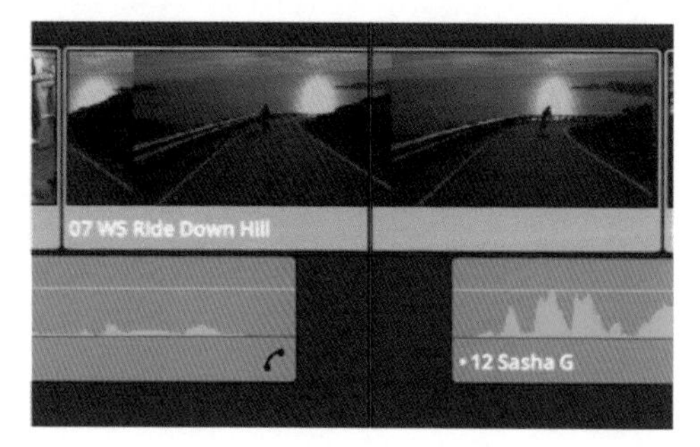

Because you are editing audio only, you don't want to edit onto the video track.

14. In the timeline header, click the V1 destination control to disable it.

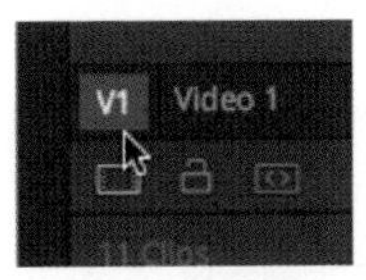

15. In the toolbar, click the Overwrite button, or press F10, to fill in the gap with your room tone audio clip.
16. In track V1, click the Auto Select button to enable it.
17. Back up the playhead before the newly added room tone, and listen to your work.

This exercise showed you how to use the Match Frame feature as an easy way to the entire contents of your source clips. It also reviewed many of the trim and edit methods that you used earlier. You'll use these features every day that you edit.

Trimming Using the Selection Tool

For some quick, basic trimming operations, you do not have to switch to the Trim Edit Mode; you can use the default Selection tool to shorten and lengthen clips in the timeline. Let's review your timeline so far and see what you have left to correct.

1. Press the Home key, or drag the playhead to the start of the timeline, and press Spacebar to play the entire timeline.
2. Position the playhead on the next to last clip in the timeline, **09 Parking**.

The clip goes on too long and the rider sets down his water bottle toward the end of the shot. It would be better to remove that final action so your audience never sees his hand and bottle. Instead of using the Trim tool, you can make this trim using the Selection tool.

3. Position the pointer over the tail of the clip.

The Trim cursor appears as usual. However, the results are a bit different for clips when compared to using the Trim tool.

4. Drag the end of the **09 Parking** clip to the left until the water bottle footage is excluded from the shot.

   Excluding frames from one side of an edit using the Selection tool leaves a gap. Sometimes this is the effect you want. For example, you might be making room to add another clip. But let's look at what happens when you add frames.

5. Reposition the pointer over the tail of the **09 Parking** clip.

6. Drag the tail to the right. Because handles were available for this trim, you were able to add about three seconds to the clip.

7. Play the timeline to review your changes.

Lengthening one side of an edit using the Selection tool overwrites the head of the incoming clip. This is the same behavior you saw when using the Rolling Trim cursor in Trim Mode. In this case, the beginning of the **10 Sunset** clip was shortened by the same length that you extended the tail of the **09 Parking** clip.

With so many options and methods available, trimming may initially seem a daunting phase of your workflow. Editors tend to use the Trim Edit Mode most often, unless they need to open a gap in the timeline; in those situations, trimming with the Selection tool is the better choice.

6 Mixing Audio

Although it often takes second place, the audio in your project is just as important as the video. To ensure that sound tells as much of your story as the visuals, DaVinci Resolve 12.5 includes a powerful, high-performance audio engine; an onscreen mixer; and audio effects that are designed to help you fully control your soundtrack.

In this lesson, you will create a balanced soundtrack by cutting in music and sound effects, and setting the audio levels to produce a perfect mix.

TIME

- **This lesson takes approximately 50 minutes to complete.**

GOALS

- **Customize the interface for audio**
- **Patch tracks**
- **Monitor, solo, and mute audio tracks**
- **Work with markers**
- **Set Level and Pan**
- **Use the Audio Mixer**
- **Change levels within a clip**
- **Add and animate audio fades**

Customizing the Interface for Audio

Throughout this lesson you'll work on the audio tracks, so let's first customize the timeline by enlarging the audio track heights so you can see the Audio Waveform displays clearly. Doing so will help you locate specific sounds and evaluate the audio more effectively. Furthermore, those waveforms are a handy visual reference to determine the volume of the audio.

1. Open **DaVinci Resolve Lessons 5-13.drp**, if necessary.
2. Select the Rough Cuts bin, and double-click the **Audio Rough Cut** timeline to load it into the timeline viewer.

3. Drag up on the horizontal divider that separates the audio and video tracks until the video track is at the top of the timeline.

You can change the appearance of the tracks in the Timeline View Options menu.

4. In the toolbar, click the Timeline View Options button to open the pop-up menu.

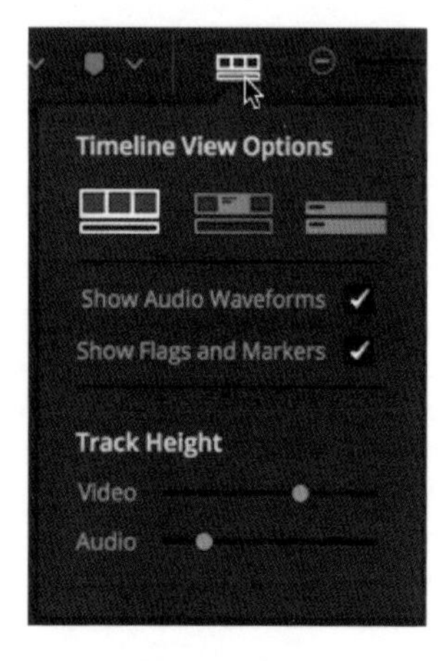

Here you can change the height of the video and audio tracks to suit your upcoming tasks.

5. Click the Track Appearance button to collapse the audio and video tracks.

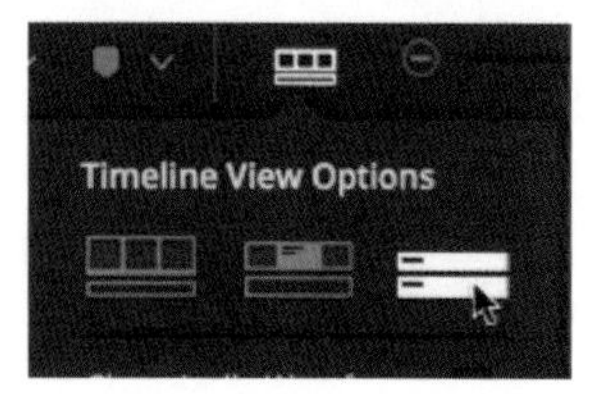

6. Click the Show Audio Waveforms checkbox to turn on the Audio Waveform display.

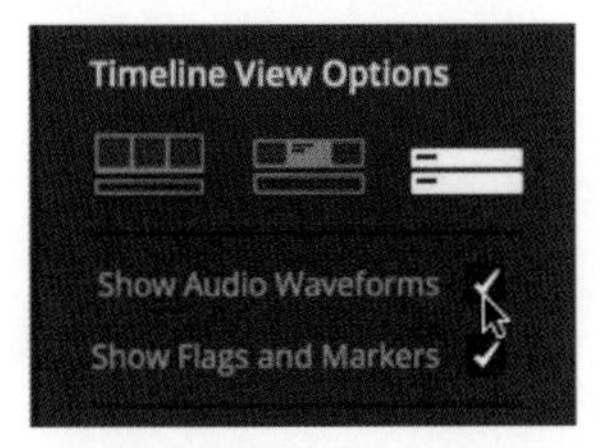

7. Drag the video and audio track height sliders all the way to the right to increase the track sizes.

8. Click the Timeline View Options button to hide the pop-up menu.

Now the timeline is set up for audio editing and mixing. You'll later add other interface elements to help control the audio; but for now, displaying larger waveforms in the timeline will help as you start to edit music, dialogue, and sound effects.

Patching Tracks

When previously previewing your timeline, you may have noticed the lack of music. With tracks A1 and A2 devoted to the interview and some sound effects, let's insert an empty audio track to accommodate some background music.

1. Select the Music and Sound Effects bin, and double-click **Marin Headlands Biking Song** to load it into the Source Viewer.

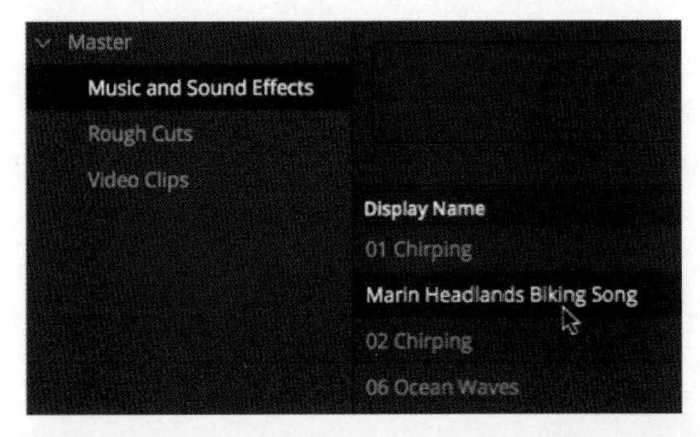

NOTE: Although the images in this book show bins in specific configurations, it is not critical that your setup match them exactly. Your bins may be in Icon view or List view, depending on your preference.

The music is longer than this scene, so you need to edit the start of the music to line up with the start of the scene, or *back-time* the edit by syncing the end of the music with the end of the scene.

2. Play a few seconds at the start of the music clip, and then play a few seconds at the end to preview which portion of the music might best fit your project.

   The ending has a good fade that will work well with the sunset shot. So let's mark an Out point on the music so it lines up with the sunset shot.

3. In the Source Viewer, press the JKL keys to locate the area in which you no longer hear the cymbal crash, and mark an Out point.

4. Mark an In point at the start of the timeline.

5. To give you room to fade out and maybe even add a title, mark an Out point roughly five seconds after the last clip ends.

   This stereo music clip needs to be cut into a new audio track. To do so, you'll add an Audio 3 track, and then edit the source clip into that track.

6. Control-click (OS X) or Right-click (Windows) the Audio 2 timeline header, and from the contextual menu, choose Add Track > Stereo.

   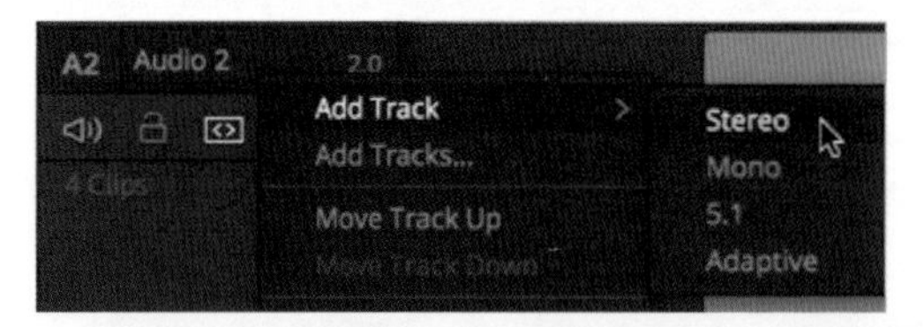

NOTE: Audio clips with multiple channels are displayed in the timeline as a single audio clip on a single track. When you first create a new audio track, you must choose its audio format (mono, stereo, 5.1 surround, or multi-channel). You cannot change track types after a track is created.

7. Drag the A1 destination control down to Audio 3 to align the contents of the A1 track in the Source Viewer with the Audio 3 track in the timeline.

8. In the toolbar, click the Overwrite button, or press F10.
9. Press Shift-Z to see the entire timeline.

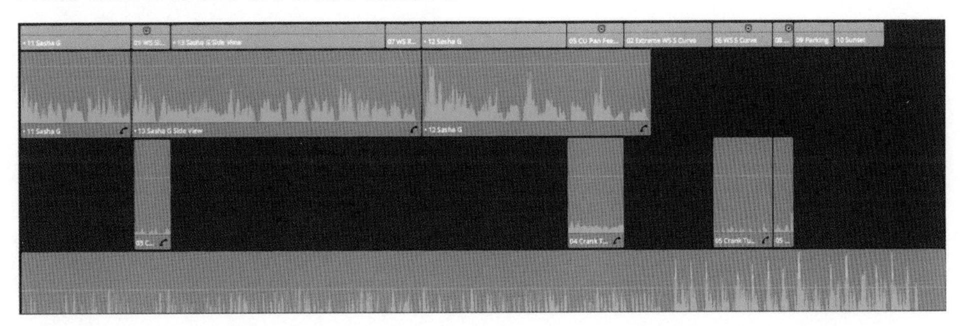

Now can see an organized track layout that places the subject's voice on Audio 1, sound effects on Audio 2, and music on Audio 3. Maintaining media organization throughout your editing stage is always important, but may be even more important when editing audio because you may find yourself managing a dozen tracks or more. The common organizational technique used here keeps similar types of audio on the same track or on neighboring tracks which makes it easier to find and edit sound effects, dialogue, and music.

Monitoring, Soloing, and Muting Audio

With your newly added music in place, you should play the tracks to hear the music in the context of the picture and interview.

1. Press the Home key to move the playhead to the start of the timeline.
2. Play the timeline to hear the newly added music.

   To get a sense of the contents of each audio track, you can listen to each independently by *soloing* the track you want to hear.
3. Press the Home key to move the playhead to the start of the timeline.
4. On A1, Option-click (OS X) or Alt-click (Windows) the Enable Track button to solo that track.

When you solo an audio track, the other audio tracks are muted and will not be heard during playback.

5. Play the timeline to hear the soloed track.

   A1 contains the interview clips. You can now mute A1 and solo A2 to audition it.

6. Click the Enable Track button for A1 to mute the track.

   To hear the A2 track, you won't have to hold down a modifier key because all of the other audio tracks are muted.

7. Click the Enable Track button for A2, and play the timeline from the beginning to hear the track's audio.

   A2 contains some sound effects for the bike-riding shots.

8. Finally, click the Enable Track button for A2 to mute it, and click A3 to solo it.
9. Play a few seconds of the timeline to hear the music in A3.
10. Click the Enable Track buttons for A2 and A1 to hear all three audio tracks.

You should now clearly understand the audio you will be working with; but before you begin mixing, you still have a few holes in your sound effects to fix.

Working with Markers

You can use markers to annotate clips in the timeline, identify a specific time in the timeline ruler, or label a range of time. Such markers are often used as reminders for a task that you want to do later. In this timeline, we've added a few sound effects and marked them using blue markers to identify them as completed tasks. However, a few shots require more ambient sounds—such as breaking waves and birds chirping—to fill in awkward silent spots. In this exercise, you'll add colored markers to identify the three clips that need additional sound effects.

1. In the timeline, position the playhead over the **07 WS Ride Down Hill** cut-away clip.

   This clip could use some ambient sound effects of ocean surf. To place a marker here, you must first select the clip.

2. Using the Selection tool, click the clip in the timeline.

   You can add markers using the Marker button in the toolbar.

3. Click the Marker button.

A blue marker is added to the clip in the timeline at the current playhead position.

> **TIP:** You also can add markers on the fly. During playback, markers are added to the timeline ruler every time you press M.

4. On the clip, double-click the blue marker, or select the marker and press Shift-M, to open the Marker dialog.

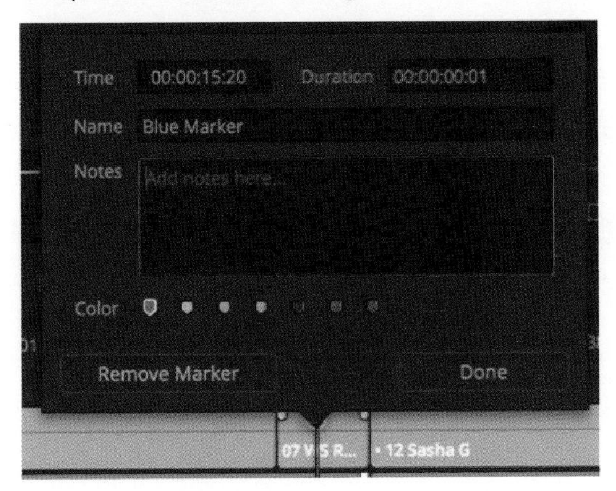

You can change the color of markers to further organize your work. For instance, you can add green markers where graphics are needed and purple markers where effects are needed. You could also add notes to markers to be more descriptive of the changes.

5. Click the red color swatch, and in the Notes section, type **Add ocean SFX**. Click Done.

You will assign the color red to markers for tasks that have not been completed, and the color blue for markers on completed tasks. With one clip completed, you have two more timeline locations that need markers and notes.

6. In the timeline, position the playhead over the **02 Extreme WS S Curve** clip.

7. Select the clip in the timeline.

   To set the color before you apply the marker, you can use the Marker pop-up menu.

8. Click the Marker pop-up menu, and choose Red.

   Selecting a color from the pop-up menu also applies the marker to the selected clip.

9. Double-click the red marker, and in the Notes section, type **Add chirping bird SFX**. Click Done.

> **NOTE:** You can apply flags in a manner similar to markers. The important distinction is that adding a flag to a clip also flags every other clip that shares the same source media. Flags highlight source media, and can be seen throughout the project anywhere the source is used.

With the red marker selected from the list of colored markers, any additional markers you add will be added with that color until you choose another.

Marking a Range of Frames

Markers can be placed on a single video frame as you have been doing, but they can also be attached to a range of frames. Doing so is useful when you want to identify a timeline area that needs attention.

1. In the timeline, position the playhead at the start of the **09 Parking** clip.

   To add a marker to a range of frames that cross clip boundaries, you must add it to the timeline ruler.

2. In the timeline, make sure that no clips are selected, and press M to apply the marker to the Timeline Ruler.

3. Press Shift-M, and in the Notes section, type **Add chirping to last two clips**. Click Done.

4. To extend the range of the marker, Option-drag (OS X) or Alt-drag (Windows) the marker to the left until the range encompasses the last clip in the timeline.

Now, with all the markers in place, you'll add sound effects to address the issues you annotated within those markers.

Finding Markers Using the Edit Index

In a small timeline such as the one you have here, navigating to each marker isn't much of a challenge. On more involved projects, however, you'll need a quick way to locate one specific marker among dozens of other markers. The Edit Index is a list view of all of the editing events (clips and markers) in the current timeline.

1. At the top of the Resolve window, click the Edit Index button.

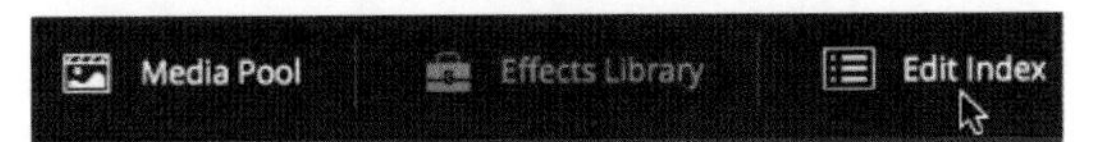

The Edit Index opens below the Media Pool, showing all the editing events and columns of metadata. This is too much information to digest even in a small timeline such as this.

2. In the upper-right corner of the Edit Index, click the Options menu.

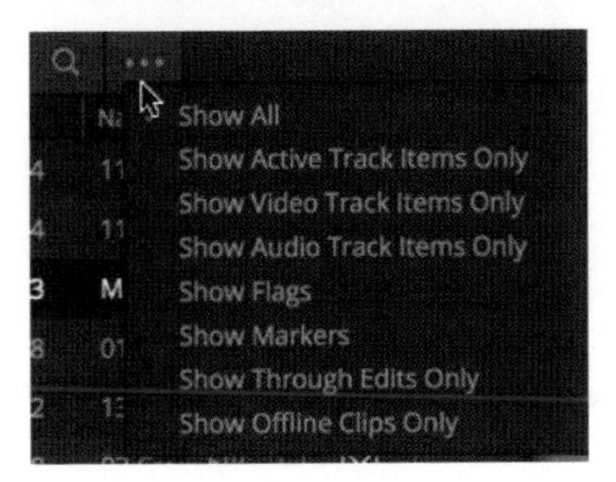

3. Choose Show Markers.

   The Edit Index changes to show only those markers in the timeline, making it much easier to review the list. But you can make it even easier. As with the bin List view, you can choose to show or hide columns of information.

4. Right-click a column header to open the menu of columns.

5. In this menu, uncheck each column except for Number, Color, and Notes.

   Now you are able to identify each marker by color and note.

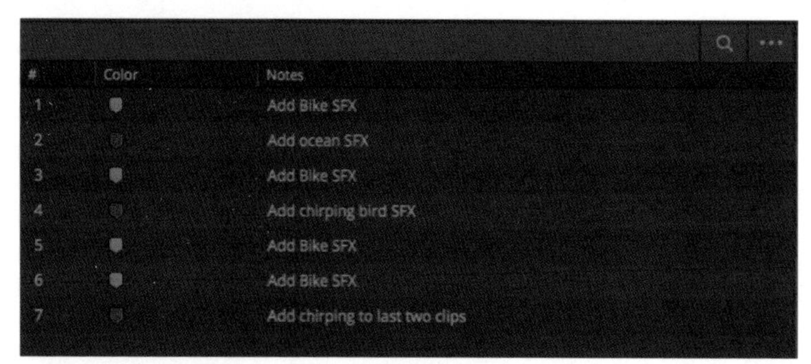

6. Click the red marker that contains the note "Add ocean SFX."

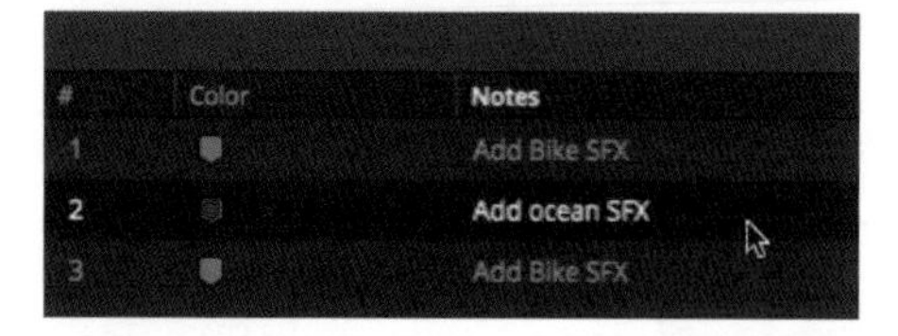

   The timeline jumps to the head of that clip. This is the first clip to which you'll add sound effects.

7. Click the Auto Select buttons for all the tracks except V1.

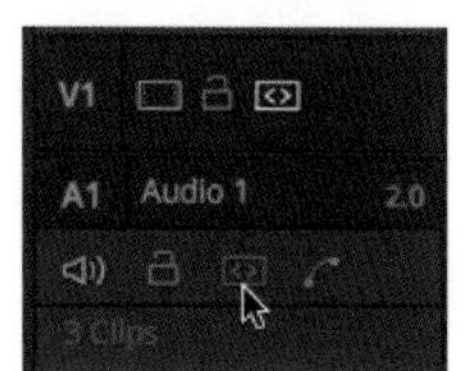

8. Tap the X key to mark an In point and Out point around the **07 WS Ride Down Hill** clip.

9. In the Music and Sound Effects bin, double-click the **06 Ocean Waves** clip to load it into the viewer.

   This clip already has an In point marked. All you have to do is patch the track and overwrite it into the timeline.

10. Drag the A1 destination control to A2, and in the toolbar, click the Overwrite button, or press F10.

    The ocean waves sound effect is cut into A2. Now you'll edit in the next two sound effects using the same method.

11. Click the #4 red marker with the note "Add chirping bird SFX."

12. With the Auto Select controls enabled only for V1, tap the X key to mark an In point and Out point around **02 Extreme WS S Curve**.

13. In the Music and Sound Effects bin, double-click the **02 Chirping** clip to load it into the viewer.

    This clip also has an In point already marked.

14. In the toolbar, click the Overwrite button, or press F10, to edit the bird-chirping sound effect into A2.

    The remaining edit is slightly different because the sound effect has to extend through the last two clips.

15. Click the red marker that contains the note "Add Chirping to last two clips."

16. Enable the Auto Select controls for all the tracks, because you'll have to mark the timeline In and Out points to include two clips.

17. Mark an In point at the current playhead position.

18. Place the playhead at the end of the last video clip, and mark an Out point.

19. In the Music and Sound Effects bin, double-click the **01 Chirping** clip to load it into the viewer.

    This clip also has an In point marked.

20. In the toolbar, click the Overwrite button, or press F10, to edit the second chirping sound effect into A2 under the last two clips.

21. Click the Edit Index button to close the Edit Index.
22. Move the playhead to the start of the timeline and play the entire timeline.

All of your audio tracks are now in place. That's the good news. The bad news is that when multiple audio tracks play simultaneously, they may compete for attention. It's your job as the editor to make sure that the most important audio content is heard and that the supporting audio tracks support the scene without detracting from it.

Setting Level and Pan

With all video and audio edited into your timeline, it's time to set the relative audio levels for the scene. You'll start by examining the tracks that contain the primary audio—in this case, it's the interview clips on A1—and setting those clips to their maximum volume levels.

1. Position the playhead at the start of the timeline.
2. Mute tracks A2 and A3 so you hear only the primary interviewee's voice.

When an audio clip is selected in the timeline, Level and Pan parameters are displayed in the Inspector.

3. Select the first audio clip on A1.
4. In the upper-right corner of the Resolve window, click the Inspector button, or press Cmd-9 (OS X) or Ctrl-9 (Windows). Then, click the Audio tab, if necessary.

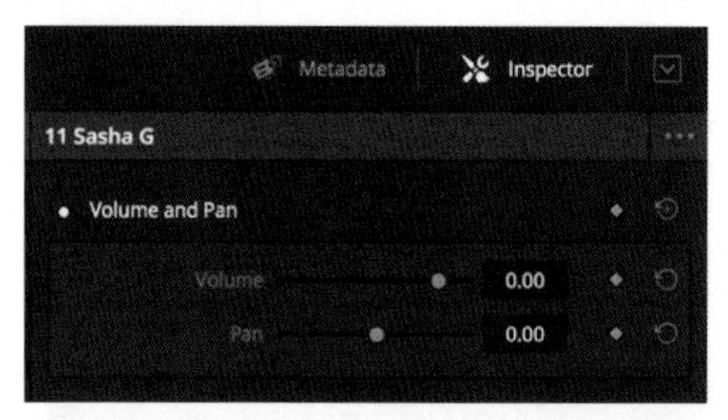

NOTE: The keyboard shortcut for the Inspector does not toggle the pane open and closed. If the Inspector is not open, pressing the shortcut will open the pane; if the Inspector is already open, pressing the keyboard shortcut makes it the active pane.

In the Inspector, the Audio tab is selected and the Volume and Pan parameters are visible.

5. Drag the Volume slider to the right to increase the clip volume. Keep dragging until the tip of the highest peak in the waveform is displayed in a lighter shade of green.

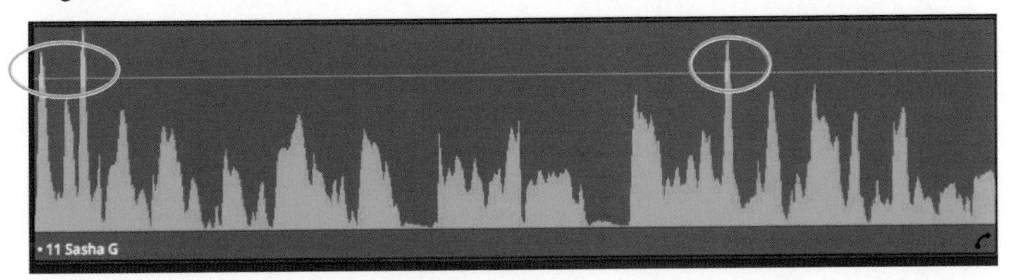

The lighter green indicates an audio peak that is above the –20 dB reference level setting. For your primary audio clips, your goal should be to set the loudest peaks below the maximum level of 0 dB. Unlike analog audio, digital audio has no *headroom*, so peaks in your audio that reach or exceed 0 dB will be distorted.

Conversely, setting the volume of your primary clips too low won't take advantage of the full digital dynamic range, which will make the audio hard to hear.

> **TIP:** Resolve uses an audio reference level of -20 dBFS by default because this reference level is the Society of Motion Pictures and Television Engineers (SMPTE) standard. You can change this in project settings if you want to use a different reference level.

6. Select the second audio clip on A1, and in the Inspector, adjust the Volume parameter so that the highest peak barely appears above the thin white audio level line.

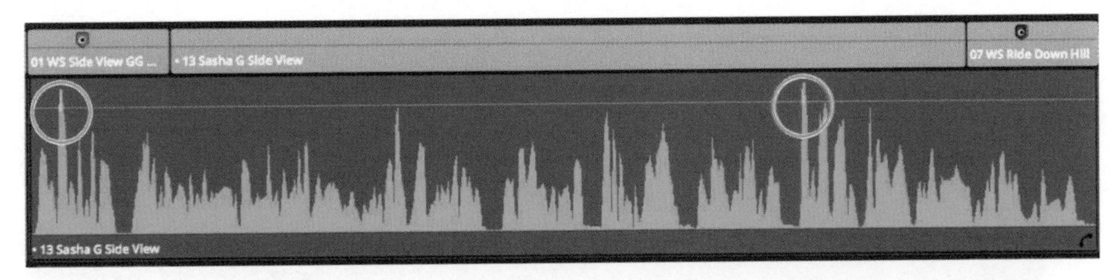

> **TIP:** After you drag the Volume slider, you can press Option-Left Arrow or Option-Right Arrow (OS X) to incrementally increase the Volume setting; or press Alt-Left Arrow or Alt-Right Arrow (Windows) to incrementally decrease the Volume setting.

As you can see, using the waveforms display to set the optimum volume level for a clip is a simple process that has the added benefit of enabling you to locate distortion problems before you even play the clip.

WHAT REFERENCE DECIBEL LEVEL SHOULD I USE?

When you're mixing digital audio, the signal peaks cannot exceed 0 dB or the sound will distort. In contrast, traditional analog audio meters are called VU standard meters that are calibrated so that a 1 kHZ tone at -10 dBFS registers as 0 VU on the meter. Analog audio has headroom so a 0 dB level signifies only the average audio level Individual audio peaks can be permitted to exceed 0 dB.

To avoid reaching a distortion point, digital audio changes the scale. As a result, reading of 0 dB on an analog meter is the same as –20 dBFS on a digital meter. However, not all countries use the –20 dBFS SMPTE standard that is used in the US. For example, the European Broadcasting Union (EBU) standardized at –18 dBFS level.

The reference setting you should use in Resolve depends upon the participating post-production facility or facilities, and the intended distribution regions and channels.

Viewing Audio Meters

In addition to the Waveform displays, Resolve includes audio peak meters that provide a more traditional way to monitor the audio levels of the combined tracks of your timeline.

NOTE: The combined level of audio tracks will peak higher than a single audio track. Keep this in mind when setting levels of individual tracks.

1. In the toolbar, click the Audio Panel button.

The master audio meters open to the right of the timeline.

2. In the timeline, position the playhead at the start of the third interview audio clip, and select that clip.

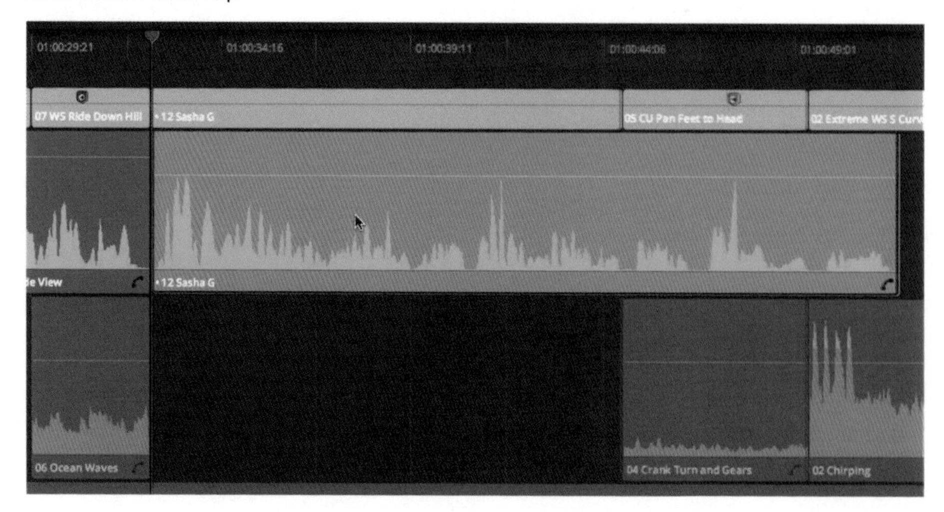

Unlike the visual feedback of Waveform displays, when checking levels using audio meters, you must set a volume level and then play the entire clip while watching for clipping or distortion. If you spot clipping, you have to lower the master volume level and recheck the meter during another playback.

3. In the Inspector, set the Volume between 4.0 and 4.5.

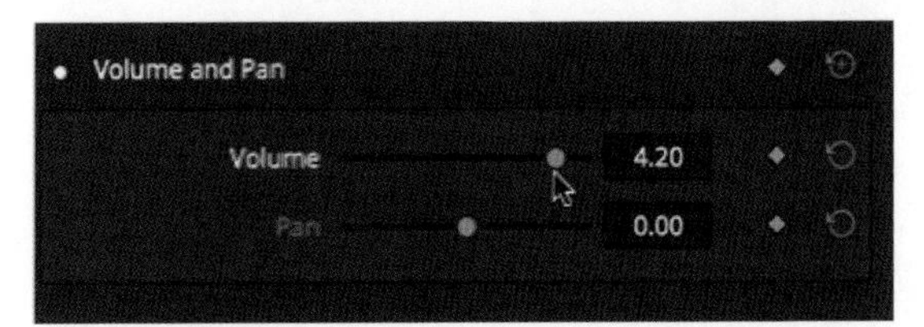

4. Choose Playback > Play Around/To > Play Around Current Clip.

   By default, the master audio levels show the average audio levels using a single pixel red line that indicates the peak level. When the audio peaks hit 0 dBFS or higher, they can distort.

5. Double-click the Volume parameter's number field, and type **2.5**.

6. Choose Playback > Play Around/To > Play Around Current Clip.

This time the audio meters display no red LED, thereby indicating that you have maximized the volume level without causing clipping.

Using the Audio Mixer

The Audio Mixer is useful when you want to see meter readings for individual tracks and adjust the volume as you play those tracks. How well it works for you depends somewhat on which mixer you choose from the Audio Panel pop-up menu.

1. Click the Audio Panel pop-up menu.

   This pop-up menu displays options for Clip Mixer and Track Mixer. Choosing Clip Mixer enables adjustments that affect only the clip currently under the playhead. Choosing Track Mixer enables adjustments that affect all of the clips on a given track.

2. Choose Clip Mixer.

The mixer opens to the right of the timeline, displaying volume sliders, also called *faders*, for all three audio tracks.

3. On the timeline track header, click the Mute button for A2 to unmute it.

4. Play the timeline to listen to the combination of the interview and the sound effects.

   During playback, the audio meter next to each track's fader shows the levels of the current clip. The master meters show the combined output of all of the audio tracks.

   The first bike sound effect is a bit low, so let's increase its volume using the fader for Audio 2.

5. Position the playhead over the first sound effect audio clip on Audio 2.

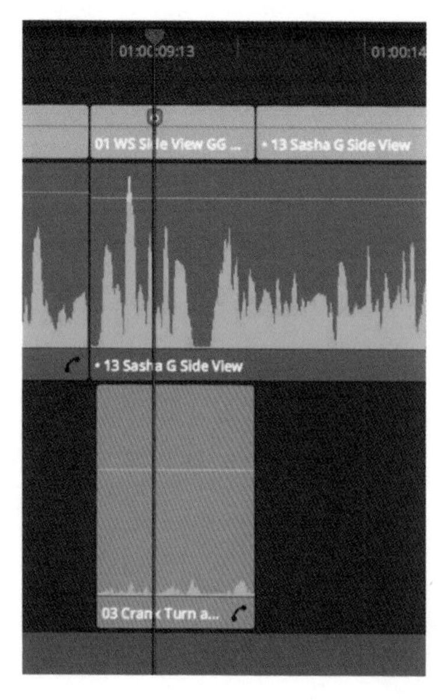

6. In the Audio Mixer, drag up the fader for Audio track 2 to between 5.0 and 6.0.

> **TIP:** Double-clicking the Volume or Pan controls in the Audio Mixer resets them to their default settings.

7. Position the playhead before the first sound effect audio clip, and play it to hear the new volume setting. That sound effect is now more prominent and easier to hear.

   Now you'll adjust the second sound effect. This time the sound of the ocean is much too loud and drowns out the interview subject. To make it easier to balance the two clips, you can adjust the fader as you play back the timeline.

8. Position the playhead before the second sound effect audio under the **07 WS Ride Down Hill** clip.

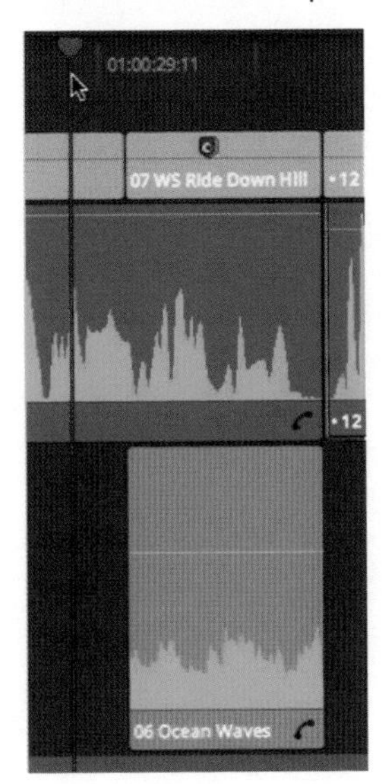

9. Press the Spacebar to start playback, and adjust the Audio track 2 fader to a level that you feel achieves an appropriate balance between the interviewee and the ocean sound effect. Press the Spacebar again to stop playback when the sound effect clip ends.

> **TIP:** The master fader can be used to reduce the overall level of the mix without changing the relative levels of each track.

If you aren't satisfied with the balance you just achieved between the two clips, you can repeat this process as many times as you like until you achieve the levels that sound the best to you.

Copying and Pasting Audio Levels

Three additional bicycle sound effects and two ambient sound effects could use adjustments similar to the ones you just performed. But instead of adjusting each clip individually, you can copy the volume adjustment from one clip and paste it to the others.

1. Click the Audio Panel icon to close the Audio Mixer, leaving more room for the timeline.

2. Select the first sound effect audio clip on Audio 2, and choose Edit > Copy, or press Cmd-C (OS X) or Ctrl-X (Windows).
3. Select the sound effect under the **05 CU Pan Feet to Head** clip.

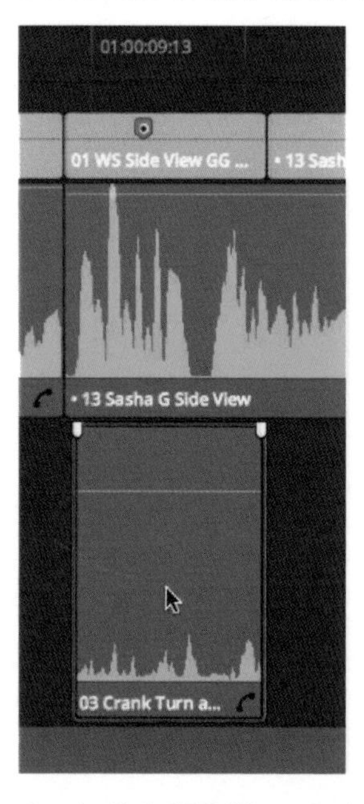

4. Cmd-click (OS X) or Ctrl-click (Windows), the remaining two bicycle sound effect clips that are under **06 WS S Curve** and the clip after it, **08 MS Riding Away**.

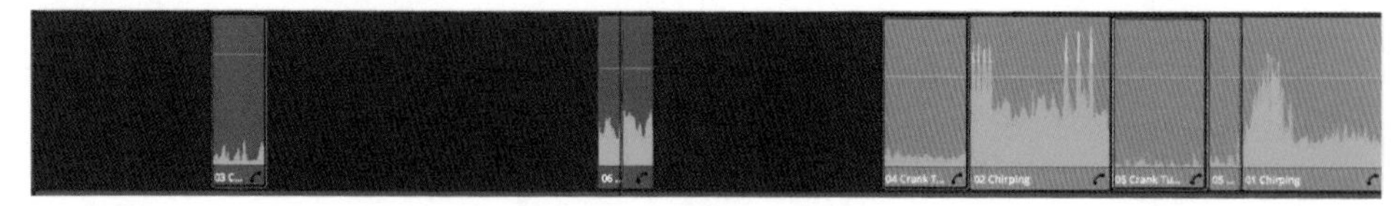

5. Choose Edit > Paste Attributes, or press Option-V (OS X) or Alt-V (Windows).

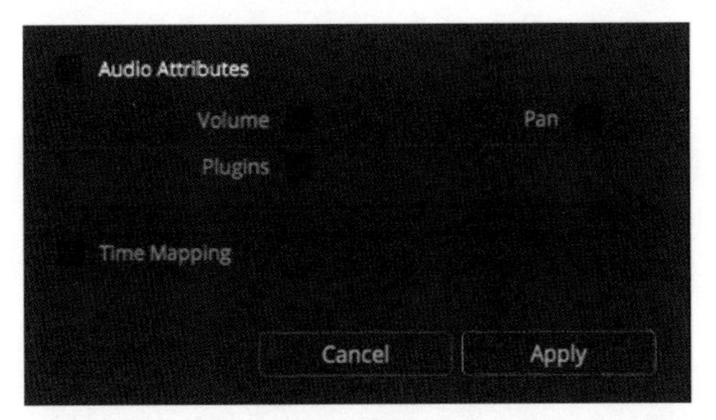

The Paste Attributes window includes clip attributes that can be copied and pasted from one clip to another.

6. Select the Audio Attributes Volume checkbox, and click Apply.

   The volume attributes from the first sound effect clip are pasted onto the three selected sound effect clips.

7. Play over the three clips that received the new attributes. Make any additional fader adjustments that seem appropriate.

   Now you'll correct the two remaining ambient sound effect clips.

8. Select the second sound effect audio clip, under **07 WS Ride Down Hill**, and choose Edit > Copy, or press Cmd-C (OS X) or Ctrl-X (Windows).

9. Select the sound effect under the **02 Extreme WS S Curve** clip, and Cmd-click (OS X) or Ctrl-click (Windows) the chirping sound effect under **09 Parking**.

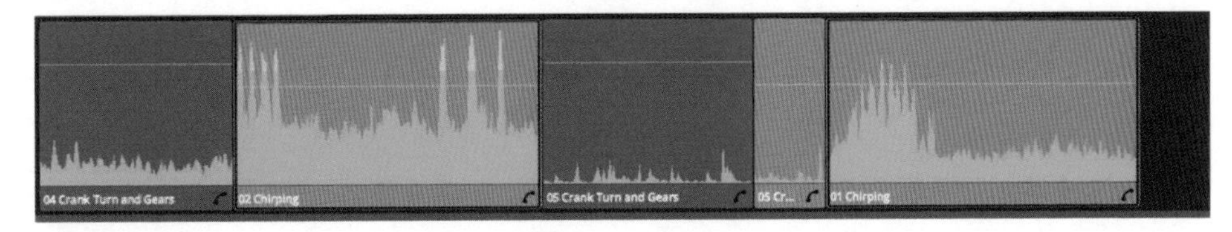

10. Choose Edit > Paste Attributes, or press Option-V (OS X) or Alt-V (Windows).

11. Make sure the Audio Attributes Volume checkbox is still selected, and click Apply.

    The volume attributes from the second sound effect clip are pasted onto the two selected sound effect clips.

12. Play the entire timeline to hear all the adjustments you've made so far.

Copying and pasting attributes to set clips at similar levels can save you a lot of time when working with a complex timeline. You can also paste other attributes, including video attributes.

Changing a Level Within a Clip

The music track is the final track that you'll integrate into your mix. Level setting is slightly more involved here than with the other tracks because you really want to set two levels for this one music clip. The music should be at a quiet level as it plays under the interview portion of the timeline and then gradually increase in volume after the interview ends.

The audio mixer is the generally best place to make adjustments when you have to ride levels and make changes on the fly to support changes within the track. For basic level adjustments, however, you can quickly set clip levels graphically in the timeline using the *level curves*.

1. In the track header for Audio 3, click the Mute button.

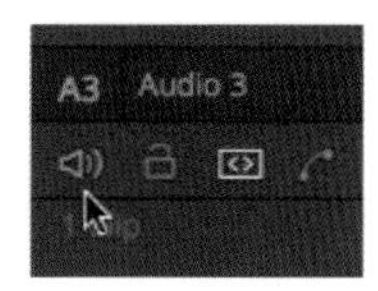

A thin white line in the audio clip represents the volume level of the clip. By default, the line starts out flat because the clip is at the same level for its entire duration. Initially, you'll set the level to remain under the level of the interview. You'll want it low enough so that it doesn't interfere with the spoken words but loud enough to add to the scene's "feel." You can set the level by changing the level curve directly in the timeline.

2. For the music clip, drag the level curve down until the tool tip reads roughly –10db.

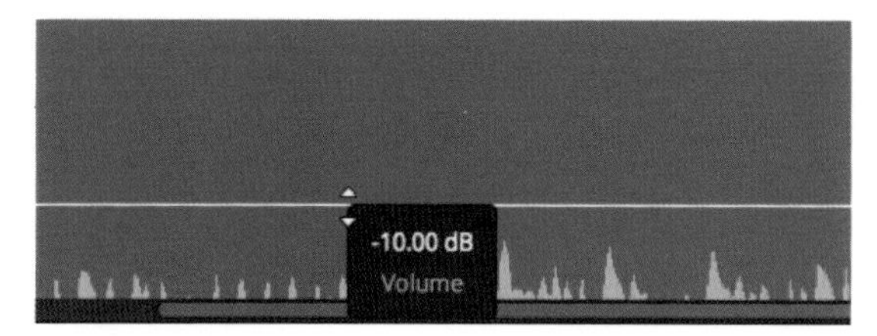

3. Play the timeline with the audio mixed in.

Dragging the entire level curve has set the clip's overall level. This level should suit the interview portion of the timeline, but it's much too low to later underscore the montage of bike-riding shots. By adding keyframes to manipulate the curve, you can change a clip's volume over time.

4. Position the playhead after the last interview audio clip.

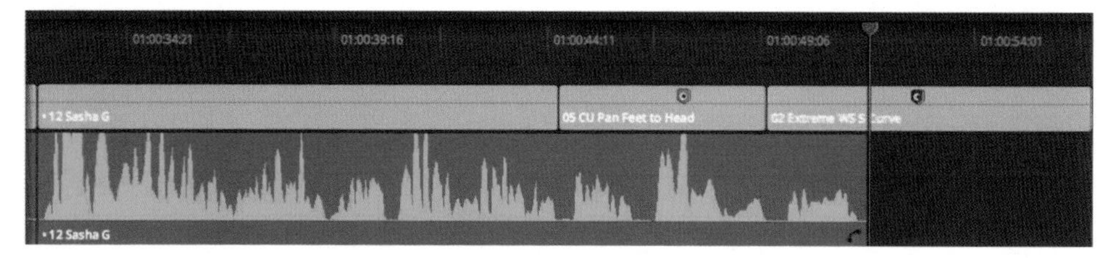

5. Option-click (OS X) or Alt-click (Windows) the level curve under the playhead position.

A faint white dot is added to the curve to indicate that a keyframe was placed at that location. (You may have to move the playhead slightly to see it.) This control point marks the point where you will begin to change the music volume. Now you'll set a control points where you want the volume to stop changing at a louder level that will play for the remainder of the timeline.

6. Position the playhead at the end of **02 Extreme WS S Curve**.
7. Option-click (OS X) or Alt-click (Windows) the level curve under the playhead position to add a control point.

> **NOTE:** You needn't reposition the playhead to add a control point. You can Option/Alt-click anywhere along the level curve to add a control point. Using the playhead, however, makes it easier to identify the precise frame in which you want to place the control point.

You've now set the duration that the gradual volume change, or *ramp*, will occur. Changing the vertical position of the second control point will cause a *ramp up* in volume.

8. Position the pointer over the second control point on the music clip.

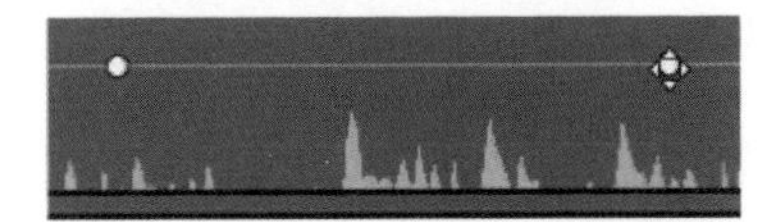

The pointer changes to a Move pointer to indicate that it is over a control point.

9. Drag the control point up until the tool tip reads roughly –5.00 db.

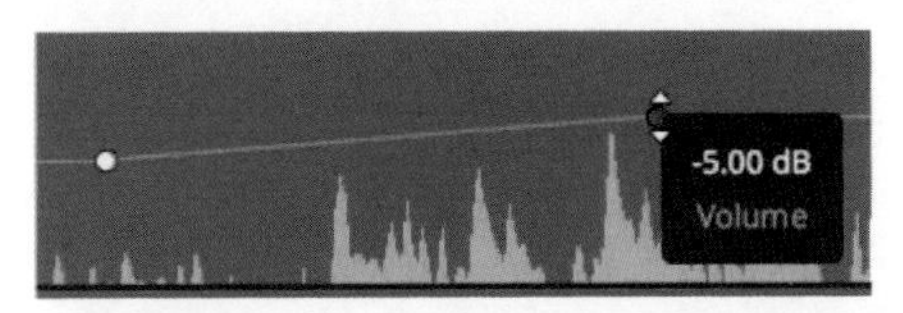

> **NOTE:** You may want to "perform" the volume changes by hand using the faders in the Audio Mixer. To do so, on the Fader Channel in the Audio Mixer, change the Automation menu from Read to Touch. Then play the timeline as you move the fader to set (and record) the level changes in real time. Resolve adds control points to the level curve as needed. When you're finished, the fader changes you made are applied to the level curve. When you have finished, however, be sure to return the Automation menu to Read.

10. Play the entire timeline to hear the mix with the music ramp at the end.

Most of the mixing done while editing can be performed more easily using the level curves than in any other way. It enables great precision with limited complexity.

Adding Audio Fades

Most audio fades are added as a corrective process to soften the incoming or outgoing audio clip. You'll find that you'll often use the obvious fade-out on music, but subtler fades are even applied to narration and dialogue when plosives, particularly those that start with P and B, are too harsh to leave unchanged.

1. Play over the **07 WS Ride Down Hill** clip with the ocean waves sound effect.

   No matter how low you set this sound, it always comes in and cuts out abruptly. It needs to be loud enough to be noticeable, but without drawing attention to itself. Adding a fade-in and fade-out will soften this sound effect.

2. In the timeline, place the pointer over the **06 Ocean Waves** sound effect clip.

   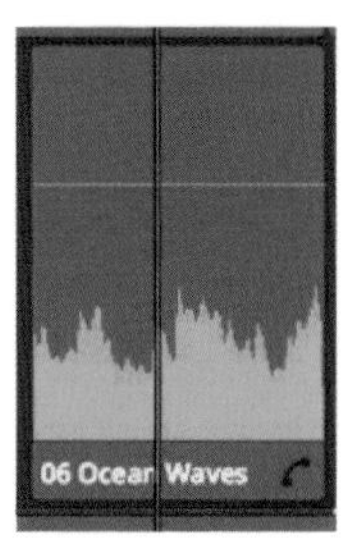

   Audio Fade handles appear in the upper-left and upper-right corners of the clip.

3. Drag the left handle in toward the center of the clip until the tool tip reads 0:12, and drag the right handle in until the tool tip reads –1:00.

   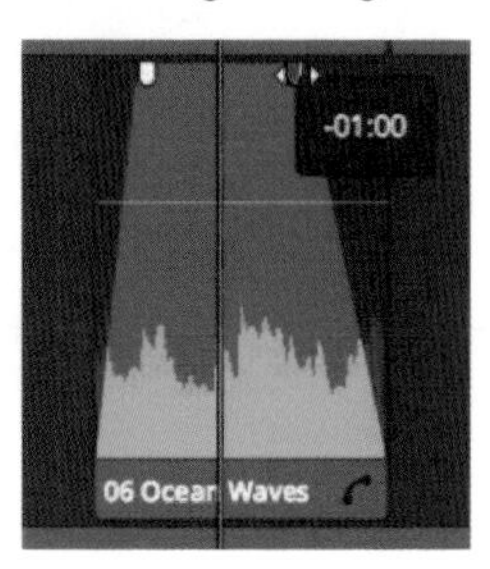

   You've added a half-second fade-in to the start of the clip and a one-second fade-out to the end.

4. Play over the ocean waves to hear the change. Feel free to adjust the length of each fade to suit yourself.

You can use any combination of fade handles, level curves, Audio Mixer tweaks, Inspector changes, peak meter adjustments, and waveform methods that you feel most comfortable with to refine your audio tracks; but these tools and techniques are ultimately just a means for you to achieve the best balance for your soundtrack. Your ear and your growing experience with audio editing should always be the final arbiter of what sounds right.

7 Applying Transitions

Ensuring the continuity between scenes and even between shots is part of the editor's job. You've learned that extending audio across shots can reinforce that continuity. In this lesson, you'll explore how visual transitions can also establish those essential connections between shots and scenes.

Transition effects such as dissolves can transport the audience between different times and places (as in the parallel storytelling of *The Godfather Part II*), and can establish metaphors for a film (as in *Citizen Kane*'s dissolve from the prison-like gate to the Xanadu mansion).

In this lesson, you'll create dissolves and other visual transitions in Resolve, and discover ways to apply and modify those transitions to best enhance continuity along with your visual style.

TIME

- **This lesson takes approximately 35 minutes to complete.**

GOALS

- **Add cross dissolves**
- **Access the Effects Library**
- **Customize transitions**
- **Saving custom transitions**
- **Replace transitions**
- **Fade video in and out**
- **Render effects**

Adding Cross Dissolves

A transition is a gradual transformation from the ending of one shot to the start of the next. You've seen them many times on TV and in films, even if you didn't consciously make note of them. The most common video transition is the Cross Dissolve, which is an overlapping fade between the end of one clip and the beginning of the next. The quickest way to add a Cross Dissolve is to create it directly in the timeline.

1. Open **DaVinci Resolve Lesson 5-13.drp** into the timeline viewer.

> **NOTE:** If the Inspector is still open from the previous lesson, close it by clicking the Inspector button to provide the viewers more space.

2. In the timeline, position the playhead over the **05 CU Pan Feet to Head** clip.

This clip starts a series of scenic bike riding shots that you'll use for your transitions. The first transition you'll add will be a dissolve between **05 Pan Feet or Head** and **02 Extreme WS S Curve**.

3. Drag the Zoom slider to zoom in to the clips you'll be working on.
4. Select the edit between **05 CU Pan Feet to Head** and **02 Extreme WS S Curve**.

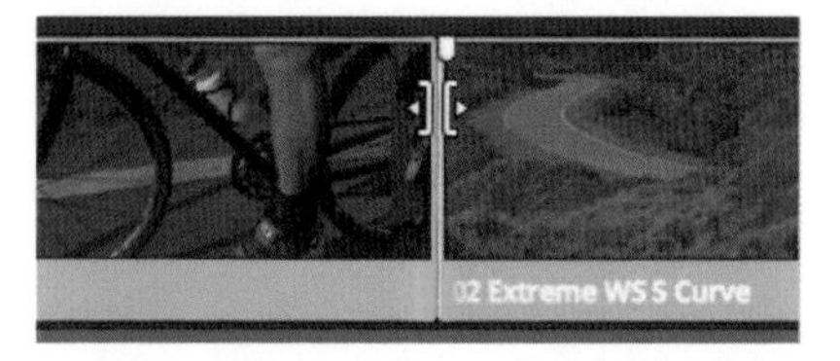

5. Choose Timeline > Add Transition, or press Cmd-T (OS X) or Ctrl-T (Windows).

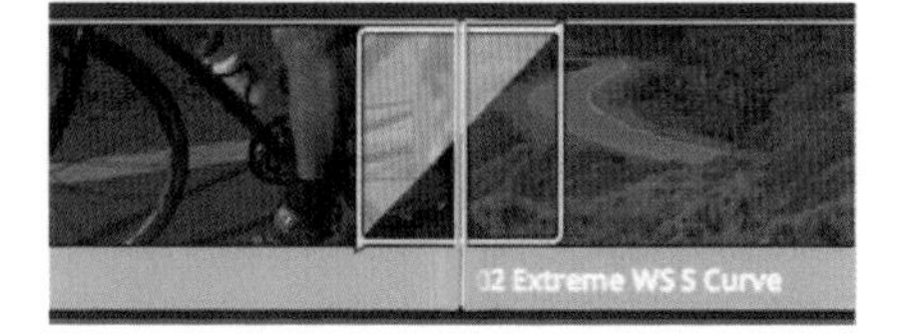

A dissolve with a one-second duration is added to the edit point.

> **TIP:** You can change the default transition duration in the Edit category of the Project Settings.

When creating a transition, frames from the two clips will overlap. That is, half of the transition frames are from the unused portions of the outgoing clip and half from the incoming clip. These handles, which you used for trimming in Lesson 5, are now used to extend clips to support the transition.

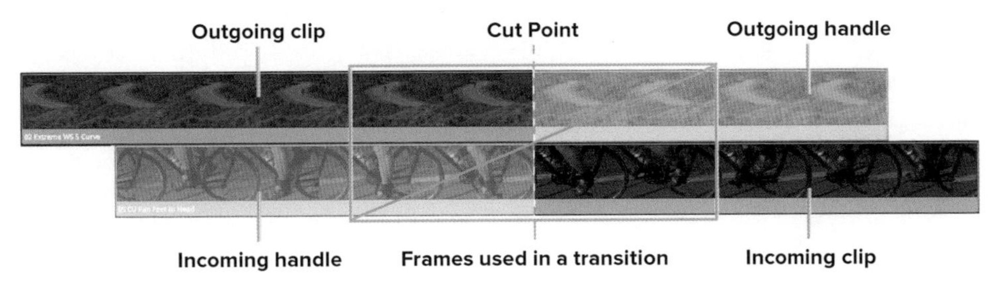

6. Play the two clips to view the dissolve.

   You can select multiple cut points across multiple clips when you want to add multiple dissolves at once. If you want to add a dissolve at the start and end of a single clip, you can do that as well.

7. Select the entire **09 Parking** clip.

8. Choose Timeline > Add Transition, or press Cmd-T (OS X) or Ctrl-T (Windows).

   Two dissolves are added to the clip, one at the start and one at the end.

Shortening and Lengthening Transitions

It would be great if the default one-second dissolve duration fit every scene perfectly, but it won't. It may cut off some of the action or extend a clip so far that you see a camera shake. Whatever the reason, at some point you will want to change the dissolve duration. The easiest and most straightforward way to do so is by dragging in the timeline.

1. Place the mouse pointer over the right edge of the dissolve between **05 Pan Feet to Head** and **02 Extreme WS S Curve**.

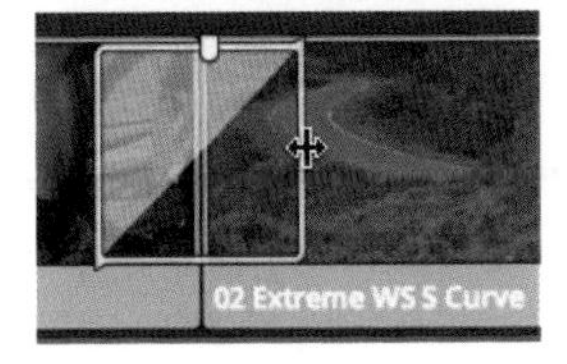

2. Drag the right edge in toward the edit until the tool tip reads -00:06.

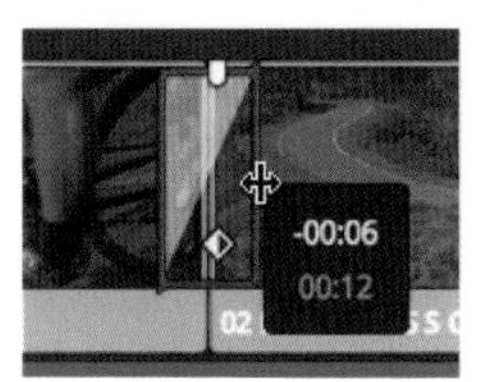

As you drag, the transition is shortened by six frames on both sides of the edit for a total reduction of 12 frames. This dissolve transition is aligned to the center of the cut, so the transition will remove the same number of frames on each side of the cut no matter how long or short you make it.

3. Place the mouse pointer over the right edge of the first dissolve of the **09 Parking** clip.

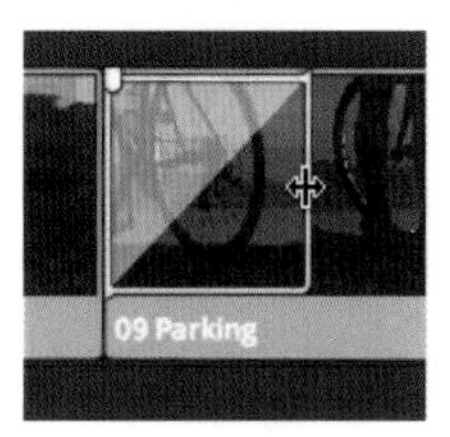

As you may see, this transition is aligned to start at the edit.

4. Drag in toward the cut until the tool tip reads -00:12.

As you drag, the transition is shortened by 12 frames but only on one side of the edit. This transition is aligned to the start of the cut, so the transition can only shorten using frames that appear after the cut.

5. Finally, place the mouse pointer over the left edge of the second dissolve in the **09 Parking** clip.

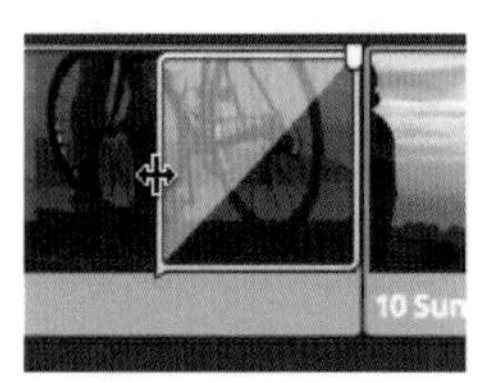

6. Drag in toward the edit until the tool tip reads +00:12.

The transition is reduced by 12 frames but only on one side of the cut because this transition is aligned to end at the cut. In a way, the edit point acts as an anchor for the transition, so the only way to shorten it is by changing the transition's start.

7. Reposition the pointer over the right edge of the first dissolve in the **09 Parking** clip.

So far you have only shortened transitions. You also can lengthen them if a clip includes enough handle to accommodate the transition length you desire.

8. Drag toward the center of the clip as far as possible.

TIP: When adding a transition using a keyboard shortcut or menu choice, selecting the left or right sides of the cut, or both sides before adding that transition determines whether the transition is added ending at cut, starting at cut, or centered on the cut, respectively.

The transition can extend only so far and then the outline turns red to indicate that you've run out of handles on the outgoing clip. That means that no more media is available to create a longer transition.

Changing Alignment

When you run out of handle, you often have to settle for a shorter duration, but if you can be slightly flexible, you can try changing the alignment of the transition.

1. Right-click the first transition on the **09 Parking** clip, and from the contextual menu, choose Center On Edit.

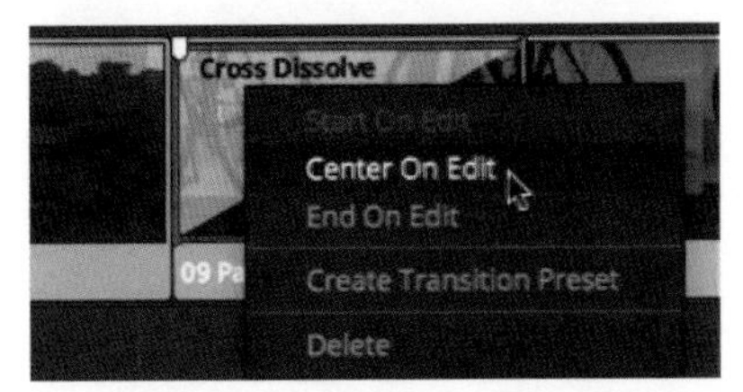

The transition realigns to be centered over the edit point. As a result, the transition will begin earlier than it was originally placed, and you will have enough handle available to extend its length. By starting the transition earlier, you moved it to the left in the timeline, so you now have room to extend it farther to the right.

TIP: If the default transition duration is longer than the available handles will allow, the duration is shortened to fit those handles.

2. Place the cursor on the right edge of the first **09 Parking** transition, and drag toward the center of the clip until the tool tip reads +00:10.

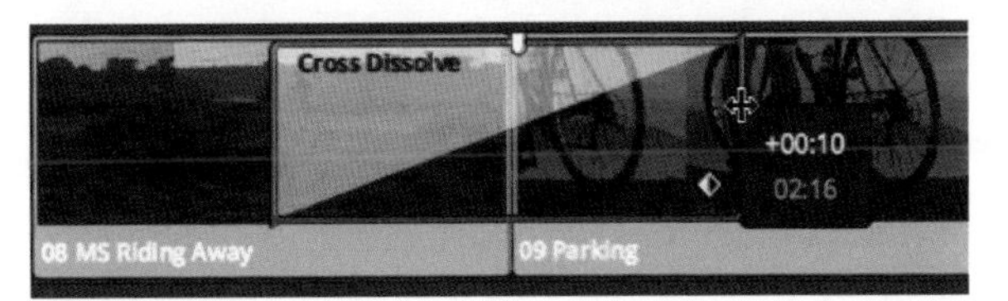

You are able to create a longer dissolve by changing the alignment and starting the transition earlier. If you had to work with even shorter handles, you could align the transition to end at the cut. Although the steps are easy, remember that shifting a transition's start or end point is effective only when it supports your shot continuity.

Copying Transitions

Within a scene it is common to use a transition of the same duration in multiple locations. Doing so helps develop a consistent pace within the scene. In this scene, you'll copy the shorter **09 Parking** transition onto a different cut.

1. Drag the scroll bar at the bottom of the timeline and the Zoom slider in the toolbar so you are able to see the last transition on both **09 Parking** and **06 WS S Curve**.

2. In the **09 Parking** clip, Option-drag (OS X) or Alt-drag (Windows) the last transition over the cut between **06 WS S Curve** and **08 MS Riding Away**, but do not yet release the mouse button.

> **TIP:** If you are finding it difficult to select a transition, use the Zoom slider to zoom in on the timeline until you can select the transition icon without accidentally selecting the cut point.

Holding down the modifier key as you drag makes a copy of the transition that you can place on another cut. Only the type of transition and the duration are copied. You can choose the alignment as you drag the transition over a cut.

3. Drag the transition to the left, so that the transition is aligned to the end of the edit point, and then release the mouse button.

> **TIP:** To remove a transition, zoom in and select it with the Selection tool, and press Delete.

4. Play the timeline to view your added dissolves.

This is a very quick way to apply a dissolve with a custom duration throughout a scene. Being able to add dissolves quickly (and faster than any other transition type) is an important technique to learn. From the drain-to-eye transition of the shower scene in *Psycho* to the openings of every Indiana Jones movie, dissolves are the most commonly used transition type in filmmaking.

Accessing the Effects Library

Resolve includes many types of transitions, each with a unique visual style. Other transitions may not be as useful storytelling tools as the dissolve, but they can be handy in specific situations. Because they are not as commonly used, you add them from the Effects Library and not with a keyboard shortcut.

1. If the Edit Index is still open from the previous lesson, click the Edit Index button to close it.
2. Click the Effects Library button to display the Effects Library.

The Effects Library opens below the Media Pool, where the Edit Index was previously. The effects library is divided into three panels: The Toolbox panel contains the transitions, titles, and generators that are installed with Resolve. The OpenFX panel contains third-party video plug-ins that you've added to Resolve. The Audio FX panel contains third-party audio plug-ins.

NOTE: OS X includes some audio units plug-ins in the Audio FX panel.

3. Drag the scroll bar and the Zoom slider to position the last interview clip and the **05 CU Pan Feet to Head** clip in the center of the timeline.

TIP: You can hold down the middle mouse button on a three-button mouse to pan in the timeline.

4. From the Effects Library, drag the Band Wipe transition over the cut in the timeline.

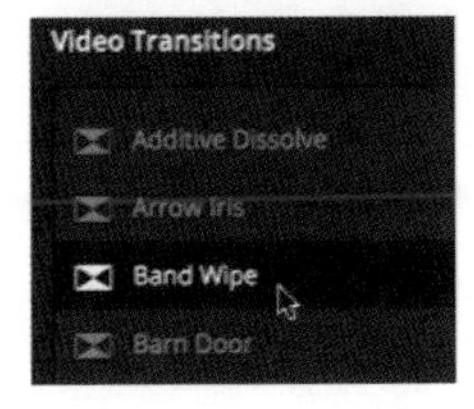

5. Release the mouse button when the Transition cursor is centered over the cut. Play back the transition that you just added.

   When you find yourself using the same transitions over and over within a project, it can be helpful to mark them as favorites, which places them in a shortlist that allows you to access them faster.

6. In the Effects Library, right-click the Band Wipe transition, and from the contextual menu, choose Add to Favorites.
7. Add the Cross Dissolve and Additive Dissolve transitions to your favorites as well.
8. From the Effects Library Options menu, choose Favorites to show the transitions you have marked as favorites.

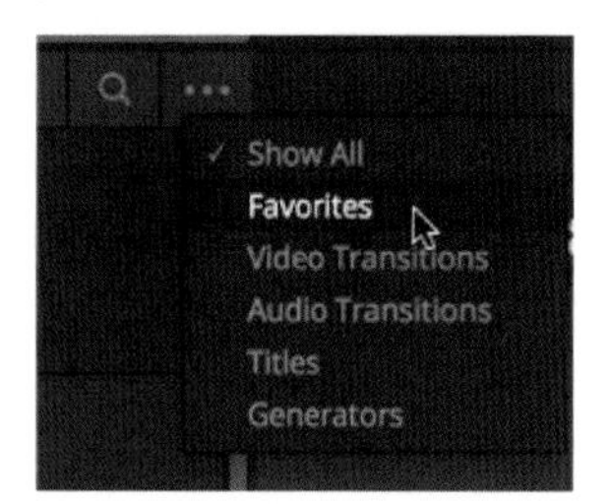

Now you have a subset of the Effects Library readily available, so you no longer have to browse through the entire library. The Favorites list is saved with your Resolve user profile, so any project you create will contain the same Favorites list.

USING THIRD-PARTY VIDEO AND AUDIO PLUG-INS

OpenFX is a cross-platform visual effects plug-in standard used by Blackmagic Design's Resolve and Fusion software. The most popular plug-in packages—such as GenArts' Sapphire, RE:Vision Effects' ReelSmart Motion Blur, and BorisFX Continuum Complete—can be added to Resolve. Thanks to OpenFX, you can use plug-ins to perform many stylized operations that would be difficult or impossible to perform using only the standard tools within Resolve, and those plug-ins can be applied in exactly the same ways you would apply other toolbox items.

The audio plug-in formats supported by Resolve are the VST Plug-in on Windows, and VST or Audio Units on OS X. In addition, OS X includes a number of Audio Units plug-ins by default. The most popular audio plug-in vendors—such as iZotope and Waves—usually support both VST and Audio Units formats. The custom interfaces used by many of these audio plug-ins are accessed from the Inspector. Note that only audio effects, such as compressors, EQ devices, and reverbs, are supported in Resolve. Instrument plug-ins are not supported.

The installation and licensing of plug-ins is managed by each vendor's installer. Once installed, OpenFX plug-ins appear in the Library and in the Open FX panel, whereas VST or Audio Units plug-ins appear in the Library Audio FX panel.

Customizing Transitions

Each transition has a number of adjustments that you can use to customize its appearance. Some of the simpler transitions, such as the Cross Dissolve, have fewer controls than specialty transitions such as wipes. In every case, plug-in customization controls appear in the Inspector.

1. Double-click the Band Wipe between the **13 Sasha G Side View** clip and the **05 CU Pan Feet to Head** clip.

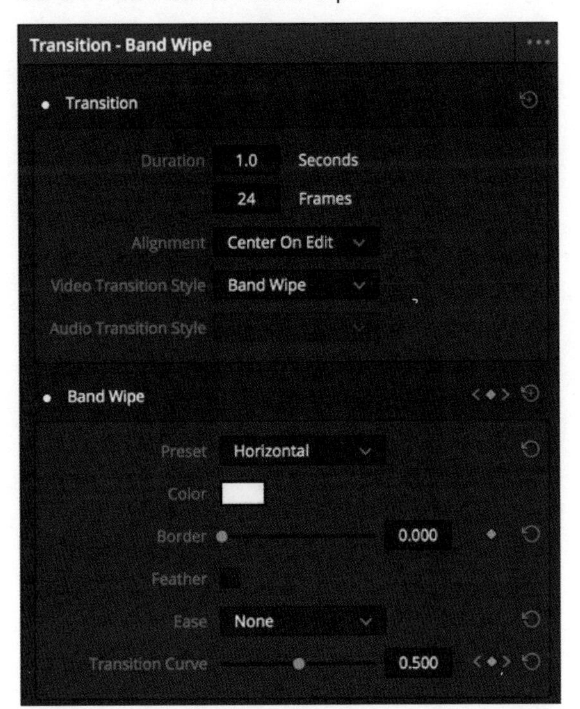

The Inspector displays the transition parameters. The upper half of the Inspector has parameters that are common to all transitions. These include Duration, Alignment, and Transition Style. The lower half has parameters specific to the current transition.

2. Hover the mouse pointer over the Duration value.

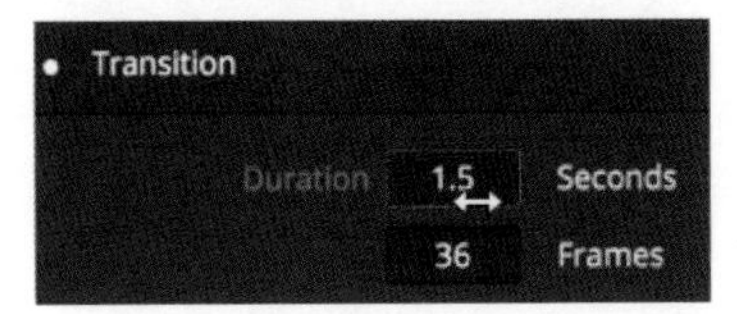

Hovering over the numeric box changes the pointer to a Slider cursor, so you can drag in the data field to change the value.

3. Drag in the field to change the duration to 1.5. The transition is now one and a half seconds long.

4. In the lower half of the Inspector, from the Preset menu, choose Horizontal Bilinear.

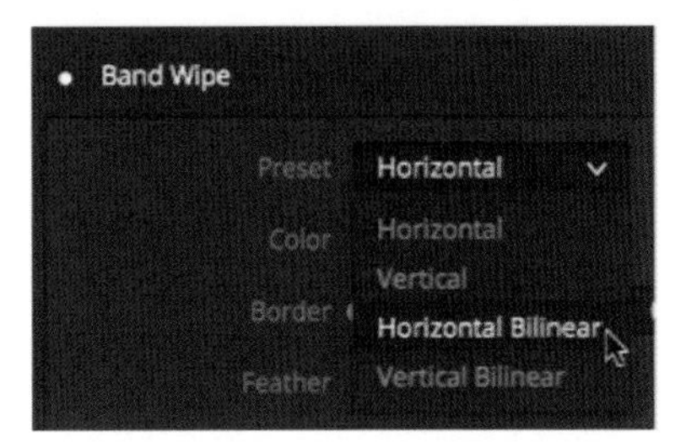

Most wipes and dissolves have variants located under the preset menu. Another common parameter for all the wipes, the Border parameter, adds a colored line to the edge of the wipe. The slider position sets the width, and the color swatch sets the color of the border.

5. Click the color swatch to open the color picker.

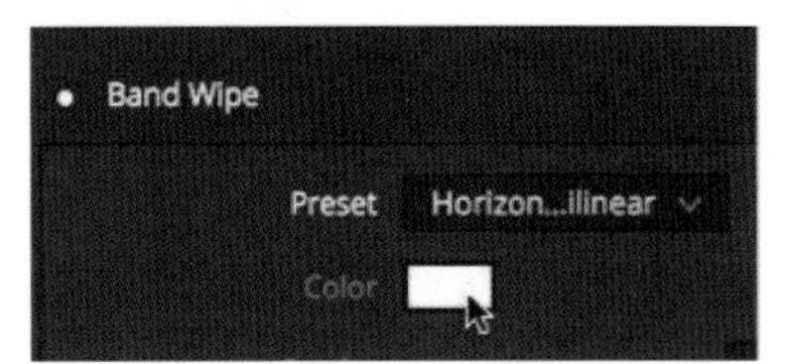

6. Select a color, and click OK to close the window.
7. Drag the Border slider all the way to 320.

   The border color and width will update with the newly selected parameters.

8. Play the modified Edge Wipe to view your changes.

Now that you have made a custom transition, in the next exercise you'll learn how to save it for ongoing use.

Saving Custom Transitions

After customizing a transition, you can save that transition and your customizations into the effects library for use on future projects.

1. Right-click the customized Band Wipe transition between the interview and the **05 CU Pan Feet to Head** clip.

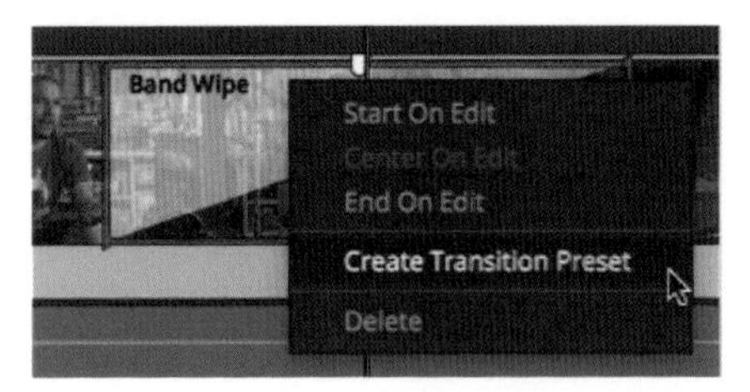

2. From the contextual menu, choose Create Transition Preset.

3. In the Transition Preset dialog, enter the name **Band Wipe with Border**, and click OK.

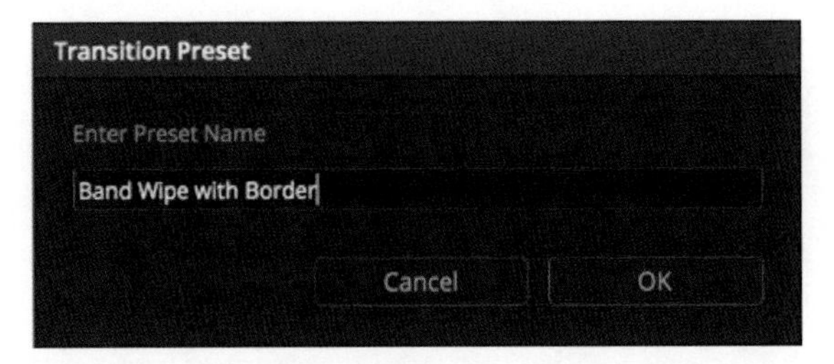

The customized transition is saved into your personal Effects Library ready to be reused in this and your other projects.

Replacing Transitions

Constant changes are a way of life when editing. You will end up making revision after revision, trimming clips here and replacing shots there. And transitions are no exception.

In the next exercise, instead of Edge Wipes, the client has decided she wants Clock Wipes. How you replace transitions can create either more or less work for you. It all depends on the techniques you use and the results you want.

1. Double-click the Band Wipe transition between the interview and the **05 CU Pan Feet to Head** clip, if necessary.

   When you are applying a new transition while trying to retain much of the appearance of the current transition, you'll want always to replace the current transition in the Inspector.

2. From the Video Transition Style menu, choose Spiral Wipe, and play over the transition to see the change.

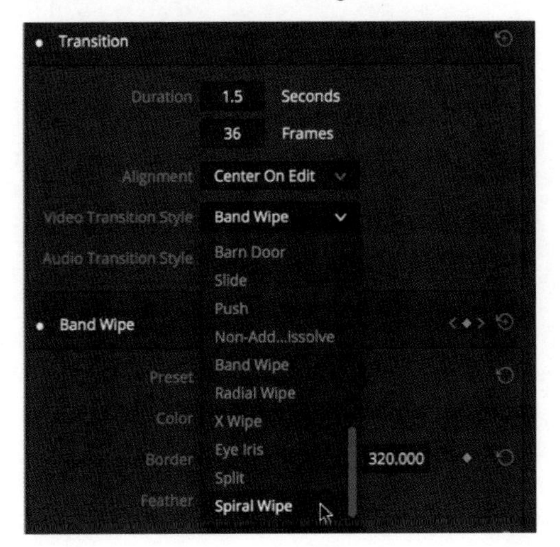

   When you change the style between wipes using the Video Transition Style menu in the Inspector, settings such as Duration, Color, and Border are retained.

3. From the Video Transition Style menu, choose Dip to Color Dissolve, and then play over the transition to see the change.

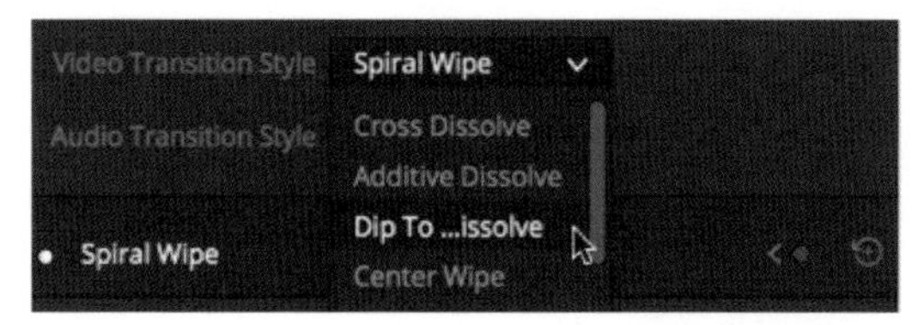

In this case, only the Duration and Color settings are retained. The Border parameter as well as other wipe parameters are not available in the Dip to Color Dissolve transition, so they do not carry over when you switch styles.

You can completely replace a transition within the Effects Library.

4. From the Effects Library, drag the Additive Dissolve transition onto the selected Dip to Color Dissolve transition to replace it in the timeline.

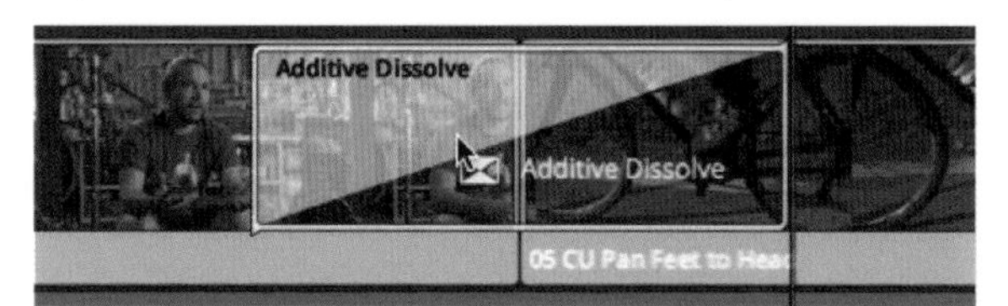

When you replace a transition using the Effects Library, all of the parameters except Duration are reset to the default.

Fading Video In and Out

Typically, a fade transition is used at the start (fade-in) and end (fade-out) of a program or scene. As with a dissolve, when you fade, you are mixing two elements. In a dissolve, both elements are a video clip. In a fade, one element is a completely black frame. So, similar to audio fading, video fading is performed on a single clip and not by using the Effects Library.

1. Position the playhead at the start of the timeline.

To begin this scene, you'll add a very quick fade-in.

2. In the timeline, place the pointer over the **11 Sasha G** clip.

As with audio transitions, two fade handles—Video Fade handles, in this case—appear in the upper-left and upper-right corners of the clip.

3. At the start of the clip, drag the handle toward the center of the clip until the tool tip reads +00:08.

You've added an eight-frame fade-in to the start of the scene.

4. Play the start of the timeline to watch the fade.
5. Place the pointer over the last clip (**10 sunset**) at the end of the timeline.
6. Drag the handle at the end of the last clip toward the center of the clip until the tool tip reads –02:00. This adds a two-second fade out at the end of the clip.

Adjusting fader handles is a fast, easily accessed method for placing and refining fades-in and -out.

Rendering and Background Caching

Depending on the speed of your computer and disk drives, as well as the media file types you are using, not all effects will play back smoothly on every system. The fps indicator above the timeline viewer shows the actual playback frame rate that your computer is achieving. If the number has a red dot next to it, you are running slower than the project frame rate.

To optimize playback performance for complex effects, Resolve automatically renders such effects to your hard disk using a *caching system*. Although Resolve can use three distinct caching systems to render files, this exercise will focus on *sequence caching*, which is the most important cache method for editors. The sequence cache operates on timeline-specific effects such as transitions, opacity adjustments, and composite mode superimpositions. Regions of the timeline that require caching have a red bar over them, whereas regions that are already cached have a blue bar over them.

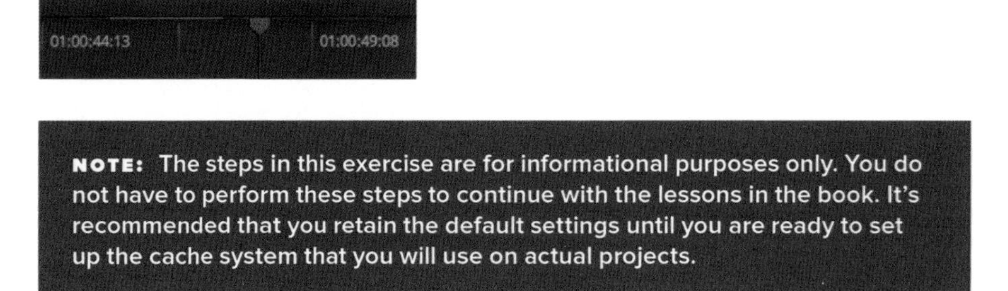

NOTE: The steps in this exercise are for informational purposes only. You do not have to perform these steps to continue with the lessons in the book. It's recommended that you retain the default settings until you are ready to set up the cache system that you will use on actual projects.

The first task when setting up the cache system is to decide where the cache files should be stored and the timing of the caching operation.

1. Choose File > Project Settings, and choose General Options.

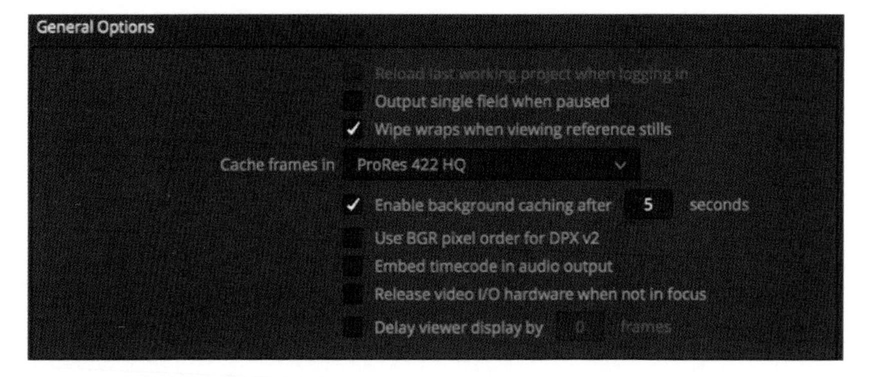

General Options include a few settings related to caching. The "Cache frames in" menu sets the compression format Resolve uses to save the rendered files. The choices common to OS X and Windows include uncompressed 10-bit and 8-bit formats, and Avid's DNxHR formats. On OS X, Resolve also includes Apple's ProRes compression format.

You can make a lot of complex choices, so you might want to retain the default settings until you're more familiar with the options. The default setting creates a high-quality 10-bit file that will look good in your final output. If you are temporarily working on a portable or a laptop with a slow disk drive, you may want to opt for a marginally lower-quality 8-bit format such as Avid DNxHR HQ or ProRes 422 to enable faster processing. For now, you'll leave this setting at the default value and move on to background processing.

2. Make sure the "Enable background caching" checkbox is selected.

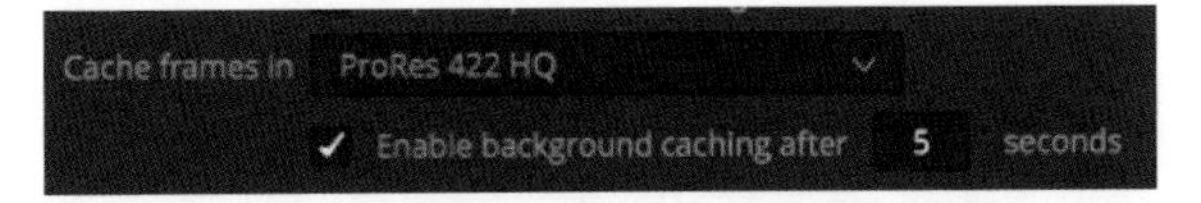

When background caching is enabled, effects rendering will begin based the length of time your computer sits idle.

3. In the "Enable background caching" numeric box, enter **3**.

Background caching will now begin to render effects when your computer sits idle for three seconds.

Selecting which hard drive is used for caching may be the most important part of your setup. If your hard drive isn't fast enough to support the playback of the cache frame compression format that you selected, you'll need to choose a more efficient compression format (usually by opting for lower quality) or use a faster hard drive. Although a cache file location can be set in project settings, it's best to use the first and permanently connected drive shown in the Media Storage setting in Preferences.

4. Click Save to preserve your settings and close the Project Settings window.
5. To open the Preferences window, choose DaVinci Resolve > Preferences, or press Cmd-, (comma) (OS X) or Ctrl-, (comma) (Windows).
6. Select the Media Storage category.

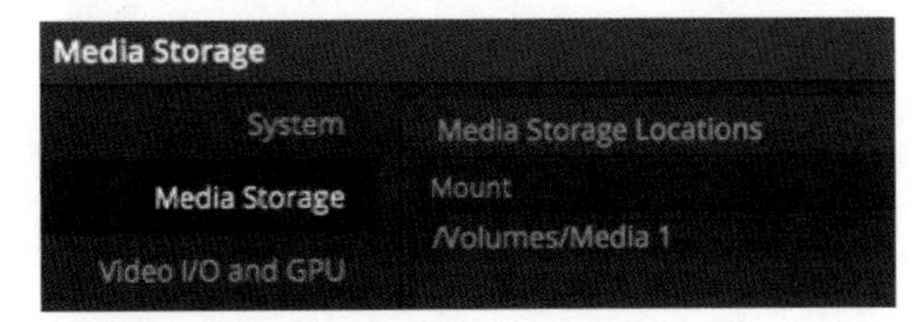

The default disk is your internal system drive, which probably isn't the one you want to select if you have faster and larger hard drives available.

The first media storage location in the list is the disk used to save cache files.

7. Select the current disk, and click Remove to remove it from the list.
8. To add a new media storage location, click Add, and select the disk drive that you want to use.
9. Click Save, and in the confirmation dialog that appears, click OK.

The last step in setting up the sequence cache system is to turn it on.

10. Choose Playback > Render Cache > Smart.

> **TIP:** To delete all of the rendered cache files for the current project, choose Playback > Delete Render Cache > All.

Sequence caching can use only the Smart render cache option. When set to Smart, Resolve automatically renders everything necessary to optimize playback. When you reopen a project, cached clips are still cached.

8 Designing Titles

The main title that starts a movie is expected to convey the tone and spirit of the upcoming film. Today, producing a good main title sequence is an art form that uses typography, color, and animation in creative ways, drawing from graphic design principles that have been used for centuries. In this lesson, you'll apply those same principles to design a lower-third title for your interview scene, and then you'll use Resolve's keyframing capabilities to animate a title on and off the screen.

TIME

- **This lesson takes approximately 30 minutes to complete.**

GOALS

- **Choose a title generator**
- **Modify text parameters**
- **Animate titles**
- **Trim titles using an Extend edit**

Choosing a Title Generator

The first title design choice you must make is to decide what kind of title you are creating. In this scene, you will create a title that explains who your interview subject is and what he does, thereby establishing his importance to this scene. Typically, titles in documentaries, news programs, or any interview program require titles such as these. The type of title is called a *lower third* because it is positioned in the lower third of the frame.

1. Open the DaVinci Resolve Lessons 5-13 project, if necessary, and load **Titles Rough Cut** into the timeline.
2. Open the Effects Library, if necessary.
3. From the Effects Library Options menu, choose Titles.

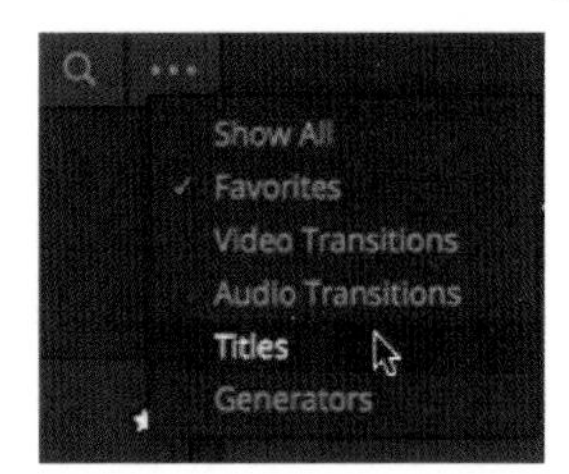

The Effects Library shows the five title generators that you can edit into the timeline. Dragging a title generator into the timeline will apply an Overwrite edit with a five-second duration. However, you can also edit in a title with the edit overlay using In and Out points.

> **TIP:** You can change the default title duration by setting the standard generator duration in the Edit category of the Project Settings.

4. Position the playhead at the start of the timeline.
5. Type **+1.** (a plus sign, a numerical one, and period), and press Return or Enter to move one second into the timeline.

   You'll now create a four-second lower third title using In and Out points in the timeline.
6. Press the I key to mark an In point at the start of the timeline.
7. Type **+7.** (plus, four, period), and press Return or Enter to move four seconds into the timeline.
8. Press O to mark an Out point.

9. From the Effects Library, drag the "L Lower 3rd" title generator over the timeline viewer. In the edit overlay, highlight Place on Top, and release the mouse button.

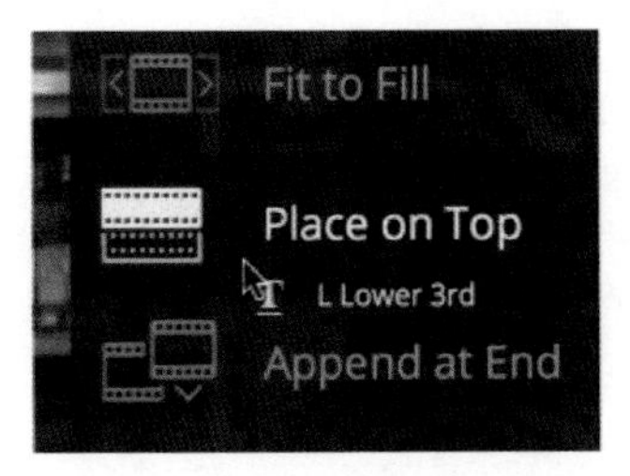

A seven-second lower third title is cut onto V2 of the timeline.

10. Press Option-X (OS X) or Alt-X (Windows) to clear the marks in the timeline.
11. Play the timeline from the beginning to view the title.

The backgrounds of all titles are transparent, so when edited on top of a video clip, the title and video are composited together.

RULE OF THIRDS

Lower third titles are located in the lower third of the screen for a very good reason—the rule of thirds. Professional photographers have used the rule of thirds for years, but it is a long-standing graphic design principle.

The rule can be illustrated by creating a simple tic-tac-toe grid that divides a frame into thirds. The rule states that if you place your subject (in this case, a title) along the lines and particularly where the lines intersect, you will end up with a more pleasing design compared to arbitrarily centering elements in the frame.

Modifying Text Parameters

Your main design choice when creating a title is choosing a mood that will complement the film. Do you choose a typeface that appears elegant, direct, loud, or friendly? To establish the look of letters, you start by choosing a typeface, and then move on to select a size, style, case, and width. You'll find the controls for all these options in the Inspector. But you will start by entering the text for your lower third title in the viewer.

1. Select the text clip in the timeline. In the viewer, double-click the larger "Title" text to select it for editing.

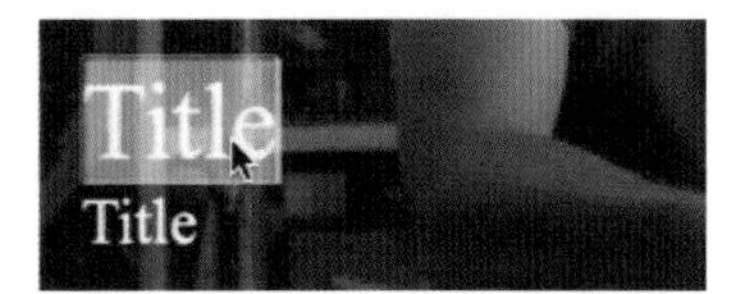

2. Type **Sasha G.**, and double-click the lower "title" text, and type **Citizen Chain Cyclery**.

   Next, you'll select a typeface and a font. Because not all computers have the same typefaces installed, you can select a typeface from those that you have available. Look for one that reflects the spirit of this scene, a slightly rustic typeface with old world charm.

3. In the timeline, double-click the Title segment to open the Inspector.
4. Above the Inspector, click the Expand button to view more of the Inspector parameters.

5. From the Font Family menu, choose a typeface; and from the Font Face menu, choose a specific style.

> **NOTE:** A font is a style within a font family, such as Garamond (the font family, or typeface) Italic (the font face).

6. Do the same for the second line of text using the Font Family and Font Face menus under the second rich text field.

THE SIMILARITY PRINCIPLE

When selecting a typeface for the second line, some people choose to use the same typeface used in the top line. This is the easy way to impose consistency; and for those not comfortable with selecting typefaces, it might be the best choice. The other choice is to use the "similarity" design principle which says that people will perceive elements as a group when they look similar. So, conversely, dissimilar elements will stand out and appear separate. Similarity relationships can come from font, color, or size. This principle is put into practice in title design when the name of the person is one typeface, font, color, or size but that person's title is displayed in another typeface, font, color, or size. These choices are then used as a template throughout the program. People associate one look with the name and another with the title. Good title design should make some use of similarity in arranging elements.

After choosing a font and typeface, your choice of color probably has the most significant impact on your title. You can easily learn the basic use of color by understanding a few simple concepts. Warm colors include variations of red, orange, and yellow and are associated with passion, happiness, and energy. Cool colors include blue, green, and purple and are the colors of calm, relaxation, and contemplation.

7. Click the bottom line's color swatch and select a warm color to reinforce the friendly nature of this sequence.

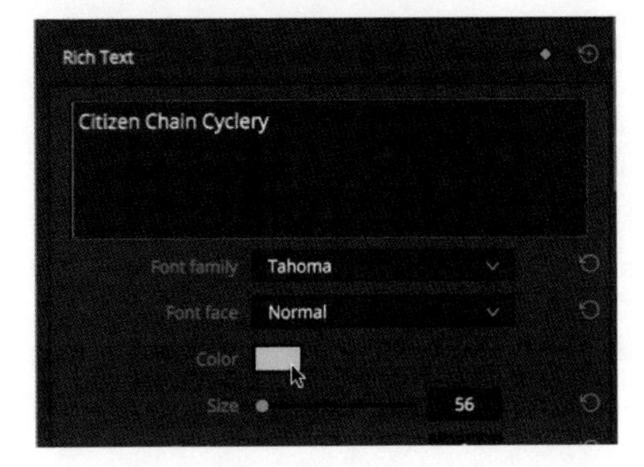

The next grouping of parameters is standard for anyone who has used email or a simple word processor. These parameters include size; tracking, the spacing between all characters in a line of text; and leading (pronounced "ledding"), the spacing between lines of text. Also here are adjustments for alignment and position.

> **TIP:** You can modify the spacing between individual characters by highlighting a character and then modifying the tracking parameter to add or remove space around that letter.

Clearly differentiating between a title and its background will help focus viewer attention. People tend to separate elements from their backgrounds based on contrast, color, and size. So adding a background to the text that contrasts well with the video clip will help bring out that text.

8. Drag the side scroll bar down in the Inspector until you see the Background parameter group.

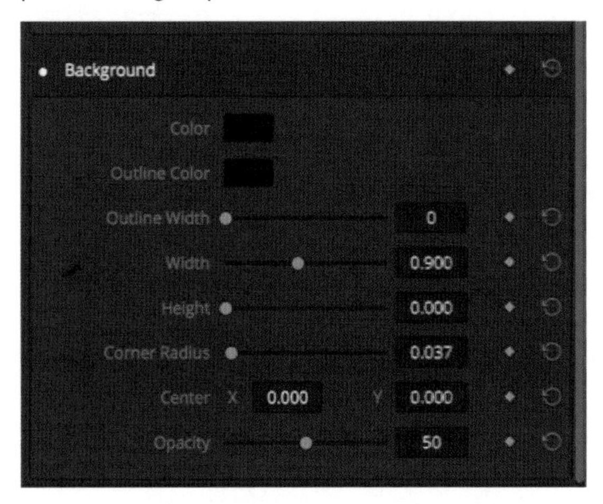

9. Set the Height parameter to 0.250 to create a background for your text that is translucent, by default. Doing so will make your text stand out from the video.

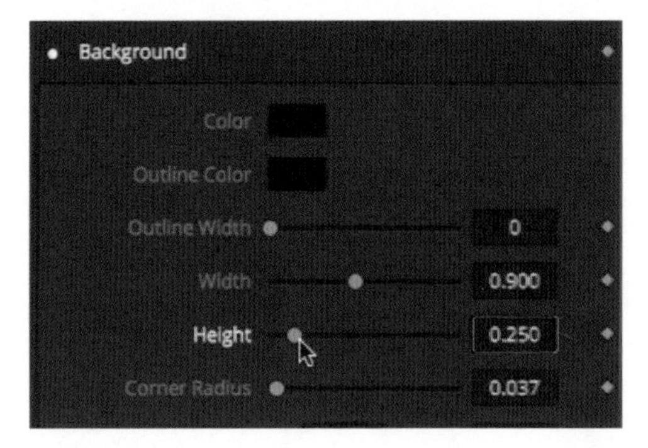

The lower third title you just created hits all the right elements in terms of creating a well-designed title. You've selected the typeface, color, and styling to enhance the mood while maintaining readability.

Animating Titles

Animated titles can raise your program to a higher and more elegant level. You do so by creating keyframes in Resolve to move and change title parameters in the Inspector over time. The first step is to position the playhead where you want to set your first keyframe.

1. In the timeline, position the playhead at the start of the title clip.

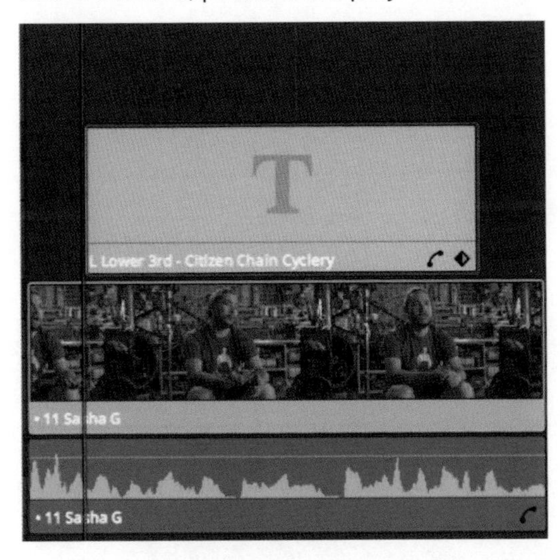

2. Click in an empty area of the timeline to deselect the title.
3. Type **+1.** (plus, one, period) and press Return or Enter to move the playhead one second into the title clip.

   This is the point in the timeline when you want your (eventually) moving title to stop moving. And when it stops, the title should look exactly as it does now. So here is where you will set position keyframes for both lines of the title.

4. Select the title to view its parameters in the Inspector.
5. In the Inspector, for the upper line of text (Sasha G.), click the keyframe button to the right of the Position X and Y parameters.

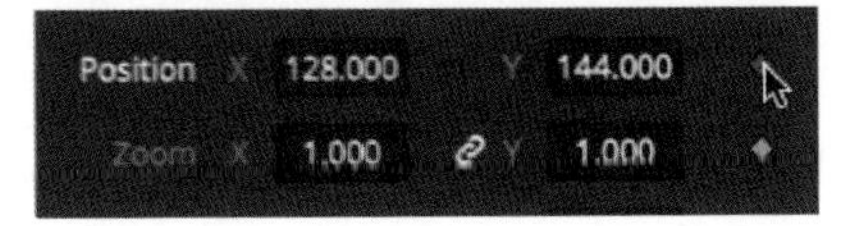

6. In the Inspector, move to the lower line of text (Citizen Chain Cyclery), and add the same keyframe to the Position X and Y parameters.

   Now you'll add keyframes that position both title lines offscreen. Because the Position X parameter already has one keyframe, you need to change only the position of the playhead and the value of the X parameter. Doing so will automatically add a second keyframe at the playhead position.

7. In the timeline, position the playhead at the start of the title clip.
8. Place the cursor over the Position X data field for the upper line of text.

9. Drag to the right until the upper line of text and background are completely off the screen in the Timeline Viewer.

> **TIP:** When dragging in the numeric value box, you may reach the edge of the screen, which will stop your dragging. If so, release the mouse button, reposition the cursor over the data field, and begin dragging again.

10. Drag in the Position X value field to arrange the second line of text off screen.

    Now both lines of text are in a starting position off screen, so you can preview your animation.

> **TIP:** To reset parameters to their default settings, click the gray reset button to the right of the keyframe button.

11. Play over the title clip to preview your animation.

    This method is the basis for animating any parameter for any title or video clip. Set your playhead, add a keyframe, and change the parameter. Once a parameter has a keyframe on it, additional keyframes are set whenever you change the playhead position and change the value of the parameter.

Editing Keyframes

Even skilled animators rarely get the timing of animations correct on their first attempt. Animation tends to be an iterative process: set the keyframes and play it back; make a change and play it again. So knowing how to adjust the placement of keyframes is just as important as setting their values.

1. In the timeline, select the title clip, if necessary.
2. In the lower-right corner of the clip, click the diamond-shaped open keyframe button to display the keyframes.

> **TIP:** If you cannot see the open keyframe button on the clip, zoom in to the timeline using the Zoom slider.

Two rich text keyframe tracks appear that represent each of the animated elements in the title. The white dots on the keyframe tracks are the keyframes for each text line. To stagger the animation and force the second line of text to animate slightly after the first line, you need to select both keyframes and drag them to the right in the timeline

3. To select both keyframes on the lower track, position your mouse pointer above and to the right of the last keyframe on the lower keyframe track.

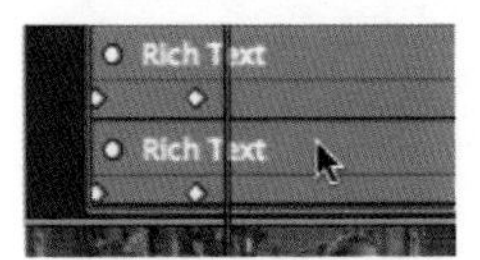

4. Drag across both keyframes to select them. When they are selected they will turn red

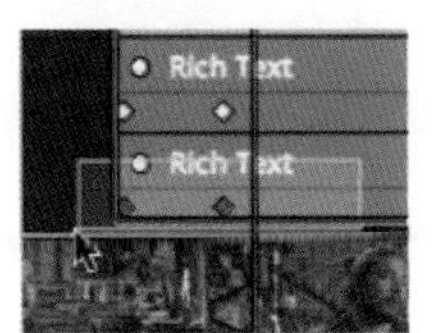

5. To animate the second title line to move onscreen later, on the lower keyframe track, drag the first red dot to the right, and stop dragging when the tool tip reads 00:08.

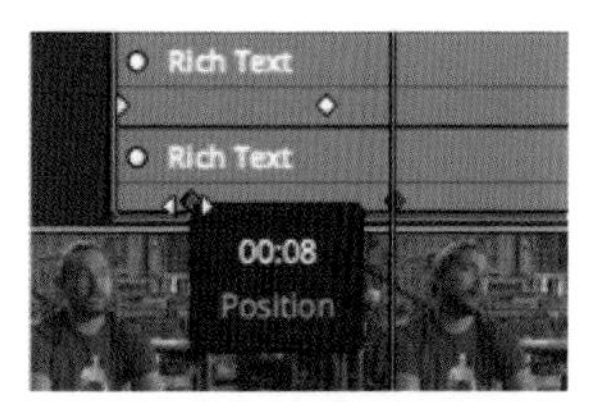

> **TIP:** When moving keyframes, press N to turn off snapping unless you want to align keyframes to the playhead or to keyframes on other tracks.

The tool tip displays the frame number from the start of the clip. By moving both keyframes eight frames to the right, you've made the animation start and end eight frames earlier.

6. Click the open keyframe button to close the keyframe tracks.
7. Play the title clip to preview your new animation.

The basic animation techniques applied here can be carried over into animating other clip parameters. You could use these same keyframe techniques to scale images, move clips along a motion path, and even animate Open FX third-party plug-ins.

Trimming Titles with an Extend Edit

A quick way to trim titles (or any other clip) is to use the Extend Edit command. Although you can use all the standard trimming techniques that you learned in Lesson 5, trimming a title often has more to do with duration than with its actual content. Using a timeline-centric trim technique such as Extend Edit can often get you more accurate results more quickly.

1. Click in an empty area of the timeline to deselect the title.
2. Position the playhead at the end of the title, and type **-1.** (minus, one, period), and press Return or Enter to move the playhead backward one second.

Using Extend Edit you can shorten or lengthen a clip by snapping its head or tail to the playhead.

3. In the timeline, click the end of the title clip, as if you were going to trim it.

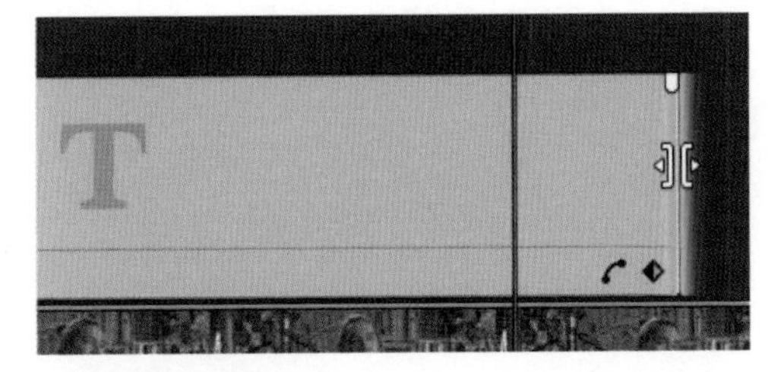

4. Choose Trim > Extend Edit, or press E.

The title is cut to line up with the playhead. keyframes remain locked to the frame, so lengthening a clip does not change their positions. They are, however, cut off when you shorten a clip using either the Extend Edit command or the Trim tool.

Whether you are creating simple slates or more permanent credits for your project, the guiding principles and techniques you have learned in this lesson will allow you to create clear and compelling titles within DaVinci Resolve.

9 Changing Clip Speed

Almost every long-form and short-form video production—including commercials, documentaries, and reality television programs—retimes clips so they play back at different speeds. Some are extreme, super-slow motion effects to heighten the action, and some are just subtle speed-ups so that a shot's timing fits better into a scene. No matter how you use them, speed changes are an invaluable tool in the editor's arsenal.

Resolve includes tools to speed up and slow down clips, play them in reverse, change their speed over time, and freeze their action completely. In this lesson, you'll explore some speed change methods and learn the many ways Resolve can process clips to realize the best results.

TIME

- **This lesson takes approximately 20 minutes to complete.**

GOALS

- **Edit with Fit to Fill**
- **Create a constant speed change**
- **Animate speed values**
- **Change how retimes are processed**
- **Freeze a frame**

Edit with Fit to Fill

All of the edits you have performed until now have been Three-point edits involving an In point, an Out point, and a third point that was either an In or Out point. The *Fit to Fill edit* is the only editing function that uses four points to create an edit. It uses the In and Out points that you mark on a source clip and applies a speed change to it based on an In/Out duration you mark on the timeline.

In the following exercise, you'll use the Fit to Fill edit to retime the speed of a clip so it fits within the In and Out marks in the timeline.

1. With the DaVinci Resolve Lesson 5-13 project open, from the Rough Cuts bin, load Retiming Rough Cut timeline into the Timeline Viewer.
2. Select the Video Clips bin, and double-click the **03 WS Up Over Hill** clip to load it into the Source Viewer.

3. Mark an In point at 16:29:37:00 and an Out point two seconds later.
4. In the timeline, disable the Auto Select buttons for tracks A1 and A2.

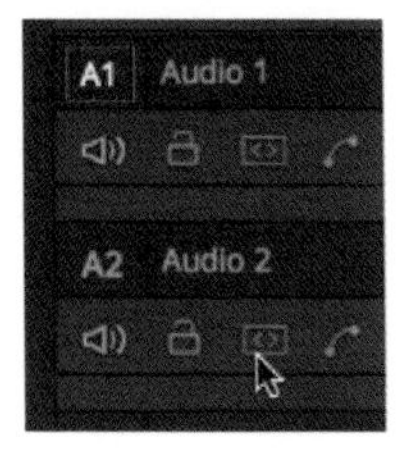

5. Disable the A1 destination control so you will not edit audio into the timeline.
6. Position the playhead over the **05 CU Pan Feet to Head** clip, and press X to mark that clip.

   Above the Timeline Viewer to the left, you can see the duration of the marked segment. The timeline has In and Out points and a roughly four-second duration. The source clip has In and Out points with a two-second duration. To fit the marked range on the source clip into the longer timeline duration, you'll need to apply a speed change so that the clip plays at half speed.

7. Drag the **03 WS Up Over Hill** clip from the Source Viewer, and hover it over the Timeline Viewer to open the edit overlay.

8. Drag the clip onto Fit to Fill, and release the mouse button.

   Fit to Fill is an Overwrite edit, so the clip in the timeline is replaced with the clip from the Source Viewer.

9. Play over the timeline to view the new Fit to Fill edit.

Using the Fit to Fill edit works well when you have assembled your first rough cut and are systematically replacing shots and trimming up your timeline. It's one of the refining tools you will use most when locking down your project.

Creating a Constant Speed Change

The most common type of speed change is a constant speed change. It uniformly alters the playback of a clip in the timeline to turn it into a slow-motion clip or a fast-motion clip of a single frame rate.

1. In the timeline, position the playhead at the start of the **08 MS Riding Away** clip.

2. Play over the clip (always a good idea before you change its speed).

   This clip goes on a bit too long after the rider leaves the frame. You could trim it, but that can often result in lots of trimming to keep all your cuts in sync with music and sound effects. When you want to retain a clip's duration and slipping is not an option, you can create a subtle slow motion effect to control which frames are played in the clip.

3. Select **08 MS Riding Away**. Control-click (OS X) or right-click (Windows), and from the contextual menu, choose Change Clip Speed.

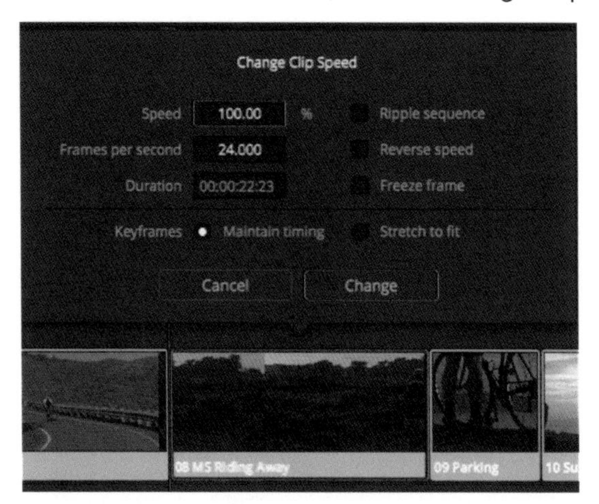

   The Edit Speed Change dialog appears with a number of controls for clip playback.

4. In the "Speed %" value field, enter **50**, and click Change to close the dialog.

   Setting this value to 50% means that the clip will play at half its captured frame rate—in this case, 12 frames per second. To indicate that the clip's playback speed has been changed, a small speed change icon is displayed next to the clip's name in the timeline.

5. Play the clip to see the speed change results.

> **TIP:** When audio is selected, changing clip speed will change the playback speed of the audio.

When creating a slow motion clip, the default settings in the Edit Speed Change dialog do not change the overall duration of the timeline. In that respect, the results are very similar to slipping a clip. Next, let's look at what happens when you apply fast motion.

Retiming with the Selection and Trim Tools

Whereas Fit to Fill edits and the Change Clip Speed dialogs are easy ways to create simple constant speed changes, the retime controls can provide more flexibility. A key difference is that a clip altered using the Retime controls can be "trimmed" in the timeline to change its speed.

1. In the timeline, select the **06 WS S Curve** clip and play it to preview its contents.

2. Zoom in to the timeline until you can see the **06 WS S Curve** clip and the two clips after it.
3. Choose Clip > Retime Controls, or press Cmd-R (OS X) or Ctrl-R (Windows).

   The Retime controls appear over the clip in the timeline. The Retime control track along the top displays blue arrows to indicate that the clip is playing forward at normal speed. A Clip Speed pop-up menu below the clip displays the current speed and provides access to other speed change controls, but the easiest way to change speed is by trimming.
4. Enable auto select for A2 to make sure that the sound effects stay in sync.
5. Move the pointer to the right edge of the Speed Change name bar.

   The pointer turns into a Retime cursor.

6. Drag to the right to lengthen the clip until the Clip Speed pop-up display reads 70%.

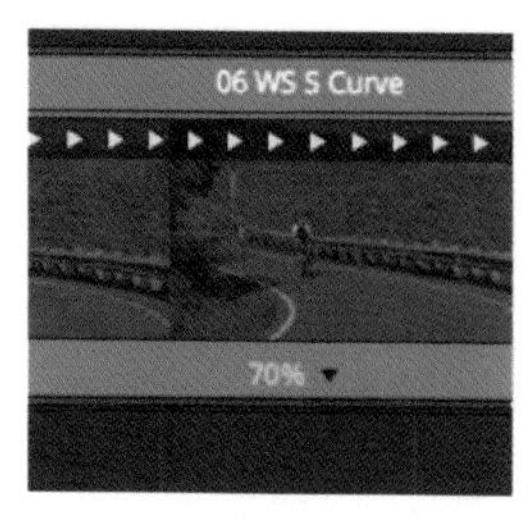

> **TIP:** To return a clip to its original speed, click the Clip Speed pop-up menu and choose "Reset to 100%".

Dragging the Retime bar overwrites the clip to the right, similar to using the Selection tool for trimming. (Dragging to the left opens a gap and increases the speed of the clip.) However, if you undo that last step, you can see how the same resizing feature changes depending upon which tool is selected in the toolbar.

7. Press Cmd-Z (OS X) or Ctrl-S (Windows) to undo the previous speed change.
8. In the toolbar, click the Trim tool.

9. Move the pointer to the right edge of the Speed Change name bar, and drag to the right until the Clip Speed pop-up display reads 70%.

10. Play the retimed clip to see the results.

With the Trim tool selected, the timeline is rippled, pushing the rest of the clips to the right. The clip's duration and the overall timeline duration are extended.

Animating Speed Values

A popular speed change these days is the retiming of a clip using variable speed. You often see it in car commercials or as transitions in reality TV shows. Usually, the first part of the clip is sped up and the rest returns to normal speed or is slowed down. To achieve this, you need to control multiple regions of a clip, much as you did with keyframing. However, to create speed changes, Resolve uses *speed points* as well as a *Retime Curve*.

1. In the timeline, select the **02 Extreme WS S Curve** clip, and play it.

2. Zoom in to the timeline until you can see the **02 Extreme WS S Curve** clip and the two clips after it.

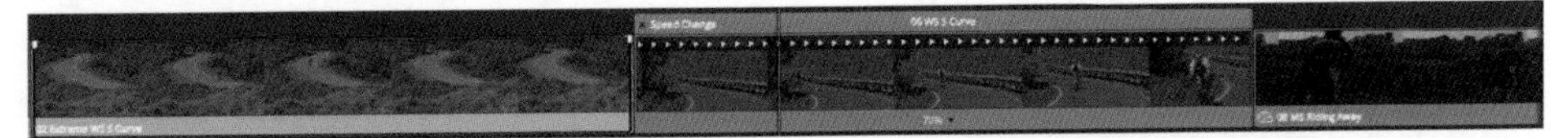

3. Choose Clip > Retime Controls, or press Cmd-R (OS X) or Ctrl-R (Windows).

   To vary the speed of a clip, you can set a speed point on the frame where you want to place a change. Then you will have control over the two regions so you can set their speeds individually.

4. Place the playhead over the point where the cyclist is at the start of the first curve.

5. From the Clip Speed pop-up menu, choose Add Speed Point.

   Now the clip is divided in two. Both sections are set to 100%, so nothing has changed visually. You'll add one more speed point when the cyclist is heading out of that curve.

6. Place the playhead over the point where the cyclist is at the end of the first curve.

7. From the Clip Speed pop-up menu, choose Add Speed Point.

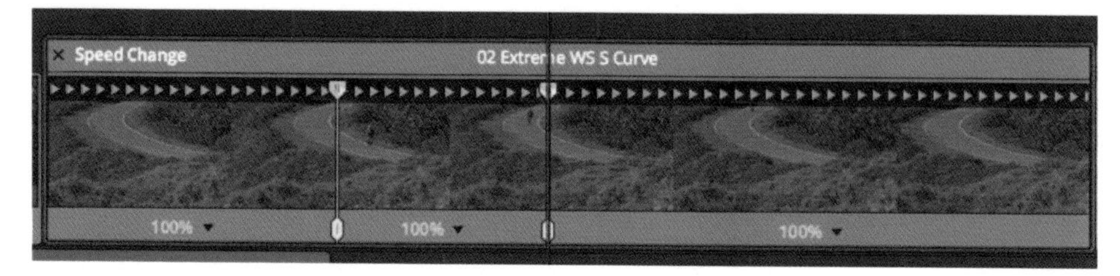

With the clip divided into three sections, you'll now speed up the first and third sections and slow down the middle section.

8. Make sure the Trim tool is selected so you can ripple the clips in the timeline.
9. Under the first section of the clip, click the Clip Speed pop-up menu. Choose Change Speed > 400% to speed up the clip.

Now you'll set the last third of this clip to play faster.

10. Under the last section of the clip, click the Clip Speed pop-up menu. Choose Change Speed > 400%.
11. Under the middle section of the clip, click the Clip Speed pop-up menu to slow down this section. Choose Change Speed > 50%.

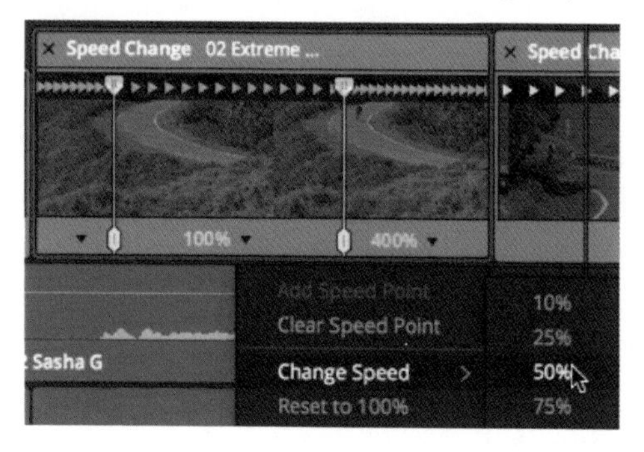

12. Play over the retimed clip to see the results.

    The first and third sections play quickly and the middle third plays in slow motion. Each speed point triggers a different speed for that portion of the clip. To smooth the transition between the speed points, you can apply a Retime Curve.

    TIP: To remove a speed point, from the Clip Speed pop-up menu, choose Clear Speed Point. Doing so will remove the speed point that is located directly to the left of the pop-up menu.

13. Right-click the clip, and from the contextual menu, choose Retime Curve.

    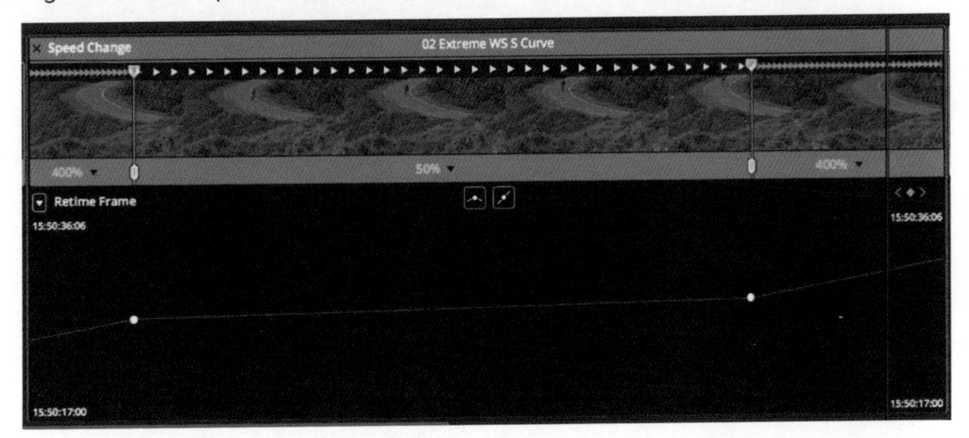

    The Retime graph opens, displaying the speed points as control points on the curve. Each point can be repositioned and the curve smoothed to create a ramping effect between speed changes.

14. Click the first white control point to select it.

    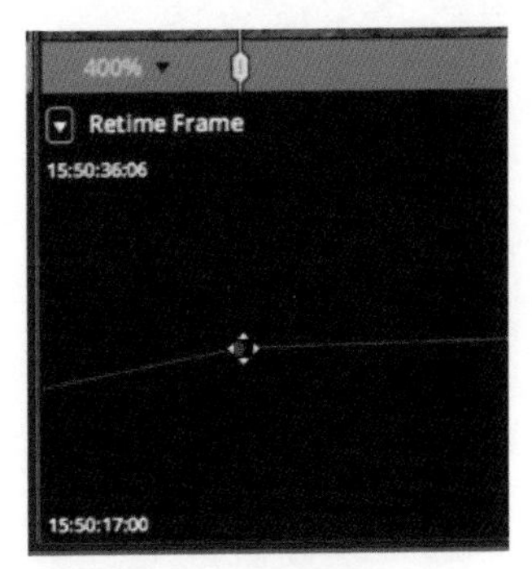

15. At the top of the graph, click the Smooth Curve button.

    Spline handles now appear on the control point. You can drag them outward to increase the ramp between speeds.

16. Drag outward on the spline handle to increase the ramp and smooth the retime curve.

17. Do the same for the second point: select it, click the smooth button, and drag the handle outward to smooth the curve.

18. Play over the retimed clip to see the results.
19. Press Cmd-R (OS X) or Ctrl-R (Windows) to hide the Retime bar, and in the lower-right corner of the timeline section, click the Curve button to hide the Retime Curve.

You do not have to use speed points to mark the sections of a clip where speed changes will occur. You also can open the Retime Curve directly and add control points just as you would to the audio volume line. It is easier, though, to control the curve using speed points.

Changing Retime Processing

You can change the way a retimed clip is processed, and thereby change how it looks. The different retime processing settings located in the Inspector trade off speed for quality. Which you choose will depend on the type of movement in your shot and how much processing time you are willing to allow.

1. Select the retimed **02 Extreme WS S Curve** clip
2. Open the Inspector.
3. Scroll to the bottom of the Inspector

4. Click the Retime Process menu to open it.

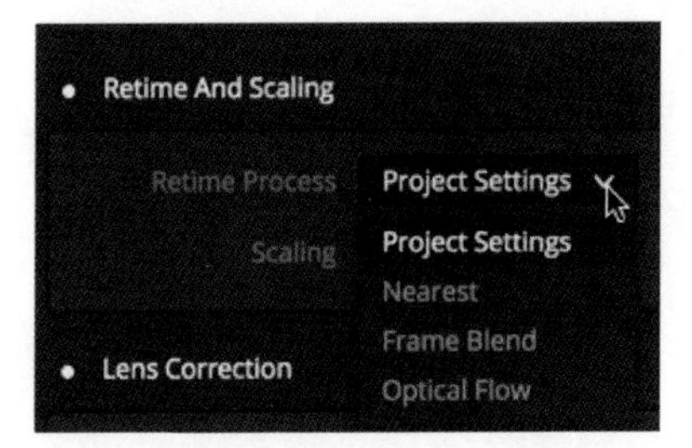

You have three options for processing clip retiming: Nearest, Frame Blend, and Optical Flow.

- Nearest is the fastest processing option but delivers the lowest-quality results. This simple operation duplicates frames to create slow motion, which often causes stepping artifacts even in clips that have just a moderate amount of movement. Nearest is the default option set on the editing page of the project settings.
- Frame Blend is a slightly more processor-intensive option that delivers better-looking results. It also duplicates frames to create slow motion but then blends them to produce smoother motion. This is the most reliable option and delivers acceptable results.
- Optical Flow is the most processor intensive and highest-quality process. It uses motion estimation and warping techniques to generate new frames from the original source frames. The results can be exceptionally smooth when the motion in a clip is unobstructed. However, if two moving elements cross in different directions (such as legs crossing when walking) or the camera movement is erratic, optical flow processing can cause stretching and tearing artifacts.

TIP: Additional controls on the editing page of the project settings for Optical Flow can sometimes improve small tears or stretching artifacts.

5. From the menu, choose Optical Flow.
6. Once the clip is cached, play over the optical flow results to see the smoother motion.

It's a good idea to first try Optical Flow processing to see if it produces acceptable results, and then revert to Frame Blend as necessary. Optical Flow, unlike the other retime processing types, requires that you cache the results. Once Optical Flow is selected, you'll see a red bar above the clip to indicate that the process needs to cache. If smart caching is enabled, the rendering will be performed in the background and you'll be able to see the results in a few seconds.

Creating a Freeze Frame

A freeze frame takes place when all of the action in a clip is stopped and held as a still image. Freeze frames can be applied in any number of creative ways. They can be used in title sequences to introduce characters in the production or at the end of a scene just before it fades out. Not every production uses freeze frames. It's a stylistic choice that you must make. In some cases, it will enhance the visual style of the show, and in some it won't be appropriate. Resolve enables you to create freeze frames easily using the Edit Speed Change dialog and Retime controls.

1. Play over the last clip in the timeline.

   You'll add a freeze frame to the last clip to end this scene. Let's start in the Edit Speed Change dialog.

2. Place the playhead just before the cyclist begins to lift his hand to take off his sunglasses.

   The first step when creating a freeze frame is to place the playhead over the frame you want to freeze. Then you create the freeze frame in the Change Clip Speed dialog.

3. Right-click the last clip, and from the contextual menu, choose Change Clip Speed.

4. In the dialog, select the "Freeze frame" checkbox, and click Change.

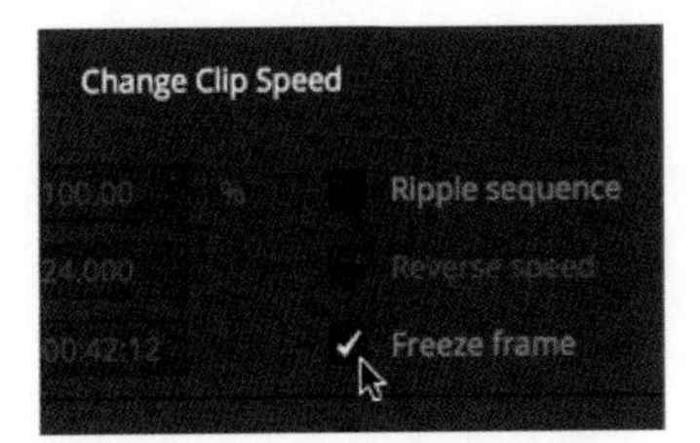

5. Play over the last clip to see the freeze frame.

   Creating a freeze frame with the Change Clip Speed dialog replaces the entire clip with the freeze frame. In some cases, this may be what you want, but you're more likely to want to play the clip until it reaches the frame that you want to freeze. To create that style of freeze frame, you can use the Retime controls.

6. Choose Edit > Undo, or press Cmd-Z (OS X) or Ctrl-Z (Windows), to remove the freeze frame and return the clip to the timeline.

7. Select the last clip in the timeline, and choose Clip > Retime Controls, or press Cmd-R (OS X) or Ctrl-R (Windows), to open the Retime controls.

8. Place the playhead just before the cyclist begins to lift his hand to take off his sunglasses.

9. From the clip speed pop-up menu, choose Freeze Frame.

   Two speed points are added to the clip to identify the range where the freeze frame occurs. After the second speed point, the clip will continue to play where the freeze frame ended. Moving the first speed point will cause the first section in the timeline to slow down. Moving the second speed point will extend the length of the freeze frame and the entire clip. To end the clip with the freeze frame, you must trim the clip.

10. Locate the pointer over the right end of the clip until it turns into the Selection Tool Resize cursor.

11. Drag the end of the clip to the left until you reach the second speed point.

12. Play over the last clip to see the new freeze frame.

    All you have left to do is add a fade-out.

13. Press Cmd-R (OS X) or Ctrl-R (Windows) to hide the Retime controls.

14. In the upper-right corner of the clip, drag in the fade handle until the tool tip reads –1:00.

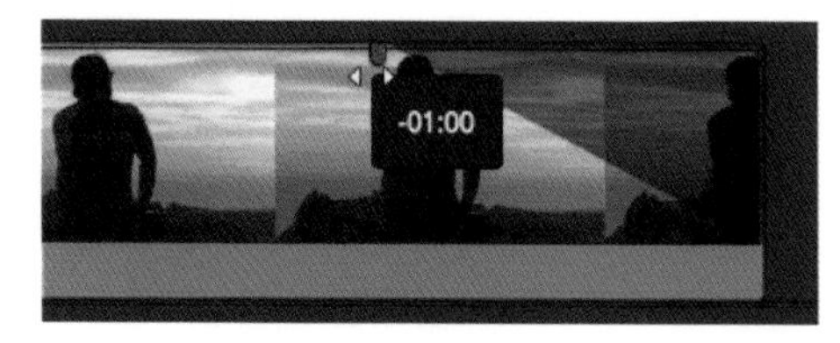

The freeze frame combined with the fade-out will also need to be cached, but the rendering is performed almost instantaneously. To experiment further, you can play back the clips you've created and try manipulating the speed points to alter the retiming and freeze frame. With Resolve, it's incredibly easy to create very sophisticated ramping speed changes and instant-replay–style retiming effects.

10 Multicam Editing

When you work on specific types of productions—such as interviews or performances that were shot using multiple cameras simultaneously—you can take advantage of the multicam editing mode in Resolve. Multicam editing allows you to group and synchronize two or more source clips showing different angles on the same performance. You can then display them simultaneously in the viewer and cut your timeline in real time. It's an incredibly fast way to edit concerts, reality TV, interviews, or any production in which several cameras recorded the same event.

TIME

- **This lesson takes approximately 10 minutes to complete**

GOALS

- **Relink clips**
- **Sync clips**
- **View multiple angles**
- **Edit in Multicam Mode**

Relinking Clips

Your multicam project is a four-camera concert of a rockabilly band. You must import this project and add it to your database from the project manager window.

1. Launch Resolve, right-click in the Project Manager window and choose Import. From the open dialog, choose DaVinci Resolve Editing Lessons Files > Multicamera Editing.

   The multicamera project is added to the Project Manager window.

2. Double-click the Multicamera Editing project.

   Because this project was initially created on a different computer, you'll first need to relink its media.

3. In the Media page, in the sidebar, select both the Multicamera Source bin and the Rough Cuts bin.

   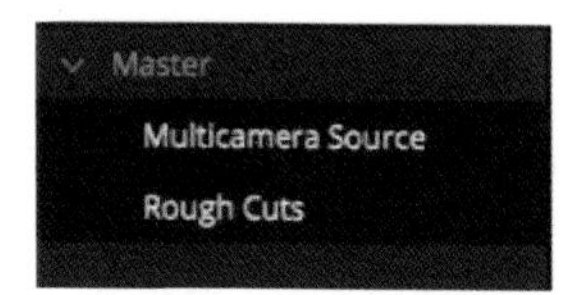

4. Right-click (or Control-click in OS X) either of the bins, and from the contextual menu, choose "Relink Clips for Selected Bins."

5. In the Relink dialog, navigate to the DaVinci Resolve Editing Lessons Files folder and select the 03 Multicamera folder. Click OK to relink the clips in this project.

The clips in the bin now have thumbnails that represent the multiple camera angles that you'll use in your multicamera project. The next step is to sync them together.

OPENING MULTIPLE PROJECTS

When you're working on one project, another project may temporarily require some immediate work, which requires you to bounce back and forth between the two. Resolve helps in these situations by allowing you to open multiple projects at the same time.

To do so, in the Resolve Project Manager window, right-click in an empty space, and from the contextual menu, choose Dynamic Project Switching.

By enabling dynamic project switching in the project manager window, your current project remains open when you open additional projects, even though you can see only one project at a time. When you enable Dynamic Project Switching, the File menu includes a Switch Project submenu that allows you to switch between those open projects.

To close a specific project, choose File > Close Project, and from the submenu, choose the project you want to close.

While multiple projects can be open at once, each open project takes up RAM in your computer. Because overextending RAM can negatively impact Resolve's performance, it is advisable to limit your open projects to a size and number that suits the available RAM in your computer.

Syncing Clips

As with every new project, you have to be familiar with your footage before you start working with it. When performing a multicam edit, the assumption is that multiple clips depict different angles of the same event, all shot at the same time. Let's look at this source material to see if you have content suitable for a multicamera edit.

1. From the Multicamera Source bin, double-click **01 Master Camera** video clip to load it into the viewer.

2. Play a few seconds of the clip to see and hear the band begin to play.
3. Do the same for the remaining three video clips in the Multicamera Source bin.

Your clips show four different but simultaneously recorded angles of the band playing. It's a classic case in which multicam editing can get the job done faster. The bin also contains a master audio file. While the sound recorded by each camera will be great for syncing clips, only the master audio file sounds good enough to use in your final project. You'll use that audio clip as the final audio track in your timeline.

To prepare the clips for multicam editing, you must sync them so that the band is playing the same part of the song at the same time on every clip.

4. In the Media page, select all four video clips, along with the master audio clip.
5. Right-click any of the selected clips, and from the contextual menu, choose New Multicam Clip Using Selected Clips.

In the Multicam Clip Properties dialog that appears, you can determine which attributes of the clips you will use to synchronize them. The Angle Sync menu is where you select these sync options.

6. Click the Angle Sync menu to view the sync options.

   The Angle Sync menu includes four methods for aligning the clips. You can choose to manually align them by marking an In point or an Out point on all the clips at a single point in time. This method is fairly easy when a clapper is present in all of the angles. If all of the clips have matching timecode, then Timecode might be the easiest sync method. The last method is to have Resolve analyze the audio on each clip and automatically sync them based on their audio waveforms.

7. Choose In to sync the clips to a common In point.

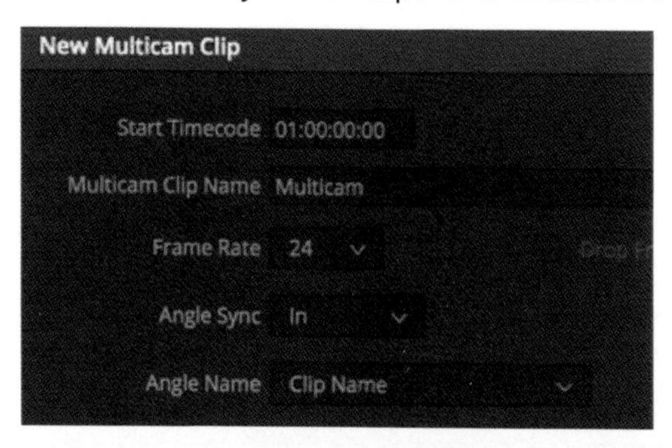

> **NOTE:** For learning purposes, these clips were already marked with an In point. Because the cameras shooting these clips were all started at different times, using a single In point will make it easier to understand resyncing angles and editing a multicam timeline.

8. From the Angle Name pop-up menu, choose Clip Name to display the clip names for each camera angle.

9. Deselect the "Move Source Clips to 'Original Clips' Bin" checkbox.

   If you were to select that checkbox, Resolve would create a bin called Original Clips and move the source clips into it, leaving the multicam clip alone in its bin and easier to find. This clip organization can be helpful when you have a large number of source clips to sync.

10. Click the Create button to begin syncing the clips.

A new multicam clip is created that contains all of the selected and synced clips.

Viewing Multiple Angles

You are now ready to edit with your new multicam clip. You can edit a multicam clip into the timeline just as you edit any clip.

> **NOTE:** Depending on the resolution of your media and how many clips you have synced, editing your multicamera source media may work best when stored on one or multiple high speed drives to achieve smooth, reliable playback.

1. At the bottom of the Resolve window, click the Edit button.

2. Select the Rough Cuts bin, and double-click the Multicamera Rough Cut thumbnail to load it into the timeline.

   This is a premade timeline that was imported with the project. You'll drag the multicam clip directly into the timeline.

3. Select the Multicamera Source bin, and then drag the **Multicam** clip into the timeline. Make sure that the start of the clip aligns with the start of the timeline.

4. Drag the playhead to the start of the timeline.

   When you edit a multicam clip into the timeline, it appears as a single clip with only one visible camera angle. To view all of the angles in a multicam clip, you must load the multicam source clip into the source viewer.

5. From the Multicamera source bin, drag the **multicam** clip into the Source Viewer.

The Source Viewer can display up to nine angles at once, although your multicam clip can contain more.

6. Drag the playhead under the Source Viewer to the end of the Source Viewer's jog bar and then back to the beginning.

   As you move the Source Viewer's playhead, all of the camera angles in the Source Viewer update to match the current Source Viewer playhead location. As usual, the timeline playhead doesn't move when you move the Source Viewer playhead. However, to perform multicam editing, you need to link the Source Viewer playhead and the Timeline playhead, so that when you move either playhead, the Source Viewer updates and allows you to see all of the camera angles for that point in time.

7. To enter Multicam Mode, from the source viewer mode pop-up menu, choose Multicam.

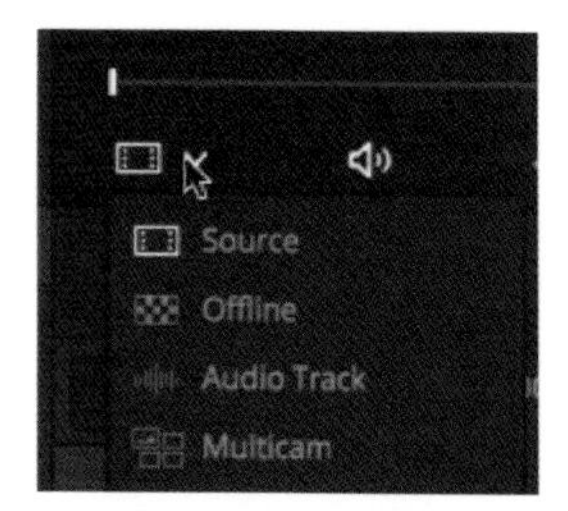

   The Source Viewer now displays controls for multicam editing. Instead of transport controls, you have audio/video selection buttons to determine whether you are going to cut audio only, video only, or both. Because the music will remain the same for the entire song (remember that master audio clip you have waiting in the wings), you will just cut video.

8. Under the Source Viewer, click the Video button.

   Any edits you make while in Multicam Mode will now be performed only on the video track. Let's also change the number of angles displayed in the viewer, because you need to view only four angles.

9. From the Angles pop-up menu, in the lower right of the viewer, choose 2x2.

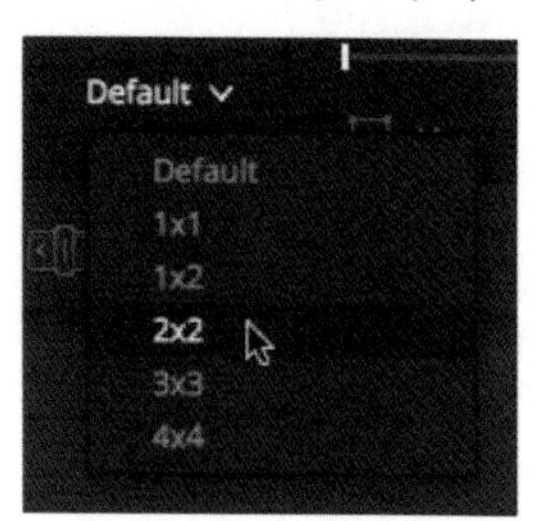

All four camera angles now fill the source viewer.

You can rearrange the angles so that the viewer displays them in an order that make the most sense to you. For instance, placing the master shot of the band in the upper-left quadrant seems more appropriate than placing it elsewhere. To do so, you need to see the timeline tracks for each angle.

10. In the timeline, right-click the **multicam** clip, and from the contextual menu, choose "Open in timeline."

The timeline expands the **multicam** clip to show each source clip on its own track. You can use this view to fix any sync issues a clip may have and to rearrange the clips' layout order. Each video track is linked to a quadrant in the view, with the bottom-most video track in the upper left and the uppermost track in the lower right.

TIP: To see all four tracks in the timeline, you may need to adjust the track height in the Customize Timeline pop-up menu.

The audio for each clip is also displayed, although all you really need is the master audio on track 5. When a multicam clip is opened, it acts just like a normal timeline, so to remove the unnecessary audio tracks you can unlink and delete them.

11. Click the Unlink/Link button in the toolbar, if necessary.
12. Select the audio clip on A1 and press Delete; then do the same for A2, A3, and A4.
13. Drag the **Music Final Mix** clip from A5 to A1.

    Now the **Music Final Mix** audio clip will become the audio that is played in the multicam clip. You can return to the main timeline.
14. Double-click the name of the timeline in the path control in the lower-left corner of the timeline to return to the Multicam timeline.

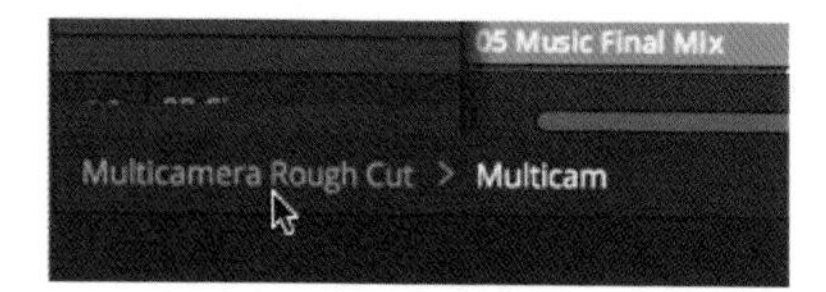

You are now ready to begin editing and enjoy the benefits of using a multicam clip.

Editing in Multicam Mode

In Multicam Mode, the Source Viewer subtly changes to allow each angle displayed in the viewer to act as a switching control. During real-time playback, clicking any angle within the viewer will add a cut to the timeline at the current playhead position and switch to the selected angle.

1. In the timeline, position the playhead about four seconds in, just before the singer turns to look toward the drummer.

2. In the Source Viewer, click the **04 Drummer** clip.

A cut is added to the timeline video track, and a blue outline appears around the drummer clip in the Source Viewer to indicate that it is the current camera angle.

3. In the timeline, position the playhead at about 9 seconds, just after the singer begins to take off her jacket, and click **01 Master Camera**, which shows the entire band.

A cut is made in the timeline and the **Master Camera** becomes the current camera angle.

4. To see the results, position the timeline playhead at the start and press the Spacebar. Stop playback when you have seen the last cut that you made.

The cuts look good, but instead of positioning the playhead and clicking in the source viewer, let's speed things up and edit as the timeline plays.

During playback, you can switch angles by pressing the 1, 2, 3, and 4 keys at the top of your keyboard or on the number pad. The numbers correspond to the frames within the source viewer. The upper-left frame is 1, the upper-right frame is 2, lower-left is 3, and lower-right is 4.

5. Position the playhead at the start of the timeline.
6. Press the Spacebar to begin playback, and then tap the desired number to switch to each camera angle in real time.

   The blue outline relocates to indicate the currently active angle.
7. Press the Spacebar to stop playback when you have finished editing.

   When you are done with your multicam edit, you can switch back to Source Mode.
8. To exit Multicam Mode, from the Source Viewer Mode pop-up menu, choose Source.

As easy as it is to edit in Multicam Mode, you'll typically want to go back and refine some cuts that you aren't happy with. The multicam timeline responds to all the same editing, effects, and color grading techniques you've already learned. So you can go back using the Rolling Trim cursor and adjust any cut as you would refine any other timeline edit.

You can also identify an angle that you aren't happy with and Option-click (OS X) or Alt-click (Windows) a replacement in the Source Viewer as you did when replacing the audio track. Resolve gives you the speed and efficiency of multicam editing while placing all of its powerful editing tools at your disposal.

11 Color Correction

DaVinci Resolve was originally designed to perform high-end color correction and feature film finishing. The Color page features the same tools used everyday by Hollywood's top colorists to color correct and finish the biggest blockbuster films, episodic television shows, and commercials!

As with editing, color correction is an art form that takes time to learn and master. It's an exciting skill, and if you give yourself the time to practice and learn, you'll be able to enhance your images and make them look amazing!

In this lesson, you'll learn the basics of color correction: Balancing the hue and brightness of images, using video scopes to guide those changes, isolating parts of an image, and even using Resolve FX for special effects. Experience is key, and with so many controls at your fingertips, this lesson will give you everything you need to start learning this creative skill.

TIME

- **This lesson takes approximately 60 minutes to complete.**

GOALS

- **Understand the Color page**
- **Modify lift, gamma, and gain**
- **Make shared adjustments**
- **Use versions**
- **Save and apply adjustments**
- **Make secondary color corrections**
- **Group clips**
- **Create a vignette using a power window**
- **Apply Resolve FX**

Understanding the Color Page

The technical and creative process of color correction takes place within the Color page in Resolve. Let's start by examining the Color page layout.

1. Open the DaVinci Resolve Lessons 5-13 project, if necessary.
2. From the Rough Cuts bin, load **Color Grading Rough Cut** into the timeline.

   One of the best aspects of Resolve is that editing and color grading are completely integrated into a single application, so you can easily move between the two with a single click.
3. At the bottom of the Resolve window, click the Color button to go to the Color page.

   The Color page is divided into seven main areas.

The Gallery includes saved adjustments that you can copy to other clips in the timeline.

The viewer shows the frame at the playhead's current position in the timeline.

The Node Editor connects color corrections, image adjustments, and effects to create unique looks.

The timeline is divided into a thumbnail timeline and the Timeline Ruler.

The left palettes contain adjustments for color, contrast, and RAW image processing.

The center palettes provide access to color curves, Power Windows, tracking, keying, and stereoscopic controls.

The lower-right area may display the keyframe, color/luminance measuring scopes, or a histogram display.

> **NOTE:** If you're using DaVinci Resolve on a computer display with a resolution lower than 1920x1080, some panels and buttons will be consolidated and not look exactly like the images in this lesson.

When you switch to the Color page, whatever was loaded into the editing timeline is displayed in the Color Page timeline. The Color page does not change or alter any cuts or transitions. It just provides a way of looking at your timeline that is more appropriate for color correction.

4. Click in the center of the last thumbnail to select it.

An orange outline appears around the selected thumbnail, and the playhead jumps to the first frame of that clip.

5. Double-click the Apple ProRes 422 Proxy name below the thumbnail to switch to viewing a display name for each clip.

   The Timeline Ruler below the thumbnails displays thin bars to represent each clip. A bar's width is proportional to a clip's duration.

6. Drag the Timeline Ruler playhead to the left to scrub through the timeline until you reach the first clip.

> **TIP:** If a track is disabled in the Edit page, it will be dimmed in the mini-timeline.

As you scrub through the timeline, the clip under the playhead highlights in orange to show that it is selected, a behavior similar to the thumbnail display outline. The transport controls under the viewer, as well as all the playback keyboard shortcuts, are the same as you used on the Edit page.

Now that you have a basic understanding of the Color page layout, you're ready to make some adjustments.

Modifying Lift, Gamma, and Gain

Among the first things you typically want to do is balance the image. You can do so in a variety of ways by adjusting the hue, saturation, and brightness to ensure that the image has bright highlights, dark shadows, and a neutral overall color tone. The most popular method is to use the Primaries Wheels. You will find that you use these controls the majority of the time you are on the Color page unless you are performing very specific corrections.

Using the Primaries Wheels, you can achieve a refined result because you can divide the image into tonal regions. The Lift, Gamma, and Gain controls broadly correspond to the darker, midrange, and brighter regions in the image. Within each Primaries Wheels region, you can make hue and luma adjustments to create a neutral-toned image. For instance, if you wanted to adjust color or brightness in the darker areas, you would move the Color Balance indicator and Master Wheel in the Lift region.

Let's make a few adjustments just to get the feel of the Primaries Wheels tool.

1. In the timeline, click the **number 08** thumbnail to locate the playhead to that clip.
2. In the Lift color balance control, drag the Color Balance indicator slightly toward blue to add blue to the darker areas.

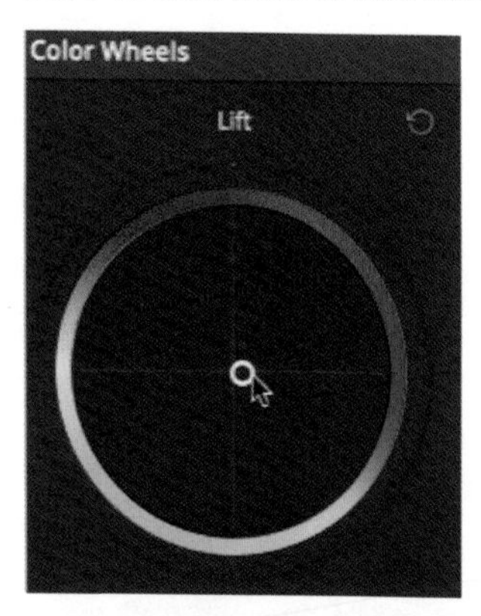

> **TIP:** Adjustments made using the Color Balance controls are subtle. In most cases, the edge of the Color Balance indicator will remain very close to or even still touch the crosshair.

The Master Wheels controls, below the Color Balance controls, adjust brightness in the lift, gamma, and gain regions. Adjusting the Lift master wheel will increase or decrease brightness in the darker areas.

3. Drag the Lift master wheel to the right until the Y luminance value reads 0.05.

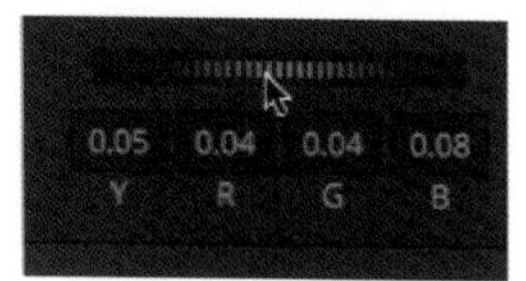

The Master Wheel under the Lift color balance control adjusts the black point for the image. When dragging it to the right, the darker areas in the image become brighter.

Let's look at the other end of the spectrum by adjusting the Gain control.

4. In the Gain color balance control, drag the Color Balance indicator slightly toward orange to add orange to the brighter areas.

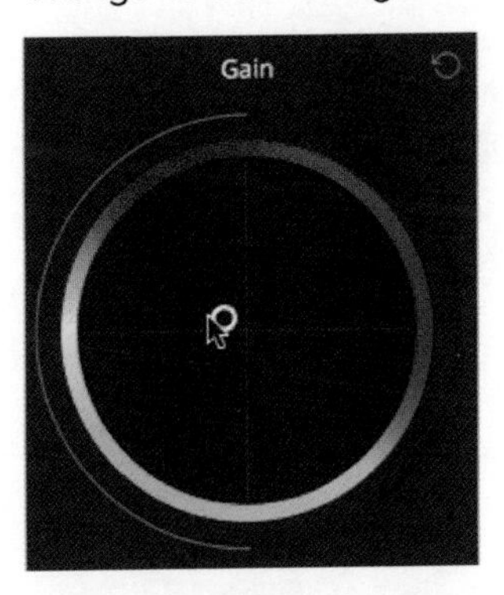

The Gain color balance control tints the brighter areas of your image.

5. Drag the Gain master wheel to the right until the Y luminance value displays 1.5.

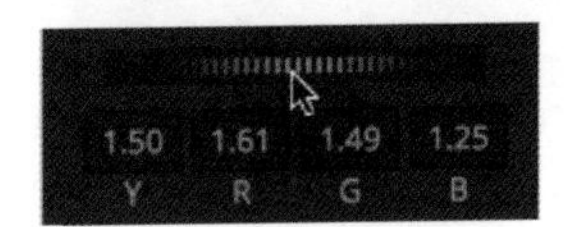

The Master Wheel under the Gain color balance control adjusts the white point for the image. When dragging it to the right, the brightest areas in the image become brighter.

By adjusting the Lift master wheel and the Gain Master Wheel, you have effectively adjusted contrast in the clip. Instead of using a simple contrast control, you have exercised greater control over the black point and white point using the Lift and Gain master wheels.

Now let's look at gamma.

6. In the Gamma color balance control, drag the Color Balance indicator slightly toward magenta.

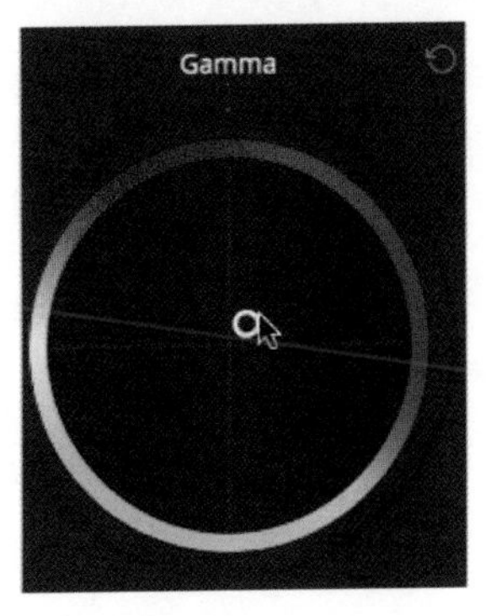

The Gain color balance control tints the midrange of your image.

7. Drag the Gamma master wheel to the left until the Y luminance value displays –0.03.

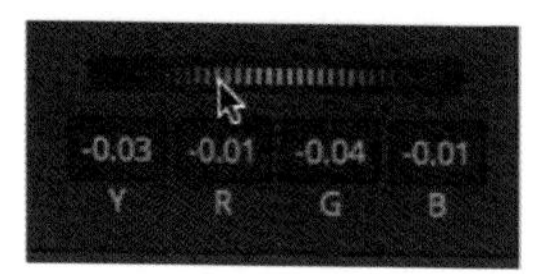

The Master Wheel under the Gamma color balance control adjusts the overall brightness while maintaining the black and white points that you set previously. When dragging this control to the left, the overall image becomes darker. Let's compare the corrected image you've made to the original image.

8. Choose View >Bypass All Grades, or press Shift-D, to see the original image. Then choose View >Bypass All Grades, or press Shift-D again, to view the corrected image.

All of these adjustments were made only to give you a feel for the controls and what they do. They clearly didn't produce anything worth keeping. You can reset each control or the entire Primaries Wheel panel using the reset button.

> **NOTE:** In the Color page, each clip has its own Undo/Redo history. That is, choosing Edit > Undo will undo previous changes depending on which clip is the current clip. The Edit page also has its own Undo history, which is separate from the Color page. The Edit page Undo/Redo commands operate on the entire timeline, not on each clip.

9. In the upper-right corner of the Gamma color balance control, click the reset button.

> **TIP:** Clicking the Reset button resets both color and master contrast adjustments, whereas double-clicking any color wheel resets only the color adjustment.

You can also reset the entire Color Wheels panel using the panel reset button.

10. In the upper-right corner of the Color Wheels panel click the reset button.

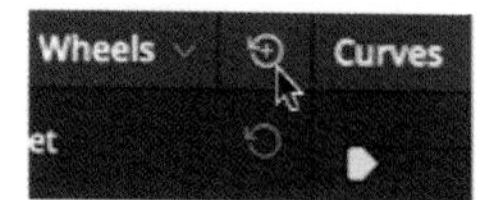

The Lift, Gamma, and Gain controls are not isolated adjustments that change only the darker, midrange and brighter areas. In fact, their ranges overlap by a considerable amount. When you adjust the lift, for example, the majority of the adjustment affects the darker areas, but the midrange and even some bright areas may be affected as well. Similarly, when you adjust gain, most of the adjustment operates within the brightest areas of the image, but you'll also see a fall-off impact within the midrange and a small amount of darkest areas. This overlap helps make more natural, smooth-looking adjustments, but it also means that you'll need to move between the three color balance controls to achieve best results because making an adjustment to one control visibly impacts the others.

Understanding Nodes

Instead of making changes within tracks using layers and effects, the adjustments you make on the Color page are performed using nodes. You can think of a node as an image-processing flow chart for each individual clip. The clip, or the input, starts at the left, flows through nodes, and ends on the right side of the screen with the corrected image output.

All of the adjustments you made in the preceding exercise were done using the first node, which automatically is provided for you in the Node Editor. As you create more sophisticated corrections, you can add more nodes that target different parts of the image or add effects.

NOTE: You'll work more with nodes as you perform more sophisticated color adjustments later in this lesson.

Using Video Scopes

As easy as those adjustments were to make, when you change brightness, hue, or saturation you always want to ensure that the resulting video signal data range falls within acceptable limits, particularly if you're preparing your project for broadcast distribution.

To analyze and measure the video signal data range inside Resolve, you have four video scopes: the vectorscope, histogram, waveform, and the default Parade.

1. To the far right of the toolbar, click the Video Scope button to display the Scope panel.

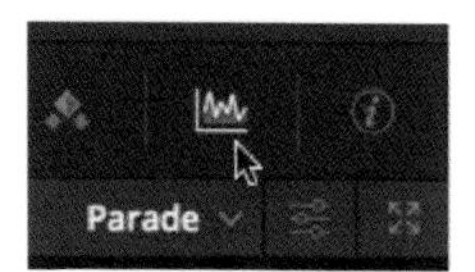

One of the easiest scopes to understand is the Parade Scope.

The Parade Scope displays the strength of the red, green and blue channels in the video signal. Since the three channels are displayed side-by-side, it is easy to compare imbalances based on their relative heights. The white point and brightest areas in the image are displayed at the top of the graphs while black point and darker areas are at the bottom. Tall Parade graphs indicate a wide or high contrast ratio, while short parade graphs indicate a narrow contrast ratio or a *flat image*.

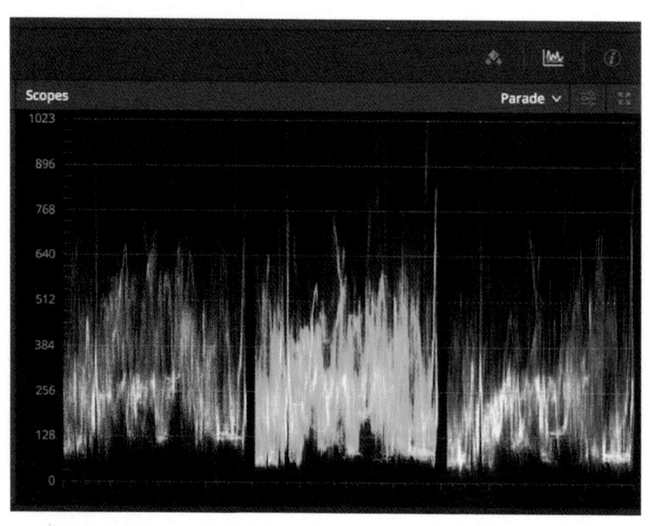

2. Click the first thumbnail in the timeline.

   In a typical shot, the bottom of the waveform for all three channels should begin somewhere between 0 and 128 on the graph. If you have something in the shot that is absolutely black, then the waveform should go closer to 0. If the darkest part of your image tends more toward a dark gray, then you might want to lean toward line 128 on the graph. In any case, that type of adjustment is made using the Lift master wheel. For this shot, you'll bring the black point close to the 0 line.

3. Drag the Lift master wheel to the left until the Y luminance value displays -0.02.

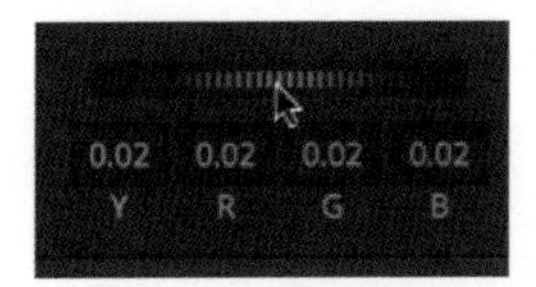

As you drag the Lift master wheel to the left, the darkest areas in the image become darker, and in the Parade Scope, the bottom point for the red, green, and blue channels are near 0.

The brighter areas in this image could be a lot brighter. Viewing the Parade, you can see the brightest highlights reach only just above the 640 line. The shiny metal items behind the person on screen should be much brighter.

4. Drag the Gain master wheel to the right until the Y luminance value displays 1.30.

NOTE: The Parade and Waveform Scopes always reflect 10-bit full-range data from 0–1023, regardless of your project's settings.

The gain adjustment now has caused some of the spikes in the Parade to reach the very top of the graph. When highlights go beyond the top of the graph, it indicates that they will lose all detail or become *clipped* because they are too bright. In most cases you do not want to clip an image.

In this case, these spikes are the *specular* highlights of the metal behind your subject. You'll never bring these highlight spikes within range without sacrificing other areas, so as you have done here, you try to maintain a good-looking overall image and limit the spike as much as you can.

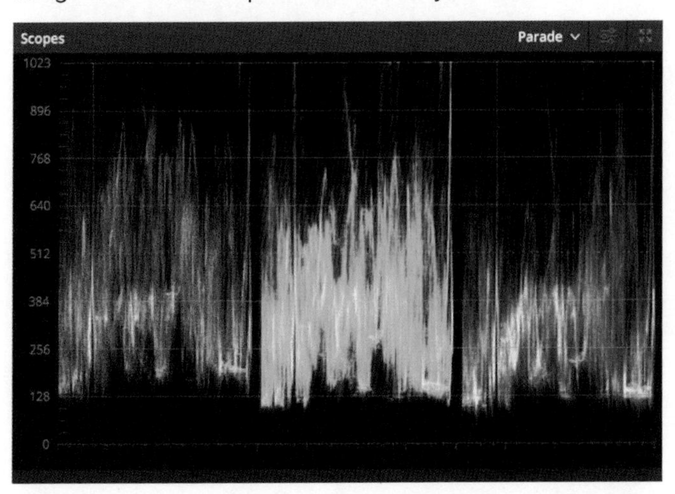

Now that you have made a good, high contrast image, you can compare those changes with the original image by temporarily disabling the correction or *grade*.

5. Choose View > Bypass All Grades, or press Shift-D, to see the original image; then choose View > Bypass All Grades, or press Shift-D, again to view the corrected image.

The image appears to have too much orange tint. While the tint is easily seen, you can also use the Parade to confirm it.

In the Parade, the red and green channels appear to be shifted higher than the blue channel. The red/green dominance is the cause of the orange tint. To fix it, you can use the Offset color balance control.

6. From the center of the Offset color balance control, drag the Color Balance indicator slightly toward teal on the color ring until the red, green, and blue channels are closely aligned at the bottom of the Parade.

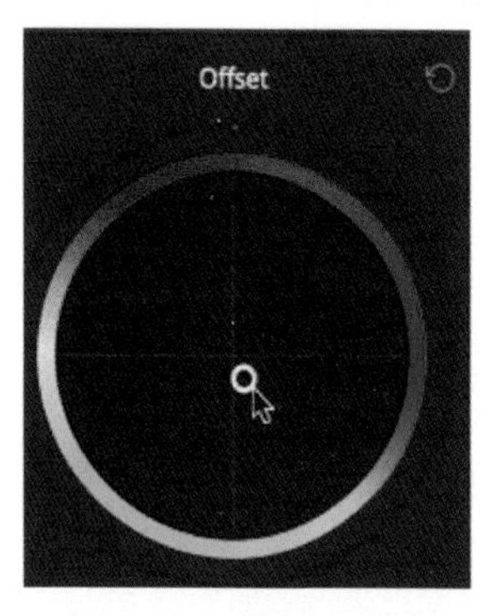

TIP: You can drag anywhere within the Color Balance control to move the Color Balance indicator. You don't need to drag the Color Balance indicator itself.

Using the Offset color balance indicator is a relatively straightforward method of quickly and easily removing color casts from a clip. For more complex color casts, you could use the other three Primaries Wheels to correct, for example, darker areas separately from brighter ones. Still, for most white balance problems this method works well.

Making Shared Adjustments

The primary color correction controls that you have used are adjusted mainly to achieve an overall look by controlling lift, gamma, and gain regions within the image. You can also make a few common adjustments that you may already be familiar with from other video or photo applications. The shared adjustment controls are located across the bottom of the Primaries Wheels panel. These global adjustments affect the entire image, not just the lift, gamma, or gain regions.

1. In the adjustment controls, position the pointer over the Sat (Saturation) value field.

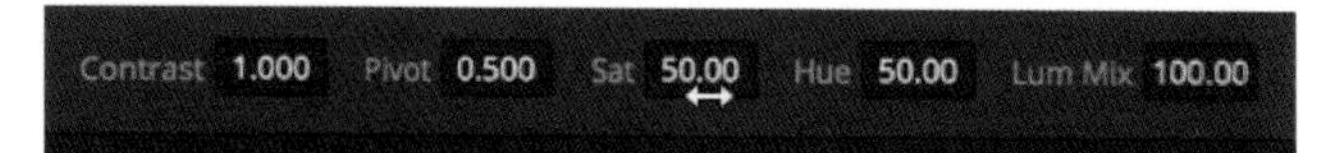

> **TIP:** Depending on your screen resolution, the names of each adjustment control may not be visible. Use the icons to identify each parameter, or hover over the icon to view a tool tip of the name.

The color in this shot appears a bit oversaturated. Dragging the Sat value to the left can decrease that saturation.

> **TIP:** As with all value fields in Resolve, when the pointer is over the value field or the parameter's name, you can drag to modify the value.

2. With your pointer in the Sat value field, drag to the left until the value reaches 40.

> **TIP:** You can reset an adjustment control by holding down Option (OS X) or Alt (Windows) and double-clicking the name or icon of the parameter that you want to reset.

The adjustment controls have a second page of parameters for globally improving your shot.

3. Click the 2 button to display the second page of the adjustment controls.

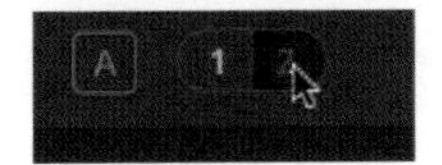

Here, you can adjust for simple white balance correction using the Temperature and Tint controls. Let's locate a shot that needs a white balance correction.

4. Click thumbnail **02** to view the shot of the Golden Gate bridge.

This shot clearly has too much blue. The clouds, which should be purely white, are the most obvious signs; but the Parade Scope also shows the blue channel rising higher than red or green, confirming that the shot has a blue color cast.

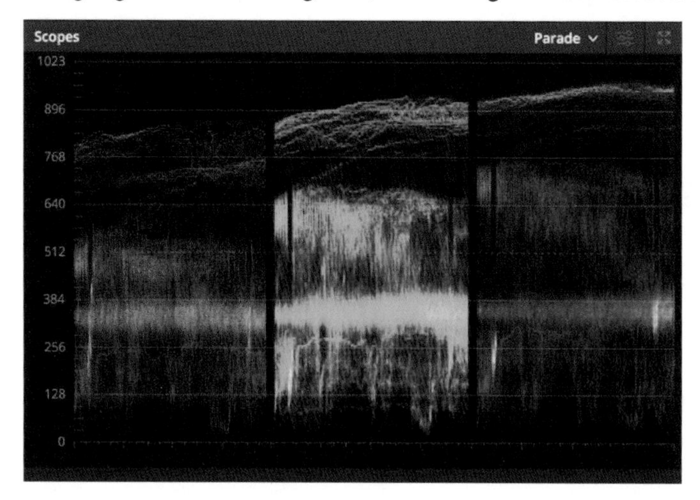

The Temperature control can shift the color in an image either warmer toward yellow, or cooler toward blue.

TIP: For off-axis color casts that come from irregular light sources, you can use the Tint control to shift an image away from magenta or green.

5. Drag the Temperature value field to the right to increase the warmer tones.

   As always when you make a significant adjustment, you should compare it to the original image.

6. Choose View >Bypass All Grades, or press Shift-D, to see the original image. Choose View >Bypass All Grades, or press Shift-D again, to return to the corrected image.

With the adjustment you have made, this image now has a much better white balance. In most color correction situations, you would likely bounce between the two images a few times while refining your adjustments. Rarely do you set a control once, compare it to the original, and move on. Color correction is an iterative learning process. It takes time; but the more you explore your options, the more you find the adjustments that work best for you.

Using Versions

Each color correction "look" that you apply to a clip is called a *version*. You can create and save multiple versions for a single clip as a way to try out different looks before you select the one you like best. Let's go back to the interview clip where you previously performed a basic color correction.

1. Click the first thumbnail in the timeline (number **01**).

   You achieved a neutral balance in this shot. It has a very natural appearance; and for an interview, this may be just what you want it to look like. Let's create a second color grade version and make some changes based on this neutral look.

2. Right-click the first thumbnail in the timeline (number **01**), and choose Local Version > Create New Version.

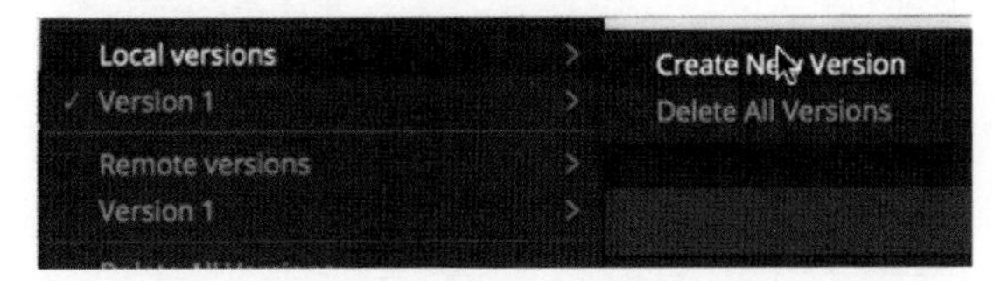

3. In the New Version dialog, type **Basic Sepia**, and click OK.

   Once you create and name a new color grade version, you can then make color adjustments that are contained in that version.

4. Drag the Gamma color balance indicator toward orange until you have a nice sepia tone on the image.

   Now you have two versions that you can switch between to compare them, or even create a third version if you want still another choice.

5. To load the original neutral-balanced version, right-click the thumbnail, and from the contextual menu, choose Version 1 > Load.

Versions come in two different types: *local versions* and *remote versions*. You've used only local versions, which are applied to a single clip that you select in your timeline. Remote versions are applied to all of the clips in your timeline that derive from the same source clip in the media pool. Local versions are a bit easier to understand initially, but applying remote versions can help speed up the color correction process if your media is captured without too many starts and stops.

Saving and Applying Corrections

Once you've established a look for your shot, you'll want to quickly apply it to other similar shots. Doing so will give your scene a sense of continuity, which is probably the single most important benefit of color correcting. The first step in copying a complete set of adjustments to other clips is to save them as a still.

1. In the timeline, ensure that the first interview clip from the previous exercise is still selected.
2. Choose View > Stills > Grab Still, or press Cmd-Option-G (OS X) or Ctrl-Alt-G (Windows).

The current frame in the viewer is saved as a still frame in the Gallery. You can compare this still image and its associated adjustments with any additional changes that you may make to this clip. It's helpful to descriptively label this still so that you'll know what it contains when you return to it, perhaps weeks or months from now.

3. In the Gallery, right-click the still, and from the contextual menu, choose Change Label.

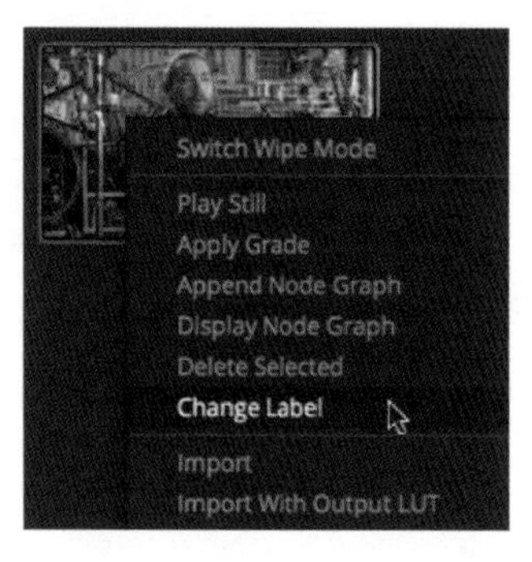

4. Assign the new label **Neutral Correction** because the correction you applied doesn't change the image dramatically, it just enhances the original footage.

TIP: When naming stills, it is best to avoid using the / (slash) character because doing so may interfere with the operating system naming conventions.

5. When you are done, press Return or Enter to close the text entry box.

TIP: To delete a still, you can right-click it, and from the contextual menu, choose Delete Selected.

Part of the color grading process involves evaluating clips side by side. Do clips in the same scene look like they belong together? Rather than playing clips sequentially and trying to recall their differences, you can compare clips side by side in a split-screen viewer.

6. In the Gallery, double-click the still to load it into the viewer.
7. Click the second interview clip to load it into the viewer.

One half of the viewer shows the still, while the other half shows the newly selected clip. You can change where the split occurs by dragging the split line left and right.

8. Drag the vertical split line halfway to the right edge of the frame to see more of the second interview clip.

Moving the split line allows you to compare different areas of the two frames. You can change the clip that you are comparing with the still, and change the type of split screen at any time.

9. In the timeline, click the third interview clip.

10. In the viewer, click the Horizontal Wipe button to change from a vertical split to a horizontal one.

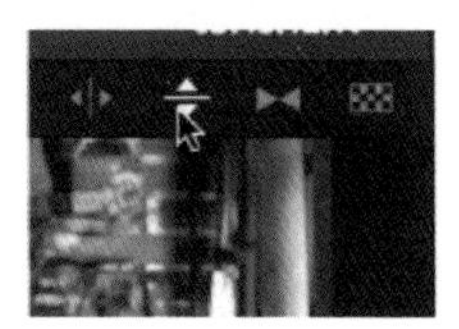

11. Drag the horizontal split line until it is over the man's face.

    With this tool, it's easy to see how very different the skin tones and the color of his T-shirt appear in a side-by-side comparison. Now, you'll add your saved adjustments to the two remaining interview clips and unify all three interview clips by applying a similar look.

12. Above the viewer, click the Image Wipe button to disable the split screen and display only the third interview shot in the viewer.

Now, you'll apply the saved grade to the other two interview shots.

13. Cmd-click (OS X) or Ctrl-click (Windows) the thumbnail **03**, the second interview clip, and thumbnail **05**, the third interview clip.

14. Right-click the still in the Gallery, and from the contextual menu, choose Apply Grade.

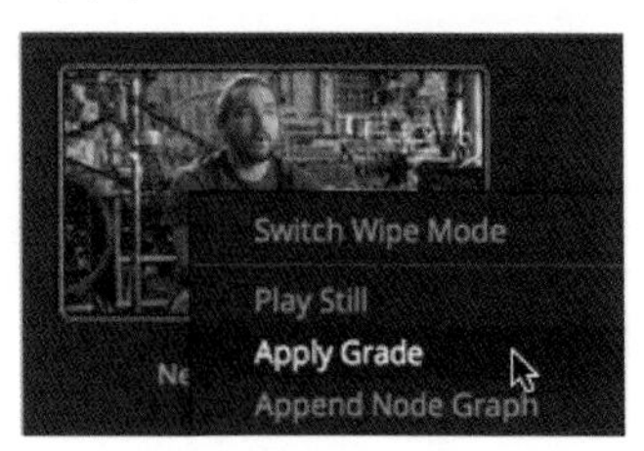

The saved adjustments depicted in the still are applied to the second and third interview clips. A colored highlight outlines the clip number on the thumbnails to indicate that the clips have adjustments applied to them.

15. Play over the three clips to view the applied color corrections.

You'll probably want to tweak each clip individually, but using stills gives you a great starting point when trying to apply a similar look to multiple clips.

Making Secondary Color Corrections

So far you've made adjustments to an entire image. These are called *primary color corrections*. *Secondary color corrections* are when you isolate parts of an image to make very specific changes to one particular area. A classic but extreme example is turning an entire image black and white except for one single object. Let's apply secondary color correction to a much more common task that you'll be able to use on many of your productions.

1. Click the second interview clip, thumbnail **03**.

2. Under the viewer, click the Loop button, and press the Spacebar to play the clip.

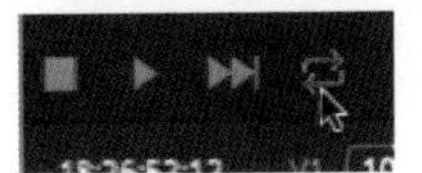

Engaging the Loop button allows you to play the clip over and over. This is desirable because the clip includes a camera movement that can influence the way you'll want to construct the secondary color correction.

3. After you have viewed the clip a few times, press the Spacebar to stop playback.

This clip looks perfectly fine except for the large bright blue pole in the middle of the room. You can't remove the pole altogether but you can dim the color to make it less intrusive in the shot.

Using Nodes and Qualifiers

The first part of making a secondary color correction on one object is to isolate the adjustment to its own node.

Using the Node Editor (located in the upper-right quadrant of the Resolve window), you can combine one or more individual corrections, called *nodes*, to create more intricate results.

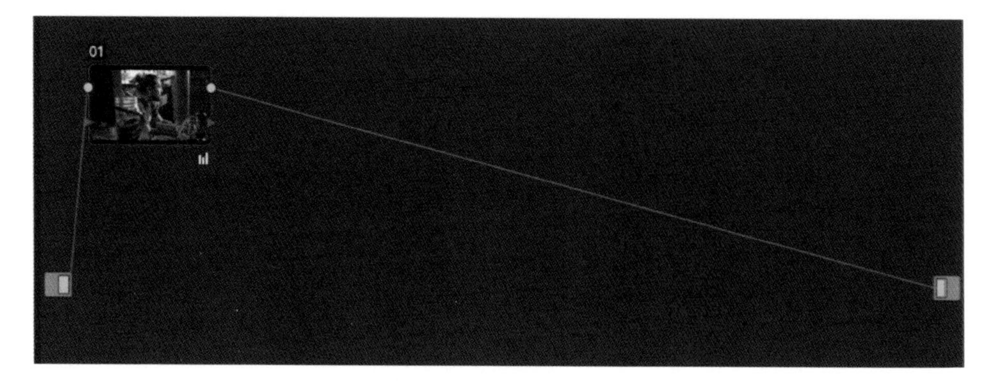

By default, every clip has one node in the Node Editor that contains the initial adjustments you made. The node shown in the current project contains all of the adjustments you used to create the neutral correction.

However, you also have the option of creating multiple nodes in which each node contains one or more corrections that affect the image. Using multiple nodes, each containing different adjustments, allows you more precise control over the order of those adjustments and an easier way to track and modify them.

Let's add a second node to the Node Editor to separate the adjustment you will apply to the blue pole from the neutral correction.

1. From the Nodes menu, choose Add Serial Node, or press Option-S (OS X) or Alt-S (Windows)

   The node is added after the initial node in the node editor. The new node is given the number 02 and has a red outline to indicate that it is the currently selected node. You can rename the node to be more descriptive.

2. Control-click (OS X) or right-click (Windows), and from the contextual menu, choose Change Label.

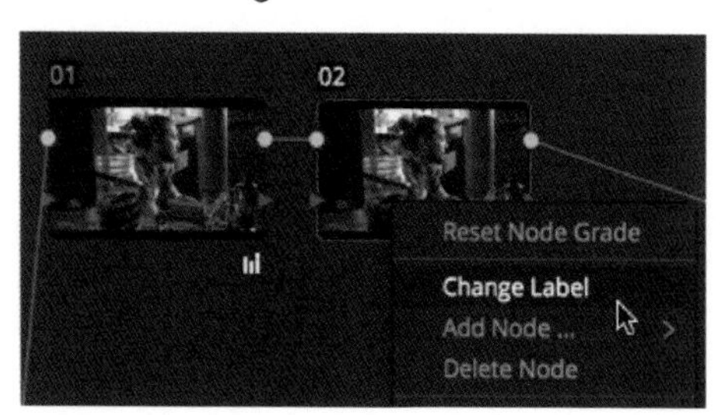

3. Type **Blue Pole**, and press Return or Enter to rename the node.

   With a new node in place, you can now use the Qualifier controls to isolate the blue pole and make your adjustment.

4. In the middle of the toolbar, click the Qualifier button to display the Qualifier controls.

   The Qualifier palette is displayed under the timeline. These controls let you isolate an area of the image based on an HSL, RGB, Luma, or 3D key. For this correction you will use an HSL key. The Qualifier controls can isolate an irregularly shaped object within a distinct range of color or lightness. Because you're generating a mask by sampling the image, there's no need for keyframing even if the object moves within the shot moves.

5. In the viewer, hover the mouse pointer over the blue pole.

   The pointer changes to an eye dropper to indicate that you can sample an area of the image you want to isolate.

6. Drag anywhere along the left side of the blue pole to sample its color and luma values.

   To see the sampled range more clearly, let's use the Highlight feature.

7. In the upper-left corner of the viewer, click the Highlight button.

   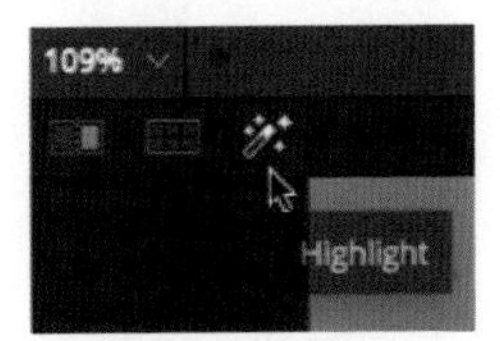

   The viewer now shows an overlay to represent the key you're creating to isolate the area. The selected area of the image is shown with the original colors, and the unselected area of the image is shown with a flat gray color. You can also view this as a more traditional black and white key.

8. In the upper-right corner of the viewer, click the Highlight B/W button to display the key in black and white.

   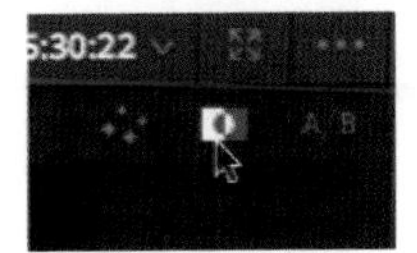

With the viewer showing exactly what you are isolating, you can refine the key using the HSL Qualifier tools: Hue, Saturation and Luminance. By adjusting the controls under each bar, you can further isolate and clean the selected area. Let's start by adjusting the blue hue selection to include a bit more of the pole.

9. Position the pointer over the hue's Width control and drag to the right until the number reaches around 8.0.

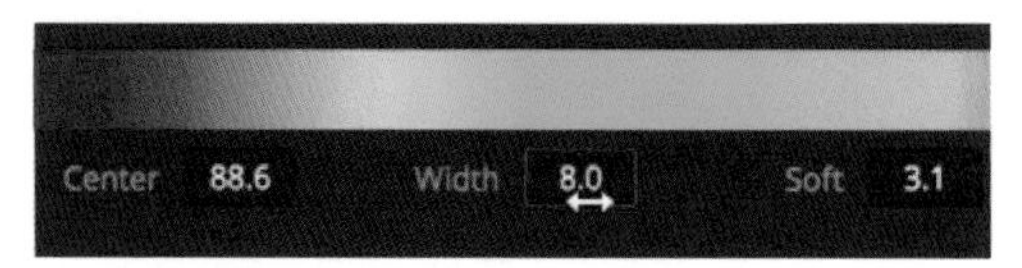

Increasing the width includes more blue hues than just the pixel you sampled with the eye dropper.

10. Under the Saturation bar, drag the L. Soft control to the right to increase the low softness and cover a wider area of the pole. Doing so will blend together more of the low saturated center of the pole.

You could continue tweaking a few other controls to further refine the selection but this looks good so far. The last step is to add just a bit of blur so the edges of the key are not completely hard. Adding too much blur can cause halo effects that are probably not desirable, but a little blur can produce a more gradual change along the edges and make the secondary correction look more natural.

11. In the Matte Finesse controls, to the right of the Qualifier controls, drag the Blur Radius to around 20.

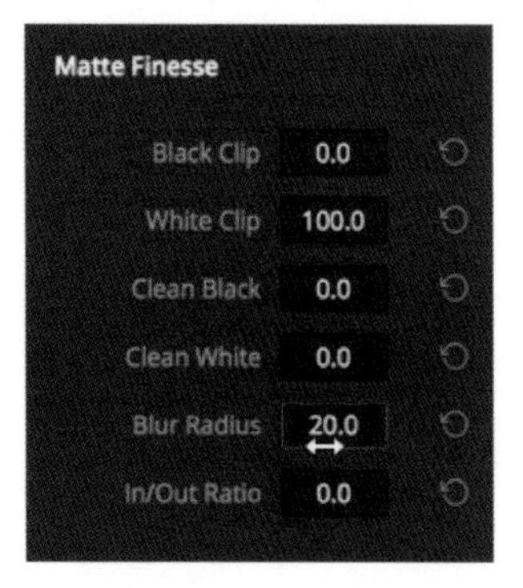

12. In the upper-left corner of the viewer, click the Highlight button to return to viewing the colored image.

Now you can make adjustments using the standard Primaries Wheels or shared adjustments palette that will apply to only the selected area.

13. Under the Primaries Wheels, in the adjustments, select the page 1 button.

14. Place the pointer over the Sat control, and drag to the left until the value reaches around 20.

As always, after you make a significant change to an image it is a good idea to compare the change with the original image. In this case you want to compare only the changes to the pole. Previously you were comparing changes to the original image. In this case, because you made the adjustment on a new node, you can temporarily disable the node to compare the change

15. Choose Nodes >Enable/Disable Current Node, or press Cmd-D (OS X) or Ctrl-D (Windows).

    Now you are viewing the neutral correction without the toned-down saturation adjustment to the blue pole.

16. Choose Nodes >Enable/Disable Current Node, or press Cmd-D (OS X) or Ctrl-D (Windows).

You may want to quickly compare before and after images a few times to review the change. You can also tweak the saturation level more if you think the image requires it.

Grouping Clips

When multiple clips in a timeline require the same adjustment, you can group those clips and apply corrections to the entire group.

1. Click the first interview clip, thumbnail **01**. Cmd-click (OS X) or Alt-click (Windows) thumbnails **03** and **05**.

2. Right-click either of the selected thumbnails, and from the contextual menu, choose “Add into a New Group.”

3. In the New Group Name dialog, type **Interview Clips** as the group name, and click OK to save the group.

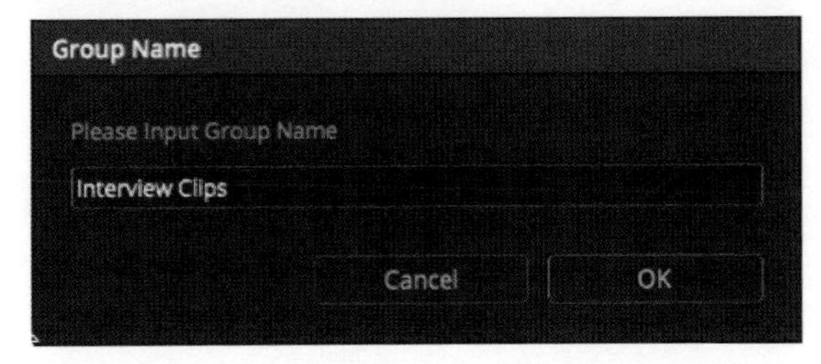

    When a clip is part of a group, you have the choice to make adjustments to all of the clips in that group or on the individual clip. You make this choice in the Group pop-up menu above the Node Editor.

4. In the timeline, select thumbnail **01**.

5. Above the Node Editor, from the groups pop-up menu, choose Group Post Clip.

The Group pop-up menu above the Node Editor gives you four choices. The Clip option allows you to apply corrections to only the selected clip. The Timeline option applies corrections to the entire timeline, no matter what group the clips are in. The two group options allow you to adjust all the clips in a group either before or after any individual clip's adjustments are applied.

Creating Vignettes with Power Windows

With multiple clips placed into a group, you can now make corrections that are applied to all of them. For your three interview clips, you can create a simple vignette using a Power Window.

1. In the timeline, make sure thumbnail **01** is still selected and Group Post Clip is chosen from the Group pop-up menu above the Node Editor.

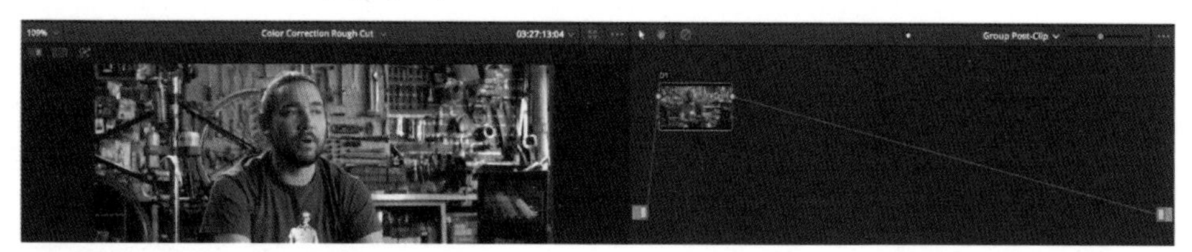

2. In the middle of the toolbar, click the Power Window button to display the Power Window controls.

Like qualifiers, you can use Power Windows to isolate a part of the frame. Unlike qualifiers, you use spline-based shapes instead of HSL or RGB selections.

3. Click the circular Power Window shape to add it to the clip.

4. Drag one of the corners of the circular Power Window so the outer circle reaches the top and bottom of the frame.

5. Drag one of the side handles to stretch the circle power window as wide as the frame.

With the Power Window creating the shape for your vignette, any color or brightness adjustment you make will use the power window as a mask.

6. Drag the Gamma master wheel to the left to about -0.05 to darken the image.

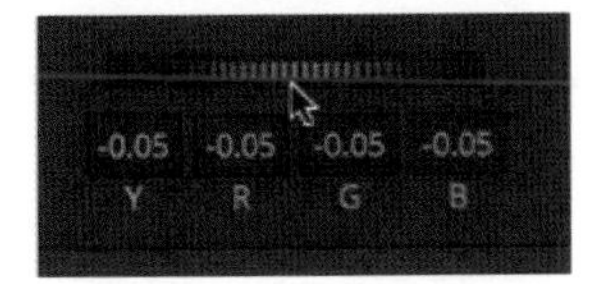

This gamma brightness change is performed inside the power window shape, but this is the inverse of what you want. To create a vignette, the brightness change must be applied outside the Power Window shape.

7. In the Power Window panel, click the Invert button.

The gamma brightness change now occurs outside the Power Window shape. You can further refine the Power Window shape using softness controls.

8. To feather the edges of the circle, in the Power Window panel, drag the Soft 1 control to around 3.00.

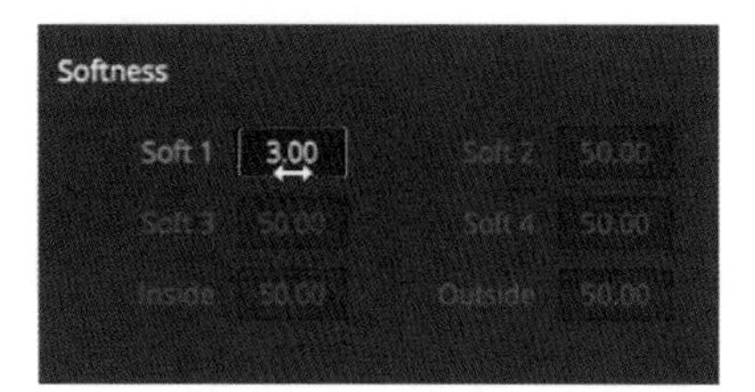

Because all the of these changes were made using the Group Post Clip setting, your soft-edged vignette is automatically applied to each clip in the group.

9. Click thumbnail **03**, and then click thumbnail **05** to view the vignette effect in all three clips.

Applying Resolve FX

Resolve includes a number of high quality filter effects called Resolve FX. They offer an incredibly useful range of filters including blurs, glows, film grain, and lens flares. You can apply these effects to an entire clip or you can combine them with Power Windows and tracking to isolate an effect to one area of the frame.

1. Click the thumbnail **06**.

2. Press the Spacebar to play the clip.

   This clip already has basic color correction on the first node, so you'll place a second node to add an effect.

3. Choose Nodes > Add Serial Node, or press Control-S (OS X) or Alt-S (Windows).

   The effect to add is a common one: Blur out the logo on the cyclist's shirt. This is something you frequently must do to avoid violating copyright laws. The first step is to isolate the area you want to blur.

4. On thumbnail **06**, drag the playhead under the viewer to the start of the clip.
5. In the middle of the toolbar, click the Power Window button, if necessary.

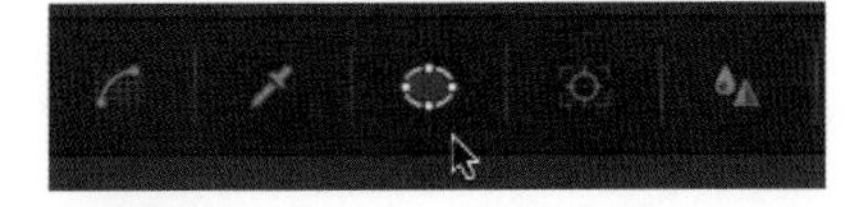

6. Click the circular Power Window shape to add it to the clip.

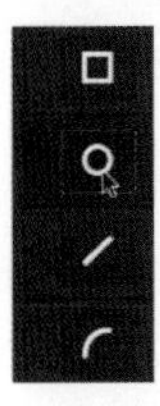

7. Drag one of the corners of the circular Power Window so that the inner circle is roughly the size of the logo on the cyclist's arm.

8. Drag the center of the circular Power Window shape to cover the logo on the cyclist's arm.

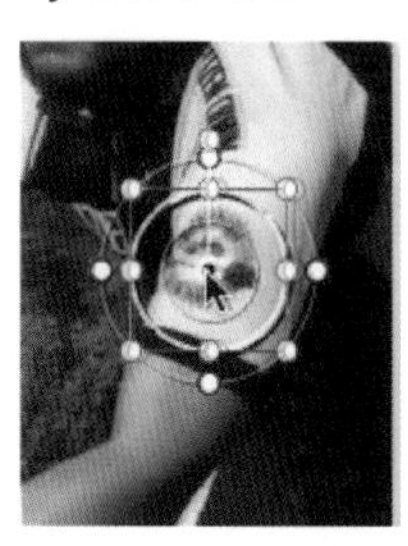

You can use a Resolve FX to "fill" the Power Window and obscure the logo.

9. Above the Node Editor, click the OpenFX button.

In the OpenFX panel, you'll typically find a list of the third-party filter effect plugins that you added to Resolve. However, it also contains a list of Resolve FX that are included with the application.

10. Scroll down the OpenFX panel to find the Mosaic Blur effect. Drag the effect onto the second node that contains the power window.

> **TIP:** Only one Resolve FX can be added to a node. To remove an effect, right-click the node, and choose Remove OFX Plugin.

When the mosaic blur is added, it fills in the power window to obscure the logo. You can modify the mosaic in the settings panel that automatically appears.

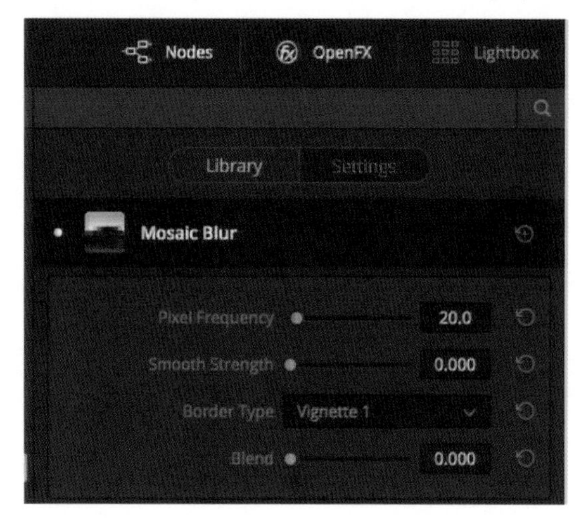

11. In the OpenFX Settings panel, raise the Pixel Frequency to around 100 to increase the number of mosaic squares used in the power window.

The mosaic is placed for this one frame only. Because the cyclist moves throughout the shot, you will need to track the Power Window to ensure that it follows the logo around the screen.

Tracking Power Windows

Resolve features an incredible 3D perspective tracker that not only follows objects, but can also determine if that object changes rotation or perspective. As a result, you can track the most challenging objects to apply Resolve FX or color correction.

1. In the toolbar, click the Tracker button.

2. Make sure the playhead in the Tracker panel is at the start of the clip.

The tracker can track various aspects of objects within a clip. You can enable and disable the transform types using the checkboxes at the top of the panel. Disabling parameters can sometimes help improve tracking, so long as you needn't track those disabled aspects of the object. For instance, in this clip, you do not care if the logo zooms or rotates; however, you do care about titling and perspective changes.

3. Click the Zoom and Rotate checkboxes to disable those transforms.

4. Begin tracking by clicking the Track Forward button.

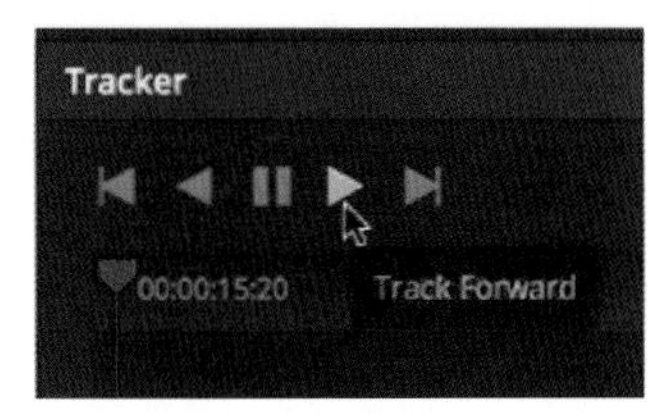

5. Once the track is completed, scrub or play through the clip to see the results.

   The tracker causes the power window to perfectly follow the logo on the cyclist's sleeve.

In this lesson, you've used some of DaVinci Resolve's basic color correction tools to apply the powerful image processing that have made Resolve the number one choice in Hollywood.

Although DaVinci Resolve takes some time to learn., its non-destructive operation encourages you to create as many versions as you want and freely experiment with its rich toolset.

12 Using the Deliver Page

Everybody's workflow is different, and the Deliver page is designed to give you flexible options from project collaboration and dailies creation to final delivery. When you are collaborating with a sound editor, Resolve enables you to send a file to Avid Pro Tools for audio mixing. You can prep a timeline for visual effects work; and even output final masters in a Digital Cinema Package (DCP) for theatrical distribution. With so many different options on the Deliver page, you're sure to find many solutions that suit your workflow.

In this lesson, you'll use the Deliver page to create three separate files: one for the web, one for further audio mixing in Pro Tools, and one as a master HD file.

TIME

- **This lesson takes approximately 15 minutes to complete.**

GOALS

- **Create a file for web streaming.**
- **Send a timeline to Avid Pro Tools.**
- **Export a master file.**

Creating a Web Streaming File

Almost every project ends up on a web-streaming service in some form, even if it's just as promotional material. To output the most common file-based output formats, Resolve includes Easy Setups, which are presets that automatically configure all the parameters for an output type that you select.

1. In Resolve, open the **DaVinci Resolve Lesson 5-13** project that you have been working on in previous lessons.
2. In the Rough Cuts bin, double-click **Transitions Rough Cut** to load it into the timeline.

   The currently displayed timeline is the one that will be exported when you go to the Deliver page.
3. At the bottom of the Resolve window, click the Deliver button.

   The Deliver page is divided into five areas.

   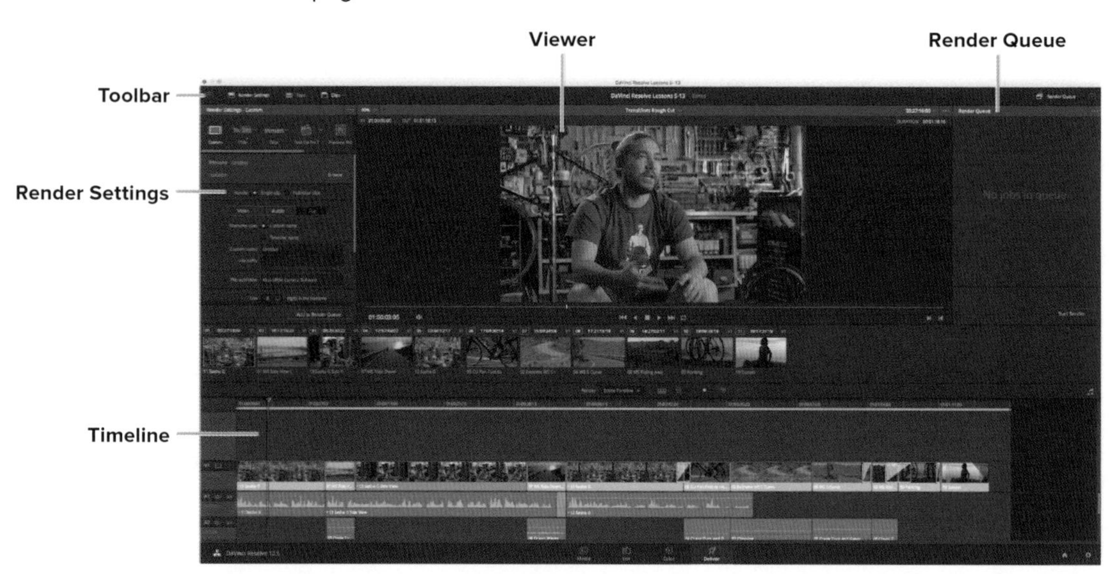

   The first step is to make sure your whole timeline is selected, which you can do by using the pulldown above the center of the timeline.
4. Above the timeline, from the Render pop-up menu, select Entire Timeline, if necessary.

   You'll use the toolbar to select tape-based output or to adjust Render Settings for file-based output. When Render Settings are selected, as they are by default, you can choose a Render Preset to configure for your output

5. At the top of the Render Settings, click the Vimeo preset.

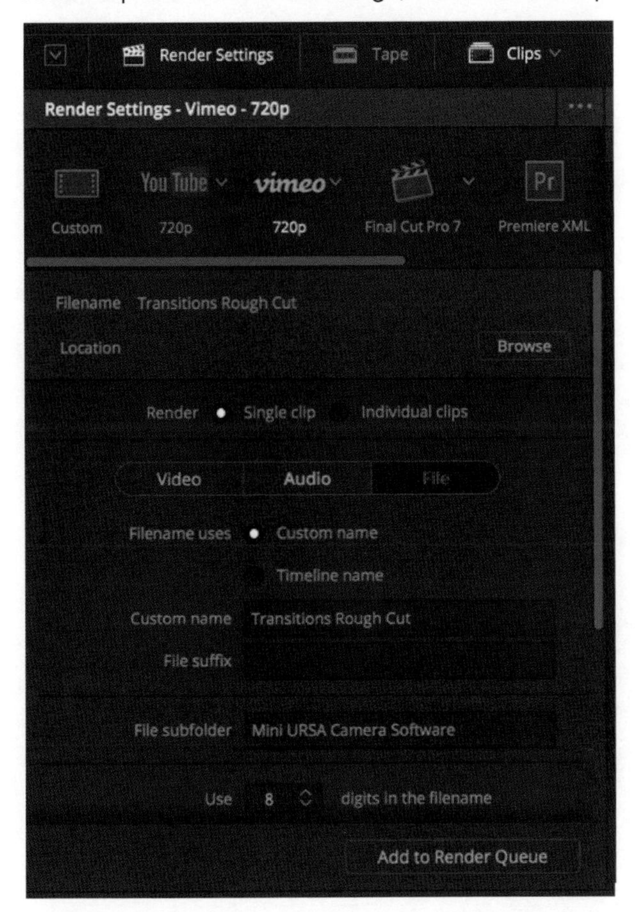

When you choose one of the presets, Resolve configures the Render Settings to output a file that conforms to the destination's requirements. If you wanted to stop at this point and output the file, you could do so. The only item you would need to set would be the destination of the output file.

6. Just below the row of presets, click the Browse button and choose a location for the output file. Then click the Close button on the dialog.

Although that is all you *must* do to output a file, you have a number of options that you can apply to presets. Let's examine options that can be useful when creating files for streaming.

7. Below the Browse button, click the Video tab to view the video-related options.

   You can customize the video compression and format in the Video tab in the Render Settings.

   The QuickTime H.264 setting is the most appropriate setting for compressing video that is intended for delivery to any of the popular web-streaming sites and services. By default, the Resolution and "Frame rate" menus are preset to the current timeline settings.

   The bit rate or data rate settings will offer various recommendations depending on the target streaming service. For example, the default 10000 kbs rate is the maximum for a 720p video on Vimeo, but it could be too high for use with other services. Let's lower the rate a bit to ensure acceptable performance on some of the other web-streaming services.

8. Scroll down and in the Quality Kb/s areas, click "Restrict to," and in the value field, enter **7500** Kb/s.

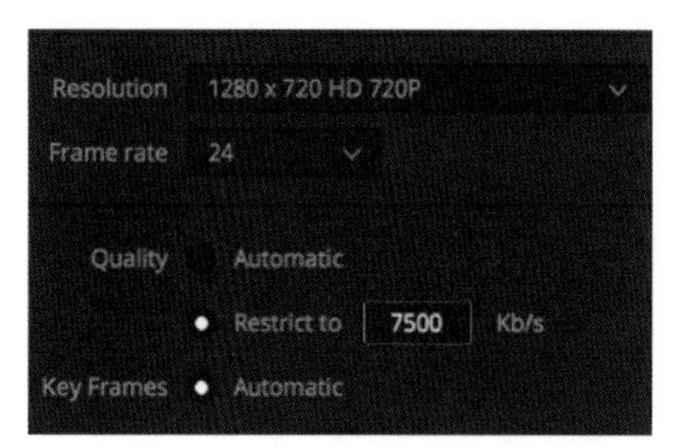

   For the most part, Quality is the only option you might need to adjust here. Now, you need only name the file.

WHAT IS A BIT RATE?

Bit rate, in terms of video, is based on the number of bits contained in an individual video frame. The higher the bit rate, the more visual information the frame contains, which usually results in higher-quality video. Bit rate is measured in megabits per second (Mb/s) or kilobits per second (Kb/s).

For efficient delivery to lower-bandwidth devices, such as older cellphones and networks, streaming files must have a lower bit rate, which is most often achieved by applying heavy video compression. For delivery to targets capable of processing higher bandwidth, like most modern Wi-Fi networks and smartphones, you can create larger files that have less compression and better video quality. Depending on the destination streaming service, you may have to output files in multiple formats with low and high bit rates to meet the demands of various streaming bandwidths.

9. Click the File tab.

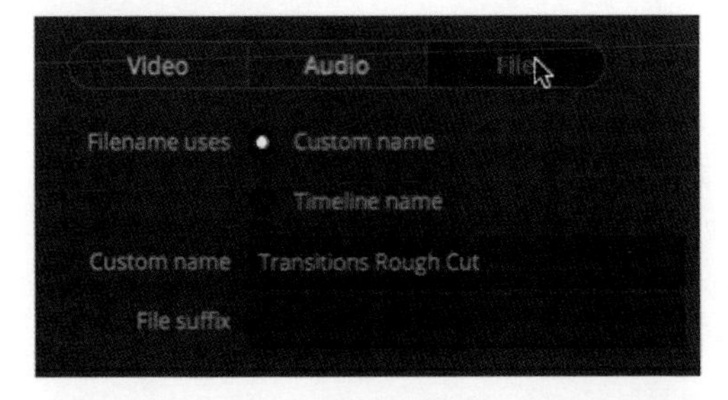

10. In the “Custom name” field type **Training Movie for Streaming**.

Once you have all of your settings configured, you add the timeline to a Render Queue.

11. At the bottom of the render settings, click the “Add to Render Queue” button.

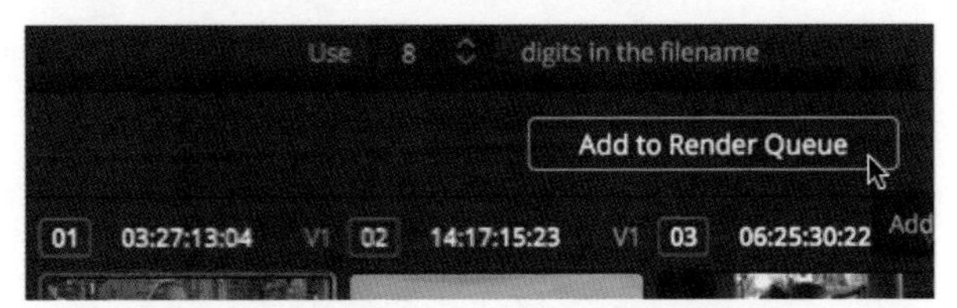

Clicking the “Add to Render Queue” button transfers that setting as a job to the Render Queue panel on the right.

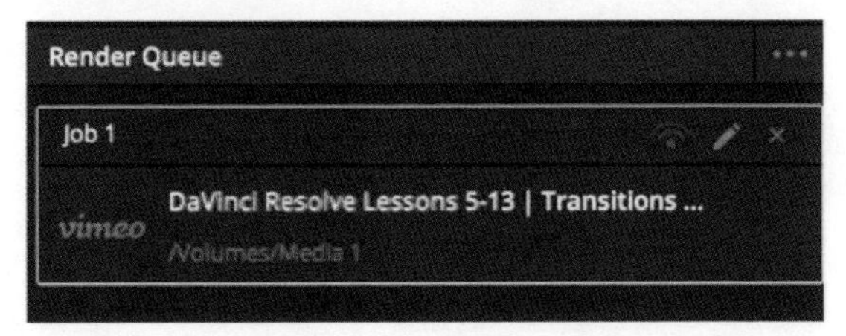

The Render Queue acts as a temporary holding area for jobs that you want to output from Resolve. You can add as many jobs to the Render Queue as you need to output. Although you could render this file immediately, let’s wait and place a couple more jobs into your queue.

Sending a File to Pro Tools

Although you can complete a lot of sound mixing tasks within Resolve, some projects may require the experienced ears and talents of a professional sound editor. For those occasions, you'll want to provide the sound editor with a project that she can import into Avid Pro Tools, a widely used digital audio workstation application for film and video.

1. At the top of the Render Settings, scroll through the row of presets and click Protools.

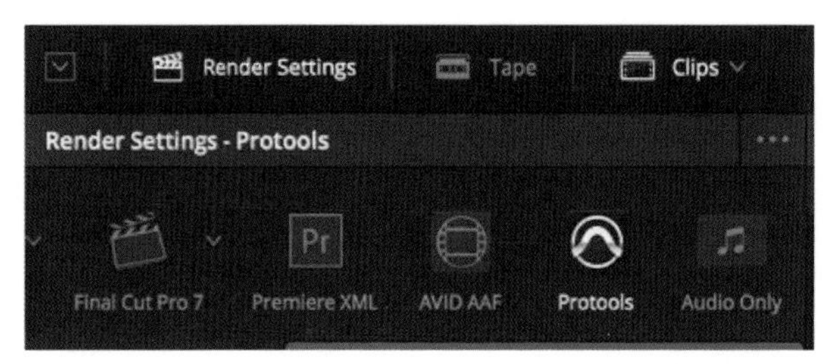

The Protools preset replaces the previously selected settings. Instead of creating a single file, such as the one you would output using the Vimeo preset, exporting to Pro Tools outputs several files. The timeline, with all your editing decisions, is converted into an AAF format file. The video track is converted into a DNxHD format file for viewing inside Pro Tools. And finally, each audio clip is output separately for editing and mixing.

2. Click the Video tab to view the video compression and format settings that are specific to Pro Tools.

A common option for outputting to Pro Tools is to include extra handles on the audio segments so the sound designer can trim and create transitions as needed.

3. Click the Advanced settings disclosure button to display more options.

4. Scroll to the bottom of the settings, and in the “Add frame handles” field, enter **12** to add an additional 12 frames on either side of each cut.

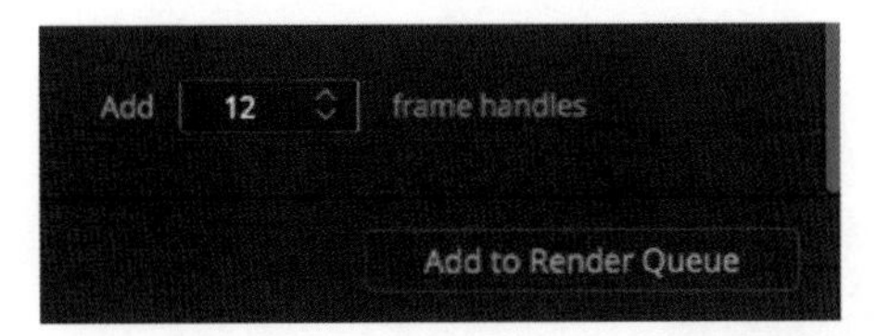

Now, you'll select a destination for the rendered files.

5. Click the File tab.

The location for the file remains the same from your previous selection. Because you will create multiple files with this preset, let's create a new folder for them

6. Click the Browse button and navigate to the DaVinci Resolve Editing Lessons Files folder. In the File Destination dialog, select the folder.

To contain all of the files that are created when you export to Pro Tools, you'll create a destination subfolder within the DaVinci Resolve Editing Lessons Files folder.

7. At the bottom of the File Destination dialog, click the Add New Folder button.
8. Name the folder **Export to Pro Tools**, and click OK.

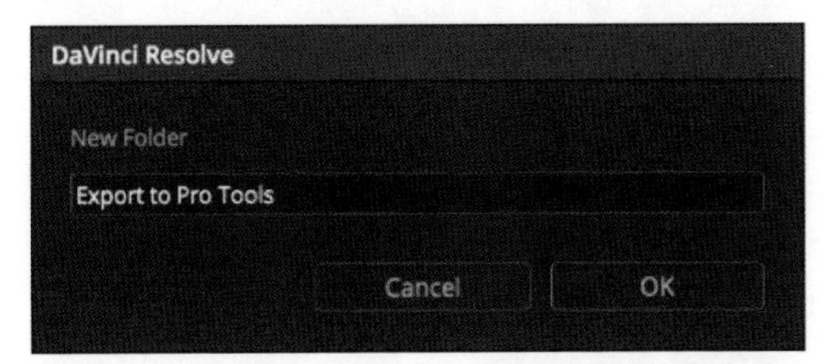

9. In the File Destination window, select the Export to Pro Tools folder, and click OK.

All of the media files created for Pro Tools, along with a Pro Tools-compatible timeline in the Advanced Authoring Format (AAF), will be saved in that one easy-to-move folder. With all of the settings configured, you can add this job to the Render Queue.

10. At the bottom of the Render Settings, click the Add to Render Queue button to add a second job to the queue.

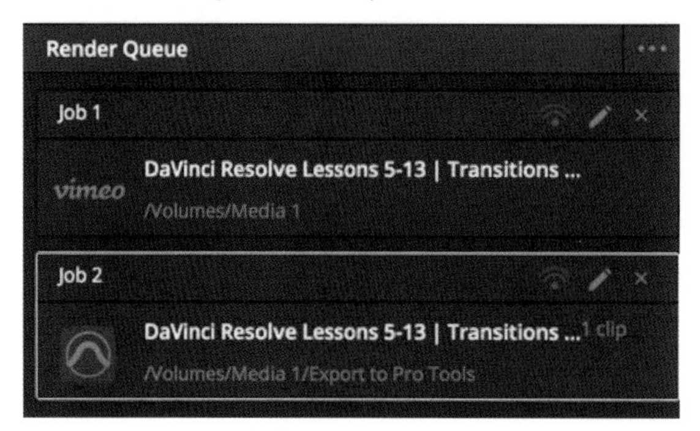

Let's create one more job to output a high-quality master using custom settings that you'll set up.

Exporting a Master File

When all of the audio and video content of your project is completed or locked, and no more changes to be made, you'll want to save that final version as a master file. A master file represents the highest-quality output possible for project distribution and will become the source from which you'll make future copies. Since each project has different mastering requirements, Resolve does not have a master file preset, so you'll want to create one of your own and save it as a preset.

1. At the top of the Render Settings, click Custom.

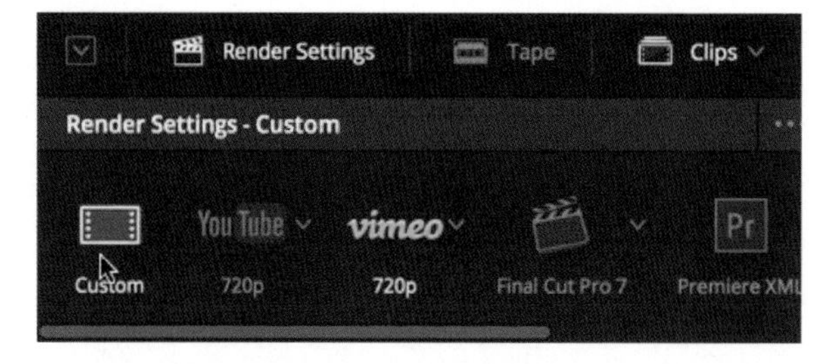

Clicking Custom makes all of the options in the Render Settings available for selection, and begins the process of creating a new preset.

2. At the top of the settings, click the "Single clip" button to create one movie file.

3. Click the Video tab, and from the Video Format menu, choose QuickTime.

   QuickTime, AVI, and MXF OP1A are video formats that output a single movie file containing both audio and video. The other choices are all image sequence output formats that contain no audio. QuickTime supports a number of codecs that you can choose from depending on the quality and file size you want to output.

4. From the Codec menu, choose Uncompressed YUV 422 10-bit.

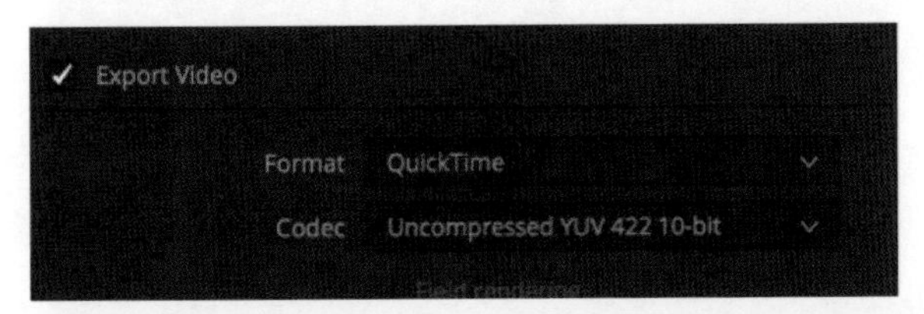

> **NOTE:** OS X users have the option to choose the Apple ProRes 422HQ, 4444, and 4444HQ codecs. Windows users can choose to output DNxHR444, DNxHR HQX, or DNxHR HQ formats. All of these formats can produce quality compressed files nearly indistinguishable from uncompressed files.

   The Uncompressed YUV 422 10-bit option will deliver the highest-quality cross-platform output in a QuickTime movie file, although it does require a powerful computer and a fast disk drive to play back.

5. Click the Advanced Settings arrow, and scroll down to view the Data Burn-in setting.

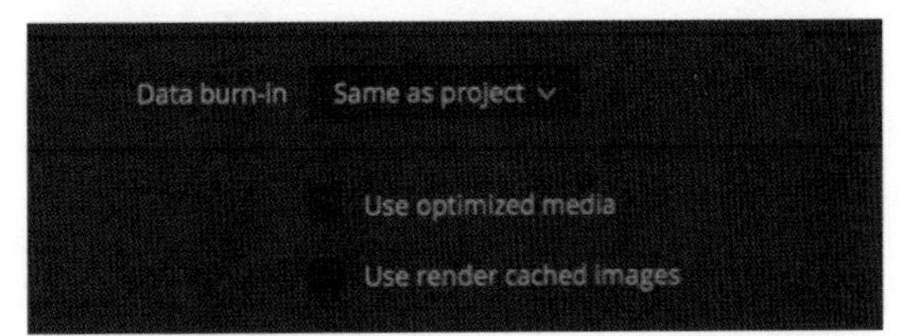

   When the Data burn-in menu is left at its default setting, "Same as project," it uses the burn in setting that is configured in the Color page.

6. At the bottom of the Resolve window, click the Color button.

7. In the center palettes under the timeline, click the Data Burn In button to open the Data Burn In palette.

   This palette lists metadata that you can superimpose over the picture of your output file as a watermark when used with the Data Burn In menu in the Deliver page.

8. Click the Custom Text1 checkbox, and in the formatting area, type **Do Not Distribute**.

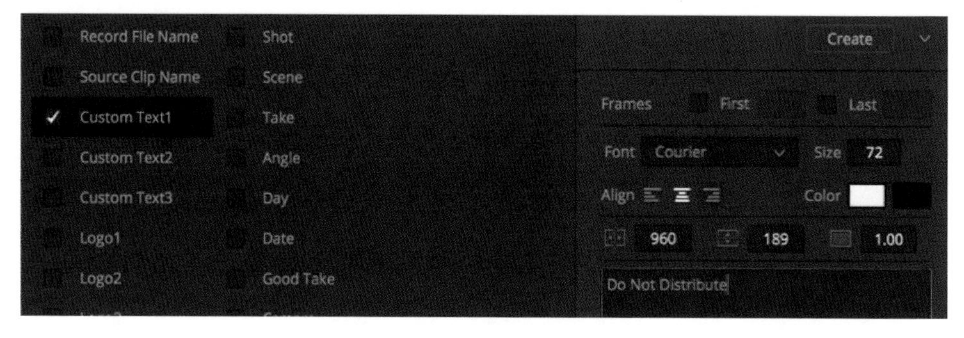

The Data Burn In text appears in the viewer.

9. At the bottom of the Resolve window, click the Deliver button to return to the Deliver page.

   Next, you will look at the output settings for your audio tracks.

10. Click the Audio tab, and select the Export Audio checkbox.

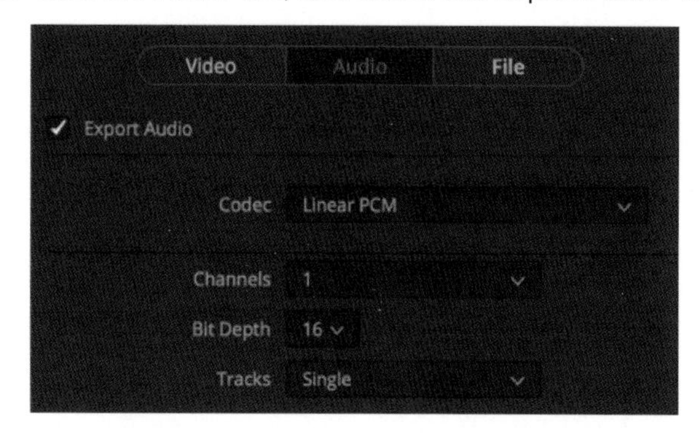

PCM linear audio is the highest-quality audio format available in QuickTime. OS X users also have the option to output audio in the compressed AAC format.

Your last task is to choose the destination where the output will be saved.

11. In the File section, under the Render To field, click the Browse button.

12. Navigate to the DaVinci Resolve Editing Lessons Files folder, and select it in the File Destination dialog. Click OK.

    Now you can save these settings as your own custom master file preset.

13. At the top of the render settings, click the options menu, and choose Save As New Preset.

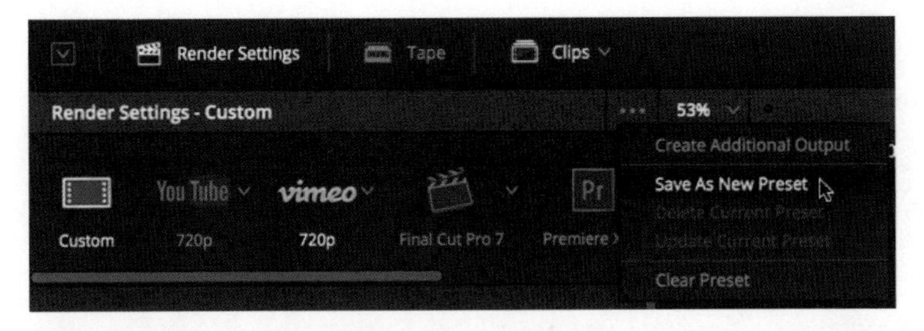

14. In the “Enter preset name” field in the dialog, type **Master File with Watermark**, and click OK.

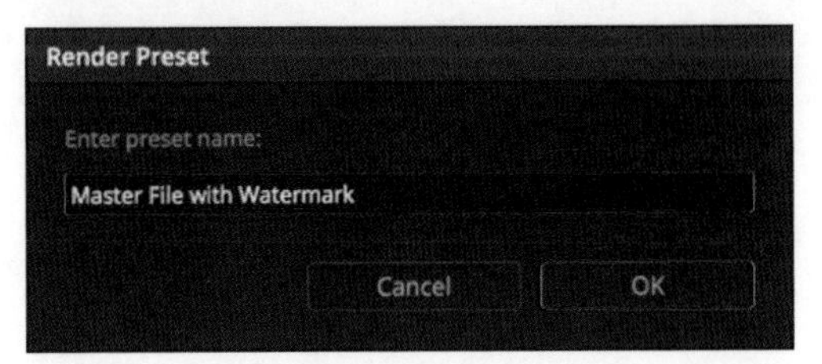

The new preset’s name appears at the top of the Render Settings, indicating that it is the currently active setting. It also is listed in the row of presets.

With all of the settings configured, you can add the job to the Render Queue.

15. At the bottom of the Render Settings, click the Add to Render Queue button to add your third job.

You now have three jobs in your Render Queue. If you save and quit Resolve now and come back at a later date, those jobs will still be in the Render Queue. Currently, these jobs, once rendered, would take up around 4 GB of space on your hard drive. Because you may not want to devote 4 GB of disk space to these lesson results, you won’t be asked to render them at this time.

16. When you want to render your own project, in the Render Queue, select the items that you want to render. Then click the Start Render button at the bottom of the Render Queue to begin the process. One by one, the jobs will render out and be marked as completed.

What you will find useful right now is knowing how to clear the Render Queue.

17. In the upper-right corner of the Render Queue, click the Options pop-up menu.

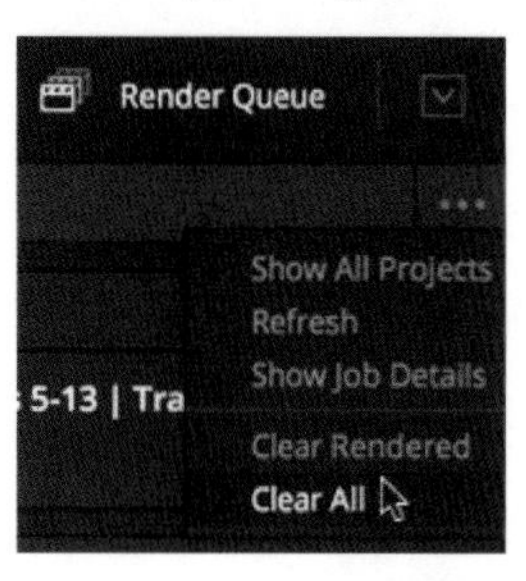

18. From the menu, choose Clear All to remove all of the current jobs from the queue.

The Deliver page has many more options for outputting various file formats and supporting a variety of workflows. If you are creating the final master file output of your timeline in Resolve, you now understand the most commonly used workflows. However, when sharing a project with a colorist or another editor, you'll find that he may use different software and other workflows. Exploring the Deliver page further, you'll discover how Resolve can flexibly address those collaborative situations.

13 Managing Projects and Media

After you've fine-tuned and rendered your timeline, you will want to back up your entire project. In fact, you should be backing up your project each day. Even before you begin editing, planning a backup strategy can save you hours if not days of work. And be aware that every project has different backup requirements.

In this lesson, you will look at ways to manage your project file and media before, during, and after editing.

> **NOTE:** This lesson uses a second hard drive for copying and transcoding media. If you do not have a second hard drive or do not want to take up valuable disk space by copying and/or moving the training media from this book, you can still read through the lesson to gain an understanding of the process.

TIME

- **This lesson takes approximately 15 minutes to complete.**

GOALS

- **Copy projects to a new hard drive**
- **Transcode to other formats**
- **Consolidate media**

Copying Projects to a New Hard Drive

Although you have many methods for doing so, the easiest way to copy a project from one computer to another is to use Resolve's archive and restore features. Archiving a project collects all of your files (even if they are on different drives) and places them in a folder in the destination of your choice along with the project file. It's all very neat and convenient.

1. Open the project manage window by clicking the Home button in the lower-right corner, or choosing File > Project Manager.

2. To archive the project, right-click it in the Project Manager window, and choose Archive.
3. In the Archive dialog, navigate to a drive where you want to save the project, and click Save.

   All of the media and the project file containing your bins and timelines are saved into a folder with the extension .dra. This folder file contains everything you need to open your project on another computer. When you bring the hard drive with the archived folder to another computer you must restore it in Resolve to begin working with it.

4. To restore an archived project, open the Project Manager.
5. Right-click anywhere in the Project Manager, and choose > Restore.

   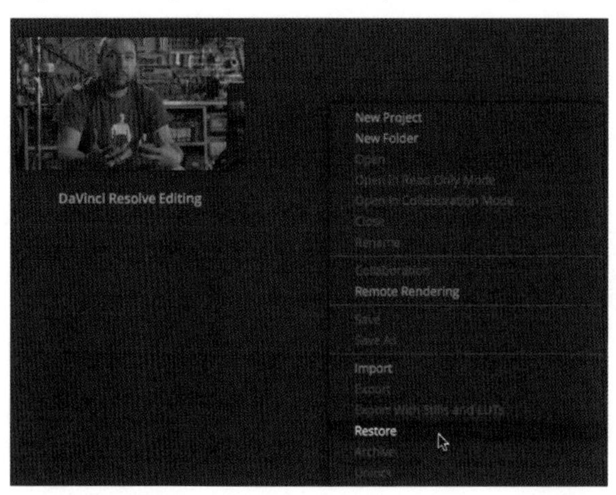

6. In the dialog, navigate to the .dra folder you archived, and click Open.

   The archived project opens into the Project Manager and you can begin working on it.

All of the archived media remains in their original locations as well as in the archive. The two sets of media are completely identical. It is up to you to decide if you want to delete the media from its original location.

Consolidating Media

Archiving a duplicate of your project and its media is a great option as long as you have the disk space to store a copy of everything. However, for larger projects that you want to put on a portable hard drive, archiving may not be the best choice.

When your hard drive cannot accommodate a complete copy of the original media, *consolidating* can help to remove media that is no longer needed. Using the Media Manager, consolidating gives you the option to copy only those pieces of media that you have actually used. For long-form projects with lots of media, consolidating is a great way to free up disk space and make backing up a project a quicker task.

1. Click the Media button; and in the Media Pool, click the Rough Cuts bin, and select all the timelines.

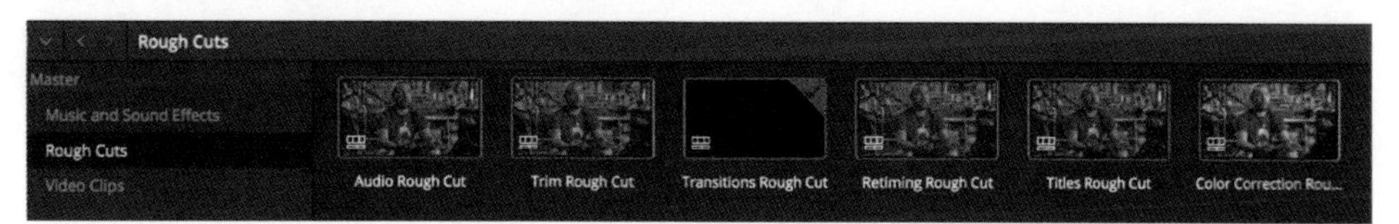

2. Choose File > Media Management.

   When timelines are selected, the Media Management window will open with the Timelines button selected.

3. Click the Copy button.

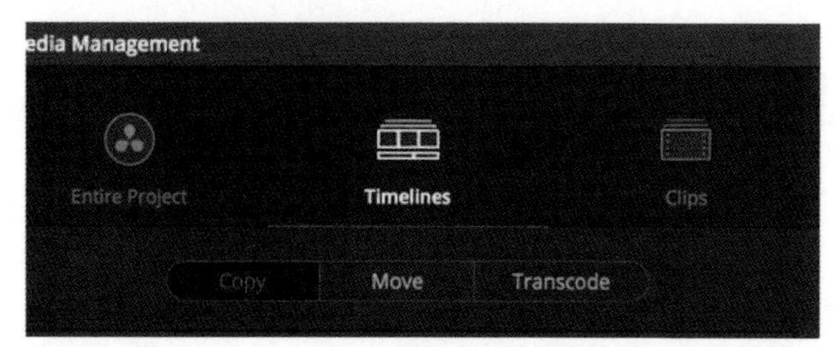

   Choosing Copy will first create a duplicate set of media files on the portable hard drive, leaving the original in place.

4. Click the Browse button, and in the File Destination dialog, navigate to a location where you want to copy the media. Click OK.

> **TIP:** You can click the New Folder button to create a folder for the consolidated files that you will create. If you don't do so, you might end up with too many files on the top level of a hard drive and no way to know which to keep and which to delete.

The option to consolidate media requires that you select one or more timelines to determine which files to keep. You have two choices for consolidating your media: You can choose to copy the clips that you have used in the selected timelines in their entirety, or copy just the portions of those clips that you have used in the selected timelines (including handles).

5. Select “Copy and trim used media keeping.”

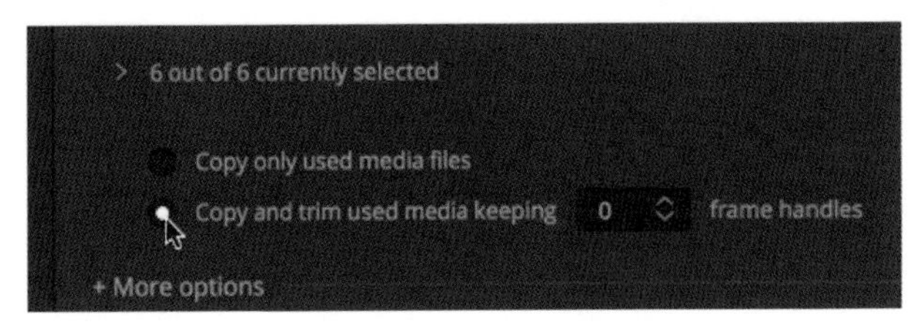

Choosing this option will trim the master clip files down to only those clip portions used in the selected timeline(s). A field is available in which you can enter the number of frame handles you would like added to each side of a clip in case you later will need to trim or create transitions.

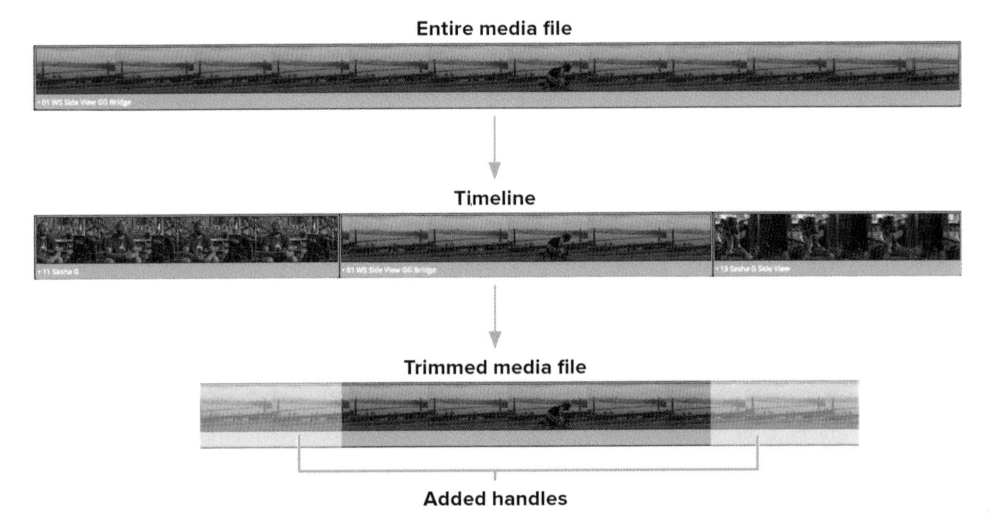

6. Enter **12** as the number of frame handles to add. Doing so will allow a half second of extra media for trimming and transitions.

7. Click “More options” to reveal additional settings.

8. Select Relink to New Files to use the new, copied media in the timeline instead of the existing media.

   You now know the primary options to consolidate media and save disk space.

   When you click Start, the files used in the timeline are copied to the destination drive, and then trimmed so that only those clip portions used—along with a half-second handle on each side of a clip—are saved to disk.

The clips in your bin will now link to these new, shorter media files, but all of the original clips still exist in their original locations. It is up to you to delete them when you are confident that they are no longer needed.

9. Click Start to begin consolidating the media.

> **NOTE:** Compression formats that use inter-frame, temporal compression, such as H.264, cannot be used with the "trim unused media" option in the Media Management window.

Transcoding to Other Formats

Whereas consolidating refers to copying and truncating media, *transcoding* refers to converting the current media to another format. Transcoding can be helpful when you need to move your project to a new location, but you are still in an early stage of editing and need access to all of the clips. Transcoding can create smaller files making moving a project onto portable hard drives faster, and making it run more efficiently on slower computers.

1. Choose File > Media Management, if the Media Manager is no longer open.
2. With Entire Project selected, click the Transcode button.

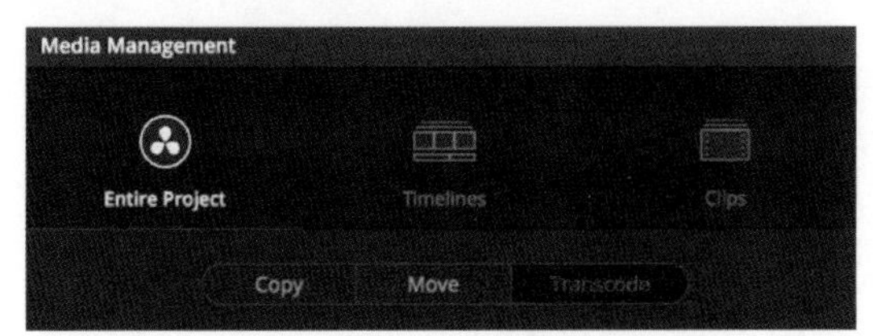

The Transcode settings have many of the same export options as Copy, allowing you to move all of your media or just some of it.

3. Click the Browse button, and in the File Destination dialog, navigate to the location that you selected in the previous exercise. Click OK.
4. Ensure that "Transcode all media" is selected.

> **NOTE:** You can also choose to transcode only the media used in your timelines. If you are moving a project to a slower computer, such as a laptop, and you still require all the media for editing, choose "Transcode all media."

Choosing the following set of options allows you to select a format type for the new media that you will create.

5. From the Video Format menu, choose QuickTime.
6. In OS X, from the Codec menu, choose ProRes 422 Proxy. In Windows, choose DNxHD 720P 100/85/55/45 8-bit. These codecs will produce the smallest file sizes suitable for editing.

NOTE: Transcoding to ProRes is not an option in Windows; so, when working with HD content, choose DNxHD.

7. Scroll down in the Media Manager window, and from the Audio format menu, choose AAC.

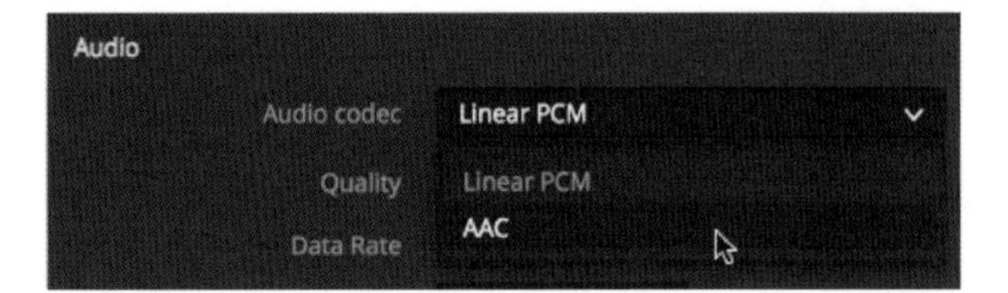

8. Click Start to begin transcoding and copying the files to the selected destination.

The files are simultaneously converted to the lower-resolution format and copied to the portable hard drive. The original files remain in their original locations, linked to the clips and timeline in your project. After you connect the transporting hard drive to another computer, import the project to Resolve and relink to the transcoded media on your portable drive. If you perform any editing with the lower-resolution files, you can export your project and relink it to the original files at a later date.

Congratulations! You have completed *The Definitive Guide to Editing with DaVinci Resolve 12.5* and are ready to explore more editing functionality on your own.

We hope that you have you have found DaVinci Resolve's professional non-linear editing and world class color correction tools to be intuitive to learn and a perfect fit as the hub of your entire creative workflow!

Index

G

I

J

K

L

M

N

O

P

Q

R

S

T

U

V

W

X

About the Author

Paul Saccone has been working in the post-production industry for over 20 years and is an editorial workflow expert based in San Francisco, CA. This is his first book, and he really hopes somebody will read it. From 1998 to 2013, Paul worked at Apple and was the product manager for Final Cut Pro versions 2 through 7, including Final Cut Studio. He is well known around the world for his dynamic and witty presentations as a speaker, demo artist, and educator. Paul currently works for Blackmagic Design and spends his free time editing with DaVinci Resolve.

Made in the USA
Lexington, KY
08 November 2016